BATTING

A COMPREHENSIVE MODERN GUIDE FOR PLAYERS AND COACHES

'This book is fantastic. It is insightful and detailed, I thoroughly enjoyed the holistic structure, weighted heavily towards tactics and the mental approach, still with accurate and simplified technical input'
SAM ARTHURS, FOUNDATION PATHWAY MANAGER,
OXFORDSHIRE CRICKET

'This book offers a complete guide to batting, explained in a way that is thoroughly engaging and intelligible to all audiences. Whether you're a player looking to advance your own batting, a parent or a coach looking to improve others, you will find everything you need in this book to develop the next great modern-day batter'
LUKE SHARPLES, TALENT PATHWAY PERFORMANCE MANAGER,
NORTHAMPTONSHIRE COUNTY CRICKET CLUB

'As technical batting coaching appears to be enjoying a renaissance following the recent fortunes of the England Test side, this book provides an accessible and comprehensive guide. The way technical and tactical aspects of batting are described makes it accessible for players of all abilities, and the drills are practical and applicable. This book is a must for all young players and coaches with a desire to understand and improve their game'
MIKE SUTLIFF, DINTON CC AND FORMER PROFESSIONAL
CRICKETER WITH LEICESTERSHIRE & GLOUCESTERSHIRE

'In touch and up to date whilst still incorporating the sound principles of batting that have lasted the test of time, this comprehensive guide is of great use to players, coaches and parents alike looking to aid the development of modern batsmanship to meet the demands of the modern game'
BEN CODDINGTON, WIMBLEDON CC AND LINCOLNSHIRE

'This is a very detailed book on batting, yet still an accessible read for players and coaches of all levels. The technical, tactical, mental and physical aspects of batting are all covered and there is a huge drills section for coaches to dip into.
DAVID RIPLEY, FORMER NORTHANTS HEAD COACH
AND LONDON SPIRIT ASSISTANT COACH

BATTING

A COMPREHENSIVE MODERN GUIDE
FOR PLAYERS AND COACHES

JAMES KNOTT & ANDREW O'CONNOR

FOREWORD BY
ADAM HOLLIOAKE

With contributions from
Sir Geoffrey Boycott, Ben Duckett, Julian Wood,
Graham Gooch & Mark Butcher

This edition first published in 2022 by

POLARIS PUBLISHING LTD
c/o Aberdein Considine
2nd Floor, Elder House
Multrees Walk
Edinburgh
EH1 3DX

Distributed by
Birlinn Limited

www.polarispublishing.com

Text copyright © James Knott & Andrew O'Connor, 2022
Photography copyright © Stowe Studio 100, 2022
Follow on Instagram #stowestudio100

ISBN: 9781913538330
eBook ISBN: 9781913538347

2

The right of James Knott & Andrew O'Connor to be identified as the authors of this work has been asserted by them in accordance with the Copyright, Designs and Patents Act 1988.

All rights reserved. No part of this publication may be reproduced, stored or transmitted in any form, or by any means electronic, mechanical, photocopying, recording or otherwise, without the express written permission of the publisher.

The views expressed in this book do not necessarily reflect the views, opinions or policies of Polaris Publishing Ltd (Company No. SC401508) (Polaris), nor those of any persons, organisations or commercial partners connected with the same (Connected Persons). Any opinions, advice, statements, services, offers, or other information or content expressed by third parties are not those of Polaris or any Connected Persons but those of the third parties. For the avoidance of doubt, neither Polaris nor any Connected Persons assume any responsibility or duty of care whether contractual, delictual or on any other basis towards any person in respect of any such matter and accept no liability for any loss or damage caused by any such matter in this book.

Every effort has been made to trace copyright holders and obtain their permission for the use of copyright material. The publisher apologises for any errors or omissions and would be grateful if notified of any corrections that should be incorporated in future reprints or editions of this book.

All names and trademarks are the property of their respective owners, which are in no way associated with Polaris Publishing Ltd. Use of these names does not imply any cooperation or endorsement.

British Library Cataloguing-in-Publication Data
A catalogue record for this book is available on request from the British Library.

Designed and typeset by Polaris Publishing, Edinburgh
Printed in Great Britain by MBM Print, East Kilbride

CONTENTS

FOREWORD BY ADAM HOLLIOAKE	viii
INTRODUCTION	xi
ONE: THE BASICS	1
Grip	2
Stance	4
Trigger movements	7
Backswing	9
Watching the ball	11
Playing late	12
TWO: THE SHOTS – TECHNICAL ASPECTS	15
Front-foot drives	16
On drives	24
Back-foot drives	27
Cut shot and back-foot ramp	30
Work to leg off the back foot	35
Pull and hook shots	37
Coming out of your crease to hit the ball	40
Sweep shots	43
Ramp shots	51
Front-foot defence	53
Back-foot defence	55
Leaving the ball	56
Running the ball to third man	61
Playing the yorker	63
Batting wagon wheel	64
THREE: THE SHOTS – TACTICAL ASPECTS	66
Front-foot drives	67
Back-foot drives	68
Cut shot and back-foot ramp	69
Work to leg off the back foot	70
Pull and hook shots	71
Coming out of your crease to hit the ball	71
Sweep shots	72
Ramp shots	73
Running the ball to third man – front and back foot	73
Front-foot and back-foot defence	74
Field placings	74
FOUR: FURTHER TACTICAL CONSIDERATIONS	79
Know your game	79
Pre-match and pre-innings – reading a pitch and assessing bowlers	80
Constructing an innings and partnership building	84

Run chases	88
Breaks in the innings	90
Different tactical batting approaches dependent on format and your strengths	91
FIVE: RUNNING BETWEEN THE WICKETS	**93**
The duties of the striking batter	94
After playing the ball	95
While running	96
The duties of the non-striking batter	97
As the ball is being bowled	98
After the ball has been played	99
General running between the wickets	100
Technical aspects of running between the wickets	103
Sprinting the run	104
Slowing down to complete the first run	105
Turning and setting off	107
Completing the last run	109
Batting with a runner	110
When the injured batter is on strike	110
When the injured batter is off strike	111
SIX: THE MENTAL ASPECTS OF BATTING	**112**
Concentration	112
Personal targets	115
The next ball is always the one that counts	116
Motivation and single-mindedness	118
Positive mindset and enjoyment	119
Confidence	121
Resilience	122
Dealing with nerves and fear of failure	123
Visualisation	125
Dealing with fielders' and bowlers' verbal distractions	126
SEVEN: ADVANCED BATTING SKILLS	**128**
The training cycle	128
Game ownership	129
Pre-match preparation	132
Hitting the gaps	133
Manoeuvring the fielders	134
Judgement of length and line, the hitting area and hitting on the up	135
Scoring off bad bowling	137
Playing swing bowling	138
Playing fast bowling	139
Playing spin bowling	144

Conditions favouring bowlers – ugly runs and attack the best form of defence	154
T20 batting – 360 scoring and power hitting	155
Reading the swing and picking slower balls	165
Limiting your game and opening the batting	169
Changing pitch conditions in multi-day cricket	171
Walking and dealing with a bad umpiring decision	171
Batting in different countries	172
EIGHT: LOOKING AFTER YOURSELF	**175**
Fitness	178
Nutrition	182
Hydration	183
Batting in the heat	184
Sleep	185
Batting equipment	186
The bat	187
Helmet	191
Batting pads	192
Batting gloves	194
Protective box	196
Thigh pads	197
Arm guard	198
Chest guard	198
Batting spikes and rubber-soled boots	199
Cap and sun hat	200
NINE: TRAINING METHODS AND DRILLS	**202**
Technical development	205
Tactical development	274
Batting games	283
Hand-eye-foot coordination	284
Training on your own	303
Pre-match	322
Waiting to bat	322
Introduction to video analysis	323
Drill and practice safety awareness	335
Useful coaching quotes to remember	347
ABOUT THE AUTHORS	**349**
ABOUT THE PLAYERS & COACHES	**351**
ACKNOWLEDGEMENTS	**354**

FOREWORD

There is something unique about the art of batting that separates it from most sports. Like the knock-out in boxing, the batsman losing his wicket signals the end of his game. It's final, brutal and beautiful at the same time.

There would be very little that would get any person to watch a game that lasts for five days (or even one day for that matter) without these little battles, these tiny victories and failures within the grand scheme of the war. It would be hard to keep people's attention for the length of time that it takes to complete any game of cricket without that massive moment of celebration for the bowler and huge disappointment for the outgoing batsman, his teammates and supporters.

I first became a professional cricketer back in 1989 and have been fortunate to stay in the game for the last 30-odd years. During that time, I have seen so many advancements, fitness fads, nuances and biomechanical changes in batting techniques to acknowledge that I will probably never know what the perfect way to bat is, as there will always be new techniques that improve the batsman's chances of scoring runs. Every time I think I have the complexities of the game covered, someone comes along and masters a new technique. At the time of writing, the off-stump guard is high on the list of debates (certainly between the players that played in my generation and the players of the current generation). One thing that I do know is that whichever technique a batsman chooses, it's important that the batsman commits to that technique and, even more importantly, does it well.

I have seen players like Shivnarine Chanderapaul average 50 in over 100-plus Test matches. When first looking at his technique you'd think he was destined for failure. If you saw a youngster batting with the same technique, there would be a lot of coaches who would tell him he could never be successful batting that way. For all the biomechanical flaws that Chanderpaul appeared to have, he made up for it with two of the more important things a batsman can possess: the ability to play the ball very late and an amazing appetite for runs born from impeccable concentration.

On the topic of concentration, I have been fascinated by the change in mindset of batsmen in the modern era. Their ability to concentrate has been elevated by a greater understanding of psychology and the use of sports psychologists who have now made terms like emotion control, pre-ball routines and arousal levels part of common dressing-room talk (within the professional game at least).

When I was a player, I would've called myself very strong-minded (I've never been one for modesty), but most of my coaches would say I was just stubborn and very hard to coach. I listened to the coaches but didn't always take everything they said as gospel; I'm not sure if this is from a) arrogance, b) ignorance, c) mistrust, d) the fact I felt I could add to things that the coaches were telling me. This last point has fascinated me in recent times. When I first started as a coach, my ego often made it hard for me to accept when a player questioned the things I would suggest to him/her. I felt that any player that didn't listen to what I had to say was 'difficult to coach and was not going to reach their potential'. I now recognise that once a batsman is at the professional stage of their career, working out new techniques is important – indeed necessary – for their game to improve. When I look back at the footage of me playing in the late 90s (bearing in mind I was probably one of the more forward-thinking cricketers at the time), I look at the naivety of my technique and feel that had I known then what I've since learned as a coach, I would have been a far better player (if I had adopted the modern techniques).

It is a new thing for me to be able to let go of the fact that modern players are superior to those of the past. It would be naïve to think otherwise. People are running faster, jumping further, have greater technology. Almost every world record has improved in every sport; it would be foolish to think that batting was the only sport/activity that has gone backwards.

With that in mind, I feel coaches need to move forward from the old-school 'tell someone how it's done' mindset and need to move towards a more collaborative approach with the player. It goes without saying that this doesn't apply to youngsters starting the game. Learning a basic and sound technique is vital. The finer nuances of the game can be developed once the player is at the professional level.

One thing that I feel remains contentious and is debated long and hard between the modern player and the more traditionalist player, is the amount of pressure a batsman applies to the bowlers. I know that it will always be the way that ex-players feel that current players aren't patient enough or prepared to wait for scoring opportunities. This argument has no finish line and will never be resolved; however, I am of the firm belief that a batsman must (by the nature of his body language and intent) make the bowler aware that if he delivers the ball into certain areas of the pitch he is going to get punished. It is this very intent that creates pressure on bowlers, and bowlers who are running up to bowl that are under pressure are far more likely to bowl a loose delivery than the one who runs in to bowl knowing that a batsman is only looking to survive.

So with this in mind I believe that batsmen need to apply pressure to bowlers; the amount of pressure is the very art of batting and if everyone had the answer to that then there would be very little need for James Knott's and Andy O'Connor's very enlightening book.

Adam Hollioake
Surrey & England

INTRODUCTION

With the variety of formats around in the modern game, cricket players and coaches need to be more flexible in their approach than ever before, developing a diverse set of skills in addition to tactical awareness. Every player will have a 'natural' game and style, but it is important now to have a variety of games to suit each format and match scenario. With practice, it is possible to develop numerous 'natural' games and different ways of playing. Ben Stokes is a great example of this. In Test cricket he can go from first to top gear very quickly, and at the appropriate time.

There are also many different styles of batting out there. No two batters are identical, and their individual style of batting will have developed through experience, watching other players and through any coaching influences they have had, whether this be from family or formal coaching. It is important to have an understanding of these to develop an all-round game, but ultimately a batter needs to know their own game and figure out what works for them. The greater this awareness, the greater the results will be on the pitch in terms of run scoring.

> *'As a player you need to realise you are your own best coach. You are responsible for your performance and your development. A coach can give you ideas and direction, but you need to select the right things that work for you and are suitable for you.;*
> **GRAHAM GOOCH**
> *Essex & England, & former England batting coach*

This book highlights and provides options on the basic fundamentals that are required for batting and run scoring, along with a breakdown of the technical and tactical aspects of each shot, coupled with the mental and physical demands of batting. Throughout this book there are many contributions from some of the game's best players and coaches, both past and present. For coaches there is a comprehensive drills chapter, with over 80 drills and practices that will help develop your player's game and keep training sessions engaging and varied. Whatever level you are currently playing or coaching at there will be something in this book for you.

> **Note for players and coaches**
> Ensure you practise thoroughly before taking any new or revised changes into a game, so that it already feels natural, thereby allowing you to concentrate on just watching the ball. So select the relevant elements that work for you. Ultimately, you need to be responsible for your own development.

Throughout this book, all technical descriptions and drill references are detailed for a right-hand batter facing a right-arm bowler, bowling over the wicket, unless stated otherwise.

ONE
THE BASICS

'The key basics to nail down are keeping your head still, playing the ball as late as possible and then practising the shots you want to perform in games over and over again.'

BEN DUCKETT

Nottinghamshire & England

It is so important for you as a batter to have a firm technical foundation and knowledge of the basics of batting early in your development, so that should you experience a slump of form and lack of runs, you always have a reference point to return back to. The more these basics are practised and repeated, eventually becoming natural and consistent, the greater success you will have out in the middle. Usually when a dip in form occurs it is a basic fundamental that is failing, so you need to go 'back to basics'.

Note for coaches

When a player is playing well and scoring runs consistently, record video footage of this for you both to refer back to if they lose form. You will then be able to highlight any differences in their game and start making the interventions to get back to their 'best' game.

'The grip, stance and backlift are the three main building blocks of a solid technique.'
MARK BUTCHER
Surrey & England

Grip

The most important aspect of gripping the bat is that your hands work together and not detrimentally oppose each other. This can potentially be a problem if the hands are too far apart on the bat handle. When working together they allow your bat to come down in a straight line, thus producing a natural flow and follow-through.

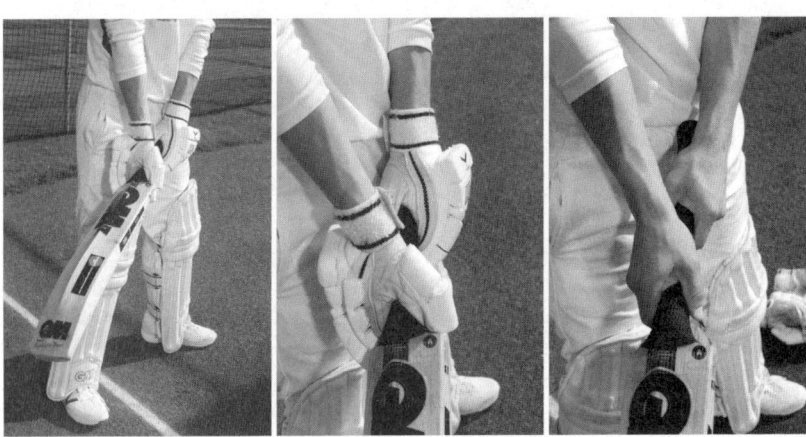

To achieve this natural flow with the hands working together, it is advised that the V shapes made by your thumb and first finger of both hands are aligned together on the bat handle as in the photo above. A good starting point is to line these Vs up down the back of the bat between the outside edge and the splice of the bat. If arranged in this manner they produce a straight line down the back of the bat. This is a good starting point for your grip, as it enables you to access both sides of the wicket more easily and contributes to you having a greater array of shots. Some of the world's best players such as Joe Root, Kane Williamson and Virat Kohli grip the bat this way.

However, there are many batters out there who line their Vs up differently to this. Remember that while this is the preferred method, some unorthodox grips work perfectly for the individual using them. It is an individual preference and should only be changed if it can be proven to be a flaw in technique, ultimately holding back a batter's development. Try an experiment. Move your Vs so they align with the middle of the bat – straight down the splice. If you take the bat back, what do you notice about the bat face? Which side of the ground will this grip assist with accessing? Which attacking shots will it help with?

The answer is the leg side, as the bat face is now more closed. With the Vs in this position, the grip can help keep the ball down when sweeping, cutting, hooking and pulling. It can also help with getting the hands high when defending. The former South African captain and now director of South African cricket, Graeme Smith, is a good example of a player who had a 'closed grip' and would often hit balls from outside off stump through the leg side.

Conversely, if the Vs are lined up more towards the outside edge of the bat, this will aid off-side play as the bat face will now be more 'open'. Former England captain and now Sky Sports commentator Nasser Hussain is a good example of a batter with a more open grip, and as a result was a good square driver.

Note for coaches

If you find a player whose grip is slightly off-side or leg-side dominant, but they are still able to access both sides of the ground scoring effectively, think hard before intervening. If this grip feels natural to the player and is effective, is there a need for a change?

Most batters will have their hands together on the bat handle, nearer the top than the bottom if the size of the bat is correct. However, some players feel they have more control of the bat if they grip it nearer where the bat handle joins the bat, and others more leverage and therefore power if they grip it near the end of the handle. As you get more experienced you may subtly move your hands lower or higher on the handle if you have premeditated a certain shot. There are even some players who have their hands slightly apart on the handle, the South African batsman Faf du Plessis being an example of such a player.

It is important not to grip the bat too tightly in your set-up if you want to achieve a natural bat flow. If you grip the bat too tightly, and your hands and arms are very tense, this can inhibit your bat swing. Having a lighter, softer grip will make it easier to produce your swing if your bat is the right weight and not too heavy. This is known as having 'a good pick-up'. You only need to grip the bat handle tightly as the bat hits the ball to ensure that the bat face does not move much on contact and you get full power into the shot.

A relaxed grip will also help you make any late adjustments to the shot you have decided to play, and if you are defending, enable you to achieve 'soft hands', where there is some give in the bat as the ball strikes it. This can help get the ball straight to ground or prevent a catch carrying to the wicketkeeper, slip or close-in fielder.

Stance

'All great players and have great footwork and balance.'
SIR GEOFFREY BOYCOTT
Yorkshire & England

The most important feature of your stance is that it feels comfortable and that you can move quickly from it, whether you have a trigger movement (also called a pre-delivery movement) or not. Trigger movements are discussed later in this chapter. A solid, balanced base, enabling your head and eyes to remain level and still as the bowler runs in, will enhance your ability to watch the ball closely as it is released.

A good starting point is to have your feet approximately shoulder-width apart, with the crease line in the middle of your feet. This ensures that your back foot will be in the crease if the keeper is stood up, thus negating any possibility of being stumped. It also provides some free distance to step safely back towards the stumps for back-foot shots. Of course, there are variations to this, and often tactical decisions may govern where the batter takes their stance. On a low-bouncing wicket, against a medium-pacer with the wicketkeeper stood back, the batter may decide to set up outside the crease, down the pitch towards the bowler to help negate lbw. If facing a very quick bowler, some stand with both feet inside the crease to give themselves more time to see, react to and play the ball.

As with grips, many batters stand differently as the bowler runs in. Some may trigger a lot, some trigger a little, and others not at all. In terms of being balanced and still with a good head position, nearly all players have their knees slightly bent in their stance, with their weight slightly on their heels, not totally on the balls of their feet. The bending of the knees puts the batter into a powerful position for movement, potentially forwards or backwards. Very much like a grasshopper ready to leap, by bending the knees slightly the batter stores up potential energy, then releases this in the movement process. If the batter's legs are stiff, straight and upright, it is very difficult to move quickly from this position. Conversely, if the knees are bent excessively, this too can hinder quick movement and can lead to coming up on contact with the ball as it is hard to maintain that very low position.

It must be remembered that the weight will be moved into the balls of the feet as the movement decision is initiated. The toes/ball of the back foot will push the batter on to the front foot, and the toes/ball of the front foot will push the batter on to the back foot.

> **Note for coaches**
>
> If a batter is often 'falling over' in their stance, with their head moving towards the off side of the pitch, ask them to bend their knees more, move more weight on to their heels and to imagine they are sitting on a stool. If you are using a bowling machine, a great way of ascertaining this is to perform a 'dummy feed', where you pretend to feed the ball into the machine. The batter will invariably continue with their movement, thus enabling you to determine the unrestrained direction of movement and balance.

In the photo on the previous page you will notice that the batter's stance is slightly open, with the back foot on middle stump, front foot on middle-and-leg stump. This slight opening of the stance can help keep the eyes level and still, by preventing the head falling over to the off side. All players are slightly different, but if you are picking up a bat for the first time this is a good starting point.

The head is also slightly forward and tucked into the left shoulder over the front foot so that the eyes are level and are presented towards the ball. This head position will also help you stay over the ball, whether you are playing on the front or back foot and will additionally help with transferring your weight into your shot and keep the ball on the ground. A useful coaching point is to ask the batter to keep their helmet grill tucked into their shoulder area while in their stance. This will help with keeping the head and front shoulder relationship together in the shot.

'Your head should be still, slightly pointed at the target, with your eyes level and on off stump. Head goes towards the ball and your head and shoulder move before your feet. Lean slightly forward – this can help you not fall over to the off side.'
GRAHAM GOOCH

How wide apart you have your feet will depend upon personal preference in terms of comfort and feel for best achieving a solid base coupled with quick movement. A good starting point is around or just wider than shoulder-width apart, similar to that of Joe Root. There are of course exceptions to this – the great England batsman Kevin Pietersen had his feet a long way apart in his stance, while players of previous generations often had their feet quite close together. Certainly, the taller you are the wider stance you are likely to need to achieve a balanced position.

> **Note for coaches**
>
> If a batter is struggling with their footwork, then a wider stance can help them as they have less distance to move forward or back, and they can simply transfer their weight on to one foot or the other. The great England opening batsman, Marcus Trescothick, is someone who admitted he never had great footwork so adopted a wider stance.

Some players also like to open their front foot slightly so that it points towards extra cover. Again, this can help with your head position and the ability to hit down the ground and to the leg side. It is also the position it should end up in for most front-foot shots, whether defending or attacking.

Many batters will open their stance up further to play inswing bowling or a right-arm bowler bowling round the wicket, so that their shoulders are aligned to where the ball is coming from. This action ensures they are not 'closed off' to the delivery, where they would have to play round their front pad to access a straight delivery. If the ball is swinging in to a right-handed batter, then this will also help reduce lbw dismissals.

Trigger movements (or pre-delivery movements)

'Timing of any trigger movement is crucial. If you do it too late you will be on the move as the bowler lets go of the ball, which will delay your footwork. On release you need to be still with your head and eyes level. The trigger movement must also be consistent, so you know where your off stump is.'
GRAHAM GOOCH

Whether you are just starting out or are an experienced player, you need to have a good understanding of a trigger movement and what it is used for.

Most batters have a trigger movement of some sort. For some it may be very small, perhaps just a small bend of the knees and lifting of the bat, while others may have a much more exaggerated movement similar to Alastair Cook, who takes large strides across the crease. The most important aspect of any trigger movement is that, whatever form it takes, it has finished by the time the bowler lets go of the ball, ensuring that your feet and, most importantly, your head are still, with your eyes level and presented towards the ball.

A trigger movement needs to be consistent and repeatable so that it is the same each ball, finishing in the same place each time. This is critical for knowing where your head is in relation to off stump, allowing you to judge whether a ball is going to hit the stumps, is moving down the leg side, or missing the off stump. This judgement is critical in determining your shot decision-making relative to each ball.

The main reason for batters having trigger movements is to activate their footwork, inducing the feeling that they are light on their feet and can move quickly into position to execute the shot. This is particularly true when playing quick bowling. Often batters can feel rooted to the spot if they simply stand dead still. If you are a successful batter, playing all types of bowling without a trigger movement, then continue to do so. However, if footwork is an issue for you, then think about adding a trigger movement to your pre-delivery routine.

Example of trigger movement

Note for coaches
A trigger movement can help footwork and speed up movement. However, if you have a batter who is committing too early when playing spin, then perhaps suggest that they do not trigger when facing a spin bowler. This will slow down footwork, but they do have more time to play the ball against a slow bowler. A lot of batters trigger against quick bowling but not when facing spin.

Backswing

As with all the aspects discussed so far in this chapter, no two batters are identical in how they pick up the bat. However, the best batters bring the bat down straight to connect with the ball, unless playing one of the horizontal bat shots discussed in the next chapter.

While in their stance, some batters start with their bat between their feet, particularly players with a wide stance. Others place the bat behind their right foot, some wide of their feet, and some may not have it on the floor at all. Some may tap the bat on the ground as the bowler runs in or move it up and down.

During the bowler's run-up it is not that important what your bat does. However, once the ball is delivered it becomes very important in two ways:

1. The bat needs to go up, so you can get power.
2. It then needs to come down straight, to give you the best chance of hitting the ball.

The bat does not have to go back straight to come down straight. Watch footage of the world's current best batters, Steve Smith, Joe Root, Virat Kohli and Kane Williamson. Their backswing initially arcs towards the slips/gully, before looping back into a straight position prior to commencing the downswing, which again comes down straight.

> *'You should pick up the bat towards first, second slip and then loop back round straight to get a natural swing.'*
> **SIR GEOFFREY BOYCOTT**

As long as your bat comes down straight, it is fine to have an arc in your backswing. However, if you do have that arc and you find you are playing around the line or 'in to out', then you will need to swing the bat back straighter for it to come down straighter. The term 'in to out' describes the motion where the bat downswing comes into your body, hits the ball, then commences to arc away from your body on the follow-through. This looping action causes batters to hit the ball mainly to the off side of the pitch.

At the point of release, most batters will have their bat between knee and waist high. The reason for this is so the bat goes back before it comes down, activating a natural pendulum motion, with the downward momentum going through the ball to give power to your shots. The bat accelerates through the ball for attacking shots and decelerates to a stop for defensive ones.

As the batter moves towards the ball the bat goes back further and then comes down to hit the ball. It does not have to move far, just enough to activate momentum to the bat. It is important that any backswing feels natural and is consistent. If you are gripping the bat lightly, this will help you achieve a natural swing, bringing the bat down straight. There is a phrase 'step and backswing'. Both occur simultaneously, hence as the batter steps forward or back to the ball, the backswing is initiated.

Like a golf swing, the golfer does not start with the club above their head. It starts low to the ground next to the ball and then goes back and up in a natural swing. It is the same for your backswing. It needs to go up before coming back down. However, most batters would find themselves too rushed to fit this in if the bat started on the ground. Therefore, the majority will have their bat between knee and waist height as the bowler lets go of the ball.

When trying to hit fours and sixes – 'power hitting' – it is useful to use another golf analogy. If a golfer wants to hit the ball a long way they use a driver in association with a very long backswing. If they want to chip the ball they use a pitching wedge with a very short backswing. Therefore, it is obvious that if you want to hit the cricket ball a long way, you have to activate a big backswing! If a batter has no backswing, their attacking shots become more of a push than a hit and getting the timing right can be a problem.

Note for coaches

There are always exceptions. Viv Richards would have his bat on the floor as the bowler released the ball, Paul Collingwood had a small backswing, and Brian Lara's bat was above his head as the bowler delivered. If your player does any of these and is making runs, then let them continue in that manner.

Watching the ball

When discussing stance and trigger movements, the importance of having your eyes level and presented towards the ball are critical. This gives you the greatest chance of seeing the ball leave the bowler's hand clearly. It is in this instance that you will receive the most information about what line and length the ball will be pitching on, and, if you are watching really closely, whether there is likely to be any movement in the air or off the pitch due to the bowler's wrist and finger positions.

The earlier you pick up the ball in its flight, the more time you will have to play your shots, and therefore make better shot selection decisions regarding whether to go forward or back, and attack or defend. If the ball has already travelled a distance before you have picked it up, the more rushed you will be to play your shot. Seeing the ball as it is let go by the bowler is crucial. Bowlers sometimes give away visual cues as to what type of delivery they are about to bowl. This is extremely useful for the batter to identify, especially against fast bowling. This is discussed further in the book.

It is most beneficial to focus on the ball as the bowler is running in, tracking it in their hand until they release it. You may be able to gain some information and evaluate what the bowler is trying to do while they are running in; for example, which side of the ball is the shiny side, or whether their grip has changed for a slower ball or other type of variation. This is an important skill to learn early on and will also aid you in picking a spinner's delivery too. This is discussed more in Chapter 3.

Next time you practise see if you can pick which side the shiny side is as the bowler is running in.

You should aim to watch the ball all the way on to the bat. A good habit when training is to exaggerate this. The aggressive New Zealand opening batsman, Martin Guptill, even exaggerates his head watching the ball in matches, so as the ball sails over the long-on boundary for 6, his head is still looking down at the spot where his bat made contact with the ball. Watching the ball all the way on to the bat will help you deal with any late movement, as well as playing the ball late and keeping it down. Additionally, as the Martin Guptill example highlights, it is also important when hitting over the top. That is developed more in the next chapter.

Note for coaches

If a batter has lost some form and is in a period of low scoring, ask them whether they are watching the ball closely before suggesting any technical changes. It maybe that they are simply not quite focused on the ball as it is released, therefore not picking up the ball until later in its flight.

Playing late

'See it early, play it late. Particularly when facing swing bowling or the turning ball.'
SIR GEOFFREY BOYCOTT

Playing late is an extremely important element of batting, as it is crucial to know where you should be making contact with the ball, in terms of its relationship with your body. Most coaches will talk about playing late, but where is that in relation to your body and head?

The answer is when the ball is beneath your head. On the front foot, if you have bent your front knee, your head will be over your left foot toes, or just inside them, so that is where you should contact the ball whether driving or defending, when aiming to keep the ball down along the ground. When playing off the back foot through the off side, this is now in line with your right leg and foot, with the ball still close to being under your head. This will obviously be dependent on the line of the ball.

If you make contact with the ball when it is under your head you will be able to keep it down and benefit from transferring your body weight into the shot, therefore maximising the power in your shots. You will also have a lot more control of where the ball goes.

Front foot contact area.

Back foot contact area.

Imagine a small box under your head that goes with you whether you play front or back foot. Any ball you hit within that box gives the maximum control and is a lower risk shot. It also enables you to keep the ball along the ground, you can angle it into gaps, increase power, as well as make any late adjustments if the ball moves.

The better the wicket, with more pace and true bounce, then the larger the box will be. The worse the wicket, slower and more seam movement, the smaller that box becomes, as you have less margin for error. Any shot you play outside of this box will bring higher risk, particularly by accidentally hitting it in the air. Your decision to play it will be determined by the match situation and the format of game you are playing.

It is essential that this simple truth be remembered. If you want to keep the ball down, upon contact the handle of the bat should be in front of the blade, and if you want to hit the ball in the air, upon contact the handle of the bat should be behind the blade. The upper half of the body – the shoulders, arms and hands – hit the ball. The lower half of the body – the legs – get you into position to do so.

Fundamentally, the feet are the servants of the body.

TWO
THE SHOTS – TECHNICAL ASPECTS

'A good technique gives you confidence and a much better chance of doing well.'

SIR GEOFFREY BOYCOTT

This chapter will cover the technical aspects of the shots you can play, whether defending, attacking or leaving the ball. A large selection of shots are available to you, wherever the bowler delivers the ball, and the length and line the ball needs to be for each shot will be highlighted. In the following chapter we discuss the tactical considerations, which will also influence your decision-making and subsequent shot selection.

The following diagram shows the various lengths the ball can be delivered on, and we will describe the ideal length the ball needs to pitch on for each particular shot.

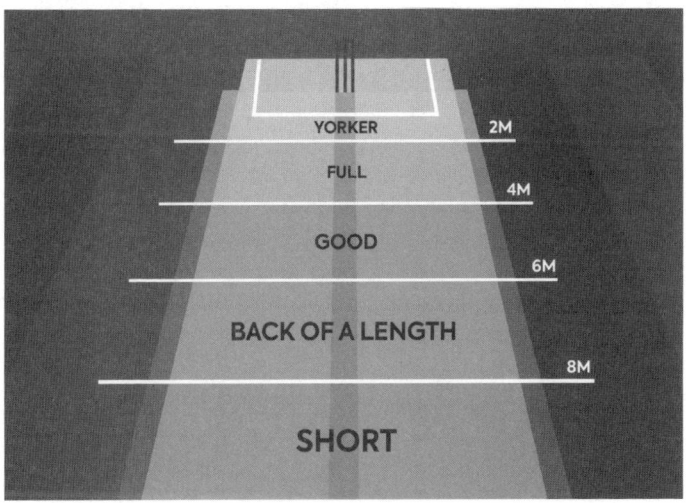

Expanding the range of shots for particular deliveries (i.e. hitting good-length balls on the up) is discussed in Chapters 4 and 7.

Player task

Once you have completed this chapter and practised the shots, highlight three attacking shots that you play well and consistently. They can be front- or back-foot. This will initiate the process of understanding your own game and what your individual strengths are.

Front-foot drives

'Footwork is an important basic to get right. If you get this right, you will get a good head position. You want the front foot alongside the ball so your bat can come through straight. If in line or off side of the ball you have to play round the front pad. That will make your head fall over.'
SIR GEOFFREY BOYCOTT

We start with attacking shots, so that if you are reading this book early in your playing career or are perhaps considering whether to give cricket a go for the first time, we want you to first of all feel the excitement of hitting the ball hard and watching it travel a long way. When in a game situation this will help you score runs, which is ultimately what batting is about.

The ideal length for playing a front-foot drive is a half-volley, or a full toss below knee height. If it is a half-volley, the ball has little distance to travel after pitching before you hit it with the bat, so there is less risk in playing the shot if there is any movement off the pitch.

Whether defending or attacking on the front foot, the first part of your body to move towards the ball will be your head and left shoulder. This will hopefully be instinctive if you have a balanced position upon the bowler releasing the ball, and your eyes are level and presented towards where the ball is coming from. Your front foot and body should then start to move just after your head and shoulder.

As you step towards the ball, your bat should be taken back higher in your backswing, as you are looking to hit the ball and score runs. You need to generate power into the shot, so this initial backswing followed by the downswing momentum will provide this.

In the photos on the previous page, the batter has taken a comfortable stride forward and bent his front knee. The bending of the front knee is crucial to allow your body weight to go through the ball, which will give you more power than just hitting with your arms, also enabling you to get your head over the ball. A bent knee also helps you to achieve a solid balanced base, encouraging the bat to come through straight, all the way from the top of its backswing to the end of its follow-through. If not balanced, there will be excess body movement restricting the bat from coming through in a perfect arc.

Note for coaches

If, despite having a bent knee, a batter is struggling to achieve a solid base, look at two potential front foot issues. After stepping forward, are they landing heel first or toes first? If landing on the balls of the feet, the front foot might not be fully planted and is trying to balance on the balls of the feet only. It is difficult to achieve a solid base like this. Encourage your batter to land heel first before planting the whole foot down. The second issue to look for is where the front foot is pointing. Ideally for all off-side drives it should not be pointing straight down the pitch. A strong base is best achieved by pointing it towards extra cover. If the batter is attempting an on drive or straight drive, their front foot can point down the pitch, while still crucially forming a solid base. Without a solid base they will fall over to the off side and the shoulders will rotate horizontally instead of working vertically.

The forward stride length that takes you to the ball should be comfortable and will vary for every player depending on how long their legs are, coupled with their natural mobility. If you are trying to take an excessively long step, it will be more difficult to get your head and weight over the ball, and harder to achieve a solid base. The length of stride is also determined by the line of the ball. If just outside off stump, it is easier to take a bigger stride. When on the stumps most players take a shorter stride forward.

In terms of the bat swing, the bat should go right through the ball and follow through in the direction you want the ball to go. Imagine if you were to let go of the bat after hitting the ball – it would go in exactly the same direction as the ball. Remember to only grip the bat tightly as you are just about to connect with the ball, so that your bat swing remains true throughout the pendulum motion. Take a look at the photo sequence below, as this highlights the perfect 'P' position that your hands and bat make throughout the swing.

Check swing.

You can swing through with a 'check swing' or a 'full follow-through'.

Full follow-through.

For check drives, it is the bottom, or toe, of the bat that should finish its swing pointing to where the ball should go. If a full follow-through drive is executed, it is the top of the handle of the bat that should point where the ball should go after the wrists have broken.

It is important that the step to the ball is in sync with the bat coming through to hit the ball. Ideally you do not want your foot planted too early then the bat coming down to hit the ball. You will lose a lot of natural timing this way, without as much body weight contributing to the power in the shot. You will just be hitting with your arms.

To keep the ball along the ground the bat should make contact with the ball on the downswing so the bat is angled:

Remember, if you want to hit the ball down, the handle should be in front of the blade when connecting with the ball. If the plan is to go over the top, then contact is slightly further out in front of the body with the bat now on the upswing:

Remember, if you want to hit the ball up, the handle should be behind the blade when connecting with the ball.

> **Note for coaches**
>
> When hitting over the top, players often try to hit the ball too hard and the shoulders start to rotate horizontally instead of vertically, leading to the bottom hand dominating the shot and the path of the bat therefore not going straight through the line of the ball. It is important to stress not trying to 'overhit'. Try to keep a side-on shape as long as possible, specifically on contact with the ball, allowing the natural swing of the bat and the transfer of body weight to generate the power required to get the ball over the top of the infield or boundary.

'Keep a strong base and keep your head still.
Don't try to overhit it and lose your shape.'
BEN DUCKETT

When hitting over the top, it is easier to hit balls that pitch just short of a half-volley length, as this length allows the bat to get underneath the ball on contact. How to 'create the length' to hit over the top from full deliveries is detailed in Chapter 7, although this of course can be used in any format of the game.

In terms of where your front foot should be in relation to the line of the ball, it will be alongside it as much as possible. Once the ball gets too wide this will no longer be possible, but it is still important that your foot goes in the direction of the line of the ball for you to still get your weight through it and have control of the shot. The three photos below show where the front foot lands in relation to the ball depending on its line:

Straight drive.

Off drive.

Cover drive.

For straight drives where the ball is hitting the stumps and you want to hit down the ground past the bowler, it is not usually necessary or possible to get a big stride in. However, it is still important to get your weight into the shot. Some players often take a shuffle forward as they play the shot to stop overbalancing. When they do this it is important to keep the knees bent so the head does not come up and the shoulders will stay in a vertical position, not rotating into a horizontal plane.

On drives

It is crucial in your batting development to have a strong on-side (or leg-side) game, with an array of scoring options. To generalise, depending on the match situation and the bowling type, there are usually more gaps on the on side to score into. It is important that when a bowler bowls into your pads you can find a gap and score. If you score consistently when the bowler strays down the leg side, you will put them under a lot more pressure. This increase in pressure is likely to cause more mistakes from the bowler, culminating in more scoring opportunities for you.

The key to any leg-side shot, except pulls, hooks and sweeps, is that it is still fundamentally a straight bat shot. The bat still needs to come down straight to give you the best chance of connecting with the ball. Just before you make contact, your wrists work to help you angle the ball into the gap.

On drive sequence.

On drive sequence.

Through mid wicket sequence.

Through mid wicket sequence.

The ball delivered above is a half-volley, so the batter is looking to drive similarly as they would a ball on the stumps or outside off stump. It is important that the contact area is still beneath the head so that you control the shot and can keep the ball down. Instead of a bent front knee, your front leg can straighten slightly to allow the bat to come through and access the ball. Often, if you try to play from a front-foot base, the bat has to come round the front pad and, instead of coming through straight, is actually coming across the ball, making it harder to get the timing right for connection. In this case the ball will likely strike the pad and you will miss out on a scoring opportunity. If your front foot strides too far to the off side, you will have cut yourself off from clean access to the ball, so once again you will play around your pad.

It is critical that if the ball is relatively straight, the front foot is taken to the leg side of the ball, ensuring that the foot is pointing straight down the pitch. This allows the hips to open up, creating a much better alignment for hips and shoulders to create a straight path for the bat to follow on its downswing and follow-through. By doing this you eliminate the possibility of playing around your pad. Do not try to overhit the on drive, as this can cause you to overbalance and mistime the ball. A good tip is to try to hit a two, and you will probably time a four. It is vital to keep your shape.

Another consideration for scoring off leg-stump half-volleys is not to aim too square. If the ball would be hitting the off side or middle of your pad you should be targeting in front of square, around the midwicket region. If the ball would be hitting the leg side of your pad or beyond then you will be aiming squarer, through square leg or even behind square on the leg side. Good-length balls that are delivered into your pads are discussed later in the chapter, when the front-foot defence is considered.

Back-foot drives

The ideal ball to drive off the back foot is one delivered back of a length, just outside off stump. If you imagine another set of stumps, the line of the ball would be in the region of fourth to fifth stump, although good footwork can allow wider balls to be driven. Players should be encouraged to step 'back and across'. The ideal height of bounce to drive off the back foot is between mid-thigh and stomach height.

As with front-foot drives, it is still important to create a solid base on your back foot, so that you can achieve a balanced position, keeping your head still. A heel-toe landing and a bent right leg will again help you achieve this base and maintain a good head position towards the ball. Ensure that your back foot stays parallel with the crease, as this keeps you in a preferred side-on position. If the back foot opens up, and points down the pitch, it is much harder to hold a solid base, and being squared-up makes it so much harder to play safely. From this position if the ball bounces higher than anticipated you can push up on to the balls of your feet, and even off the ground, to get on top of the bounce of the ball.

> *'When driving on the back foot, your head should still be 'forward', and try to maintain a sideways-on position.'*
> **MARK BUTCHER**

Keeping your hands high is a very important facet of this shot, as this is essential in keeping the ball down. You are playing back because you are expecting the ball to bounce relatively high, so it is essential that the hands are high above the ball, allowing the bat to remain vertical, with the handle in front of the blade on ball contact. Similarly to the on drive, a good tip is to try to hit a two, and you will probably time a four. It is vital to keep your shape.

> **Note for coaches**
> Look out for players moving straight on to the ball of their back foot. It is very hard to keep balanced and batters tend to 'fall back' on to their heel, which takes their body weight away from the ball towards the leg side. Try to encourage young players to get into the habit of moving 'back and across', so that when the ball is hit you cannot see the stumps because their pads are covering them totally, having successfully moved into the correct position.

A good starting point for back-foot drives, defence and leg-side work off the hip is to get your back foot in line with off stump, ideally moving backwards as well as over to the off stump, back and across.

This position ensures that your head is going towards the ball for deliveries outside off stump, improving the drive, that your head and body are in a solid position behind the ball when defending, and that it is easier to open up the body to work off the hip into the leg side. The step back towards the stumps gives you extra time to play the shot.

The back-foot defence and work off the hip are detailed later in this chapter.

It is important as you move back and across that the front shoulder remains side-on to the ball and that it is dipped to assist in taking the bat back to create extra power in the shot. As you initiate the downswing to hit the ball, most players will slide their left foot towards their right foot to help stay side-on, to remain balanced and to ensure that their head and body weight are still and balanced. It is important that as you step back towards the stumps, you keep your head forward, tucked into your left shoulder, with your weight on your back leg so you can stay upright and not fall backwards. Remember to keep your back foot parallel to the crease whenever possible.

It is critical that you let the ball come to you and play late, ensuring the ball is kept down, and maximum power is attained in the shot. You should aim to make contact beneath your head, in line with your right leg.

A full follow-through or check drive follow-through are personal preference, but the same rule of thumb applies – if you were to let go of the bat after playing the shot, would it finish up where you want the ball to go?

The faster the bowler, the harder it is to create time to execute your footwork. Some players will simply push off their front foot to transfer weight on to the back foot to give themselves time. As long as you can achieve a solid base and a still head you will have a great chance of connecting with the ball. Remember, to play forward you have to load up your back foot to push you forward, and to play on the back foot, you have to load up your front foot to push you backwards.

Cut shot and back-foot ramp

If a back-of-a-length ball is too wide to play with a straight bat, you may still be able to attack the ball in the form of a cut shot. Where the ball is shorter with higher bounce, the ramp shot can be played, where the ball can be deflected up and over the slip cordon.

We will look at the wider balls first. Here it is important to get your head as close to the ball as possible, so to achieve this your back foot needs to move back and across beyond the width of the stumps.

Cut shot sequence.

Ramp shot sequence.

Late cut shot sequence.

Your right foot should be parallel with the crease, pointing towards point. Your knee should be bent to achieve a base, and your head as close to the ball as possible. Think of it like a front-foot drive position but on your back foot. As you step across, lift the bat back round your back ready to attack the ball. There is no need to slide your front foot across for this shot, the body can remain open.

You now have three options. The first is to make contact slightly in front of your right leg, hitting the ball in front of square in the cover region. The second is to make contact in line with your right leg, hitting the ball square or towards backward point. The third option is to make contact after the ball has gone past the line of your right leg, guiding the ball through the third-man region. This is often referred to as a 'late cut'. Your decision will be based on tactical considerations, influenced by the pace of the bowler, the pace and bounce of the pitch, the field that is set and where your own personal strengths lie. The sequence below shows the varying contact points:

Late cut. Cut. Ramp.

When initially practising this shot, start with making contact in line with your right leg and punching the ball square of the wicket using the pace of the ball to give you power. It is important that as you make contact with the ball that it is a 'punch' with the right hand, not a swat and that you 'roll' the wrists on contact to keep the ball down. If you achieve a punch the bat should naturally finish on the right shoulder. If yours is more of a swat, your bat will not finish on your left shoulder, it will be lower down your body.

Remember, as this is a back-foot shot, it is assumed that the ball will bounce quite high. Therefore, it is essential that your hands are high as you commence the downswing on to the ball. Together with the roll of the wrists, this will ensure the ball is kept down. If after pitching the ball bounces chest height or higher, it can become difficult to keep down. Therefore, instead of trying to keep the ball down, another option is to go up and over the fielders. This can be a safe option if practised regularly. It is essential that, just prior to ball contact, the weight is shifted back towards the front foot, enabling the body weight and momentum to add power to the shot.

The cut shot can also be played close to the body, to balls bouncing chest high or above. Here you can use the splice of the bat, the part of the bat closer to the bat handle, to make contact with the ball. The bat is still quite strong in this area, so if you use the pace of the ball to your advantage, you can still gain power in the shot.

The other option for these high-bouncing balls just outside off stump is to play a back-foot ramp shot over the wicketkeeper or slips. As with a late cut, contact is made after it has passed your right leg, and the bat is placed at an angle so that as the ball hits the bat it is guided over the slips and wicketkeeper. The bat is held so that the handle is lower than the blade at point of contact, forming a ramp to elevate the ball over the fielders. As with any shot it is important to keep the head watching the ball closely all the way on to the bat. To get full value for this shot it can only really be played to fast bowlers, where there is enough pace to ensure the ball carries over the wicketkeeper and fielders.

Work to leg off the back foot

This shot is ideally played to a ball pitching short of a length, bouncing between mid-thigh and stomach height, although it is often played to a ball getting up into the rib cage area. This shot is an important one to add to your repertoire because it opens up the leg side for scoring, where there are often fewer fielders. It also allows you to rotate the strike on a regular basis, keeping the scoreboard ticking over. The bowler becomes frustrated every time they stray off line, allowing you to score off more balls, which subsequently adds more pressure on them to put the ball in the area on and around off stump, otherwise known as the 'corridor of uncertainty'.

Similarly with the back-foot drive, your back foot should go both back and across towards off stump, but this time do not bring your left foot towards it. Ensure that the back foot has turned into a slightly open position, allowing the hips and body to be open when contacting the ball, as in these photos:

Dip the head and front shoulder to help keep your weight over the ball, ensuring it is kept down. The ball should be hit as late as possible, or close to you, literally taking it off your thigh pad. When starting out practising this shot do not look to add power, simply get the feel of the ball hitting the bat just before it is about to hit your thigh pad or body. As you are about to make contact, slide your front foot back towards the stumps so that you open up further, allowing the bat to access the ball. You should be pivoting around your back leg. Look to use the pace of the ball, whether seam or spin. You will regularly get singles or twos this way, making contact regularly. Your target area for scoring is just in front of square leg, around to fine leg.

Once you get adept at this shot, you can progress to adding more power by incorporating a punch of the bottom hand. This can allow you to access a greater scoring area in front of square on the leg side, as well as hitting the ball to the boundary. It is vital that the contact area is still below your head, just before it hits your thigh pad or body, guaranteeing you control the shot and keep it down. The side-on sequence below highlights the key points throughout the shot:

Pull and hook shots

The pull shot is played to a short ball that is usually bouncing stomach high or above. It is a horizontal bat shot, played to balls outside off stump, in line with the stumps, or even slightly down the leg side. For balls pitched outside off stump and in line with the stumps, your target hitting area is in front of square leg, and if down the leg side, the ball can be hit behind square leg.

When facing quick bowlers it is rare to have enough time to step backwards towards the stumps. You should aim to transfer weight back though, but keep your head forward, in a still and balanced position. If you have a strong base, with your head still, you will increase your chance of making regular powerful contact with the ball.

Hook shot.

Hook shot.

Pull shot.

As you are targeting an area in front of square do not slide your front foot back or away to the leg side. Aim to keep a side-on position throughout the shot with a controlled swing of the bat. As the shot is completed, it helps if you finish with your chest facing the direction the ball has been hit as this ensures that your shoulders were engaged fully in the hitting process. Ideally the bat should be lifted high as the ball gets to you so that you have the bat parallel with the height of the ball, which will help you keep the ball down. Rolling your wrists on contact will also reinforce this. As you improve, you can experiment with having a lower backswing and come up from underneath the ball to gain elevation to hit over the infield and potentially over the boundary.

The hook shot is almost identical to the pull, but usually played to a higher bouncing ball, heading down the leg side of the stumps, past your left ear. You are simply helping it round the corner, anywhere behind square leg. This time your left foot can slide back to open up the body as you make contact.

With both shots it is vital you keep watching the ball at all times. Also, once the ball gets further away from your body and head, the greater risk there is in playing the shot. If it is too high, above the eyeline, it becomes hard to keep the ball down and control it. Similarly, if the ball is beyond your body width down the leg side, and you play the hook incorrectly, it can result in a catch off your glove to the wicketkeeper.

With both shots, if you need to gain more time but are struggling to do this with footwork, then bring your elbows in as you contact the ball rather than having the arms locked straight out in front of you. 'Short-arm' pull shots can still generate plenty of power and give you control of the swing of the bat. When facing very quick bowling, you may find that these shots just become a matter of reaction and instinct rather than a focus on technique. As long as there was a successful outcome to the shot, or leave, you can continue with your innings, taking on learning to the next delivery.

Note for coaches

A good practice drill for the pull and hook is to kneel on one knee, where the ball would pitch, and throw underarm balls, hard or soft, into the hitting area. Ask the batter to simply keep a solid base, transferring weight on to the back foot, remaining as still as they can as they make contact, keeping their head forward, intensely watching the ball on to the bat. Most errors occur in this shot when the player takes their head and weight back too far, losing balance and a strong head position, thus minimising their ability to keep watching the ball closely.

Coming out of your crease to hit the ball

'The most important aspect when coming down the wicket is QUICK FEET. This gets you to the pitch of the ball as quickly as you possibly can, so you are not rushed in the shot.'
BEN DUCKETT

It is very common when playing both spin and seam bowling, particularly in the shorter forms of the game, for batters to use their feet to come down the pitch towards the ball. It will almost certainly be premeditated, therefore it is important to get the timing correct so that you do not come down too early. If you do, the bowler has advanced warning of your intentions and can therefore alter their delivery accordingly. Conversely, if your advancement is too late, you will be unable to get to the pitch of the ball, which could have dire consequences. Most batters come down the wicket to play a form of drive, either along the ground or over the top, using the forward momentum to add power to the shot.

Other shots are possible, even pull shots. This can occur when a fast bowler puts in a short ball, having seen the batter advancing early down the pitch. It can also happen if you misjudge your premeditated movement down the pitch!

We will focus on the technique for coming down the wicket to drive. You are simply using your feet to turn a good length ball into a half-volley or full toss, enabling you to attack it with a drive shot. The sequence is literally MOVE-STOP-HIT.

When first practising this shot, think about your first movement being your head and front shoulder going towards where the ball is coming from. This allows you to retain a side-on shape, keeping your head and eyes going towards the ball. It is important that your knees remain bent, so that the head is kept in a level, horizontal plane, not bobbing up and down. This will enable you to fully watch the ball, not having to continuously refocus as your head keeps altering its viewing height.

Note for coaches

It is common for batters to move their back foot forward first, but if a player is often falling short of reaching the pitch of the ball, encourage them to take the front foot forward first. Another common feature is for batters to 'stand up' as they come down the wicket. Encourage them to stay low, keep a side-on shape, and although the body is moving, see if they can keep their head as still as possible.

After this initial first front-foot movement, your back foot will naturally join up with your front foot as in this photo:

Try not to bring your back leg behind your front foot, so they cross over. This is not a good balanced position and it is harder to push on from there with your next stride towards the ball. However, for more advanced players this is an option for opening up the off side of the ground.

Your next stride, pushing forward off your back leg, will be towards the line of the ball, but if it is not quite where you anticipated it would be, you will have to adjust accordingly. If you have kept your head level with bent knees throughout the movement, you should now be in a perfect position to drive the ball with the technique described earlier in this chapter. If you can hit the shot from a relatively stationary position, you massively increase your chances of hitting the ball powerfully. If your base is unstable, you will find the power and control reduce drastically. Look at televised matches. Where the batters' bases are stable, the ball disappears into the crowd. Where they are unstable, the batter is invariably dismissed. Remember MOVE-STOP-HIT! This principle actually applies to every shot you ever play when batting, albeit the STOP may only be evident for an instant! Young players respond well to the analogy of a car accelerating from standstill, then slamming on its brakes!

However, if you have not managed to get the ball on the half-volley or full toss, you still need to play the ball on its merits. So, having come down the pitch, if you have now accidentally turned the ball into a good-length delivery, you still need to play a good defensive shot or attempt to work a single. Just because you have come down the wicket does not mean you have to attack that delivery.

Further detail and discussion on using your feet is discussed in Chapter 7.

Sweep shots

'The execution of sweep shots varies so wildly these days but, generally, a low base with the back knee on the ground is helpful. In the absence of that, watch the ball hard!'
MARK BUTCHER

There are several types of sweep shot, with roughly three each side of the wicket. Sweeps are mainly played to spin bowlers but are equally productive to seam bowlers too. A sweep is often a premeditated shot, where the batter decides to play the shot before the bowler releases the ball. When the shot is played on instinct, it is usually when the ball is delivered down the leg side and the batter goes with the ball to sweep it behind square.

The sweep shot, whether played conventionally or reversed, is a great scoring option to a good-length ball, one that you would usually be playing a forward defensive shot to. It can be played 'hard', where you are trying to hit the ball for four, or 'softly', when you are simply looking to get the ball into a gap or taking runs to a fielder sweeping on the boundary. It is a great strike-rotation shot.

A strong back leg kneeling position is recommended for most sweep shots, and a high to low downswing is preferable for keeping the ball down. To attain a balanced position, it is advisable to go towards the ball as straight as possible, as if replicating a lunge. The widest part of your body should be your shoulders. If, however, you approach the ball at an angle, your body profile could increase to the distance from the right shoulder to the ankle of your back foot. Add to this the weight of your bat reaching out in its backswing and you make an inherently unstable base, possibly culminating in missing the ball and falling over.

An interesting question is: if you played six forward defensives, could you have played six sweep shots?

We will look at six types of sweep shot:

1. Fine or paddle sweep
2. Orthodox sweep
3. Slog sweep
4. Fine reverse sweep
5. Orthodox reverse sweep
6. Slog reverse sweep

Fine or paddle sweep

A fine sweep is nearly always premeditated, where you are looking to get the ball behind square on the leg side. To hit that part of the field you will need to position your feet so they are in line with the ball. It can be played to a full-length, half-volley or full-toss delivery. The important technical aspects are to get into position early, with a good stride out with your front foot, the bat out in front of the pad, with your arms fully extended.

The photos above show the length of the front-foot stride and how far forward and low the head position is, enabling you to watch the ball all the way on to the bat. There is no backswing, you simply allow the ball to hit the bat and skim off the face. The pace of the ball will dictate how fast it travels after hitting it. You can generate more power by getting further across the off side of the crease so the ball is beyond your eyeline and your front pad. This has greater risk, because if you miss it your stumps are likely to be exposed. However, the reward is more power in the shot.

Orthodox sweep

Once again, the orthodox sweep is often premeditated or played on instinct to a ball travelling down the leg side. When premeditated it is important to get your front pad covering your stumps so that if you miss the ball it hits your front pad and not the stumps. The front foot and body position are very similar to the fine sweep except this time you will be taking the bat back to create a backswing. Once again, kneeling down on the back-leg knee is highly recommended for stability. As with any attacking shot, a solid base with a still head is vital.

Because of the front-foot position and backswing/follow-through direction, the ball will now travel fairly square on the leg side. Control of the bat swing is dependent on how much power you look to generate and, as in the pull or hook shots, you can roll the wrists and control the angle of the bat face to keep the ball down. Commonly a batter will open the bat face slightly to get the ball up into the air to clear fielders. Rolling the wrists is a safer option, because even if the ball hits near the toe or splice of the bat, not being hit as cleanly, at least the ball will stay down and not go in the air.

Slog sweep

It is important to understand that, although called a slog sweep, the shot is not a cross-batted slog. It is an attacking sweep shot that you are trying to hit in front of square, usually over the midwicket area. Like any other attacking shot it is best played with control, through a stable base and a strong head position, watching the ball hard. There is one major difference to the orthodox sweep, and that is in the position of the front foot, which now moves inside the line of the ball, usually on or outside leg stump. By opening up the hips and clearing the body, a better body shape is created to get the ball over or through midwicket.

Fine reverse sweep

For the fine reverse sweep, you are now looking to get the ball well behind square on the off side of the pitch. Once again the shot is usually premeditated and should be played in a similar fashion to the fine sweep, except now the wrists are rolled so that the bat face is angled off side and the ball can run off the face of the bat towards the third-man area. Unlike the other two reverse sweeps, this type of reverse sweep can be easier to play if you step forward with your front foot rather than your back foot. Playing reverse sweeps can be a very individual thing. Whether a batter reverses their hands or their feet is totally up to the individual, as what works for one might not work for another. It pays to experiment, trying all methods until you are confident in playing the shot successfully your way.

Orthodox and reverse slog sweep

For both the orthodox reverse sweep and reverse slog sweep, it is best to switch your body round and bring your back foot into the forward front-foot position, but both can be played with the front foot stepping forward.

Position the foot in line with the ball to hit it square towards point, or inside the line of the ball to hit towards or over extra cover. As with any other sweep, try to get your head low and towards the ball, as this will increase the chance of striking it cleanly. You will need a strong backswing to generate power, but here the bat goes back and round your left shoulder.

Reverse sweep reverse feet

Reverse sweep normal feet

Reverse sweep normal feet

Slog reverse sweep reverse feet.

Note for coaches

With all premeditated sweep shots it is important that batters have a 'plan B'. If the ball is not the right length or line, they need to adjust the shot in some way to hit the ball in a controlled manner. It is almost impossible to resort to a completely different shot, as the batter is already committed, so a safe version of it must be found. This is often achieved by not trying to hit the ball too hard, just concentrating on hitting it somehow.

To negate the possibility of being stumped by the wicketkeeper, it is essential that you do not drag your back foot out of the crease when playing any sweep shots, so a solid and stable base is essential. A batter should be discouraged from coming down the pitch, then attempting to play a sweep shot. There is a very high possibility that they will miss the ball and be stumped.

Ramp shots

'Head position is crucial when setting yourself to play a ramp shot. As soon as you lift your head or don't get in line with the ball, the harder it is. Practise this. Lots of people lift their head or they don't get in line. If you do this you are far more likely to miss it. Watch the best who do it (Jos Buttler); his head is always in line with the ball.'
BEN DUCKETT

A ramp shot is played mainly to seam bowlers, where there is pace on the ball to work with. It is nearly always premeditated and used to hit the ball with power, as these shots can often go for six against a quick bowler, in a V between third man and fine leg.

Like any other attacking shot, a strong base combined with a still head can lead to a higher success rate of execution. Although you move your body into position prior to the bowler releasing the ball, it is essential to be in position, with your head totally still, just before release. England batsmen Jos Buttler and Ben Stokes are two of the world's best exponents of this shot. It is worth viewing clips of them playing this shot, to see the technical points inherent in their execution.

This photo shows the ideal body position prior to ball release:

You will see the player is chest-on with bent knees and the head forward, in line with and looking at the ball. The bat is out in front of him at an angle, handle above blade, so that when the ball hits it will go upwards. If the ball is delivered straight at you, you need to move inside or outside the line of the ball, depending on whether you are attempting to hit off side or leg side. This photo sequence depicts a batsman moving outside the line to angle the ball towards the fine-leg region.

Note that the bottom hand can add some extra power on contact.

Note for coaches

This can be a difficult shot for young players to practise as it needs pace on the ball. Underarm full-toss tennis ball feeds are a safe option if practising this for the first time. If using a bowling machine, light orange balls are the best initially, as the batter has the pace to work with, but the ball will not hurt much if they miss it, or top edge the ball into their body or helmet.

Front-foot defence

'You have got to have a good defence to bat for long periods of time. You have to learn to have a good defence so you don't get out and then you can still attack when the right ball comes along. Like Liverpool – they have a great goalkeeper and centre-back – they have to have a good defence. But it doesn't mean you have to play defensively.'
SIR GEOFFREY BOYCOTT

Although the front- and back-foot defence have been left until later in this chapter, it is important to emphasise how vital these shots are to master, because whichever format you play there will be deliveries that you simply cannot attack. In this instance, you will need to defend to make sure that you do not get out, remaining at the crease to face the next ball. The higher the level of cricket you play, the more regularly bowlers will deliver the ball into these areas.

The stronger your defence, including leaving balls, the longer your innings will be, and you will score more runs when the conditions favour the bowling team. Similarly to the frustration felt by a bowler when a bad ball is hit for four, so it is when a batter consistently defends their best deliveries. The more frustrated they become the more likely they are to lose patience and bowl loose balls.

After scoring over a thousand runs in a calendar year, including a triple hundred in a Test match, the former New Zealand captain Brendon McCullum attributed this sustained success to improvements in his defensive game. He felt that with a stronger, trusted defence he did not have to attack the bowling as often and could therefore bat with less risk attached to his innings. There have not been many better attacking batters in the history of the game than Brendon McCullum, but he became a more consistent run scorer once he improved his defence.

The forward defence is usually played to a good length ball that you judge will be hitting the stumps. As with the front-foot drive it should be the head and shoulder that lead the way into the shot, with your front foot following shortly after. The movement is forward and generally across. The stride should be comfortable, but you may want to consider a bigger stride if there is a lot of seam movement in the pitch. In most cases, the bottom half of the body (legs and feet) make exactly the same shape in defence as they do in attack. The only real difference is the top half, which decelerates for a defensive shot until stopping, while for an attacking shot, the top half accelerates through to completion of the follow-through.

On contact with the ball the bat should be under your head and at an angle so the ball will go down into the ground. Once again it is good to remember the simple theory: bat handle in front of blade on contact keeps the ball down. To help this it is important to relax both elbows so that the arms are not straight, enabling you to get your hands high to get on top of the bounce. Your bat should not be touching the ground. Higher hands make it easier to create the angle of the bat to get the ball to ground as well as counter any high bounce and protect your fingers. You should be able to see the number 9 created by your bat, hands, arms and shoulders.

Most batters defend the ball just in front of the line of their pads, rather than alongside it. However, there should not be a gap between bat and pad for the ball to go through. If the ball does come into you off the seam and misses the bat, it should be hitting your front pad. This protects your stumps, so if you have executed a positive stride into the ball, hopefully you will have got outside the line of off stump, reducing the possibility of an lbw decision.

Note in the photo that the batsman has the full face of the bat to the ball, it is not angled in any way. The straighter the bat, the fuller the face you present to the ball, the less you will edge or miss it.

The final point is to have both hands as relaxed as possible when gripping the bat, when contact with the ball is made. The top hand is fully gripping the bat handle, and the bottom hand only grips it with the thumb and first two fingers. This also helps to keep the ball down and takes pace off it, so if you were to outside-edge the delivery, there is less chance of it carrying through to be caught behind the wicket.

Back-foot defence

A back-foot defensive shot should be played to a back-of-a-length delivery that is in line with the stumps. Similarly to the back-foot drive, your right foot should move back and across towards the off stump. Your head and shoulder should remain dipped and forward so that you can keep the ball down on contact. Once again, remember to keep the handle of the bat in front of the blade if you want to keep the ball down. You should be able to take the weight of your body on your back foot. If you keep your head forward you will not overbalance. It is vital to keep your back foot parallel to the crease to ensure you do not get into a squared-up position, hence a less stable base. Your front foot can slide towards the back foot to help keep you side-on as the bat comes down towards the ball.

One of the reasons batters can often outside-edge a back-foot defensive shot, is they do not slide the front foot alongside their back foot, so as their bat comes down it moves across their body instead of coming down straight. It is possible to be slightly more open-chested for this shot, as this can help get your hands higher to cover any steep bounce, but it is vital that the bat is held in line with the ball if you use this method. To begin with, try to keep as side-on to the ball as possible.

As with the front-foot defence, relaxed elbows and hands are important so you can play high and get the ball to ground easily. Once again, a full face is presented so the ball is hit straight back down the pitch. Similarly to the front-foot defence, you should be able to see the number 9 created by your bat, hands, arms and shoulders. A successful way of coaching young players to get their hands high is to ask them to 'smell their gloves'. This simple comment immediately gets them to put their gloves near their face, producing high hands, with a straight bat. The top hand is fully gripping the bat handle, and the bottom hand only grips it with the thumb and first two fingers. Another good instruction is to ask them to hide their bottom forearm and elbow behind the bat.

If the match situation dictates that you need to score off as many balls as possible, you can use your wrists to open the face to these deliveries, for both your front- and back-foot defensive shots, attempting to find a gap to get a single. Running the ball to third man is discussed later in this chapter.

Leaving the ball

'The leave is one of your shots. It is a profitable shot in the long run to you as it

tells the bowler you know where your off stump is and tells him you know what you are doing. Like any other shot – you have to practise it to get good at it.'
GRAHAM GOOCH

If you are a young player just starting out, it may be hard to understand the necessity to sometimes leave the ball, offering no shot at all, allowing it to travel through to the wicketkeeper. However, to become an established run scorer it will become much more significant the older you get and the higher level of cricket you play.

At the time of writing, two Australians, Steve Smith and Marnus Labuschagne, have been dominating Test match cricket, scoring big hundreds regularly. In his first 14 tests Labuschagne scored nearly 1,500 runs with four hundreds and eight fifties. At the time of writing, he is averaging over 63. Steve Smith averages the same over 73 Test matches. Both Smith and Labuschagne have many scoring shots but they also have the best defensive techniques. For all his idiosyncrasies pre-delivery, Smith plays very straight in defence with 'soft hands'. Both of these batsmen make excellent decisions about whether they need to play at a ball or not. They are brilliant leavers of the ball. They leave so well that bowlers lose patience and bowl straighter to make them play. This opens up scoring opportunities on the leg side, where both batsmen are very strong. It is a simple game plan but highly effective. You will not see many leave shots on a highlights package of these two batsmen, so you will have to watch them live to study their defence and leave techniques.

A front-foot leave is usually played to a ball pitching on a good length, one that you judge will not be hitting the stumps. It is also a ball that would be dangerous to play at, whether defending or attacking, with the distinct possibility that you may edge a catch behind the wicket, so it is safer to let it go through to the keeper.

While you are learning to judge the line for a leave, these two questions may help you:

1. As the ball reaches you would it be in line with your head or going past your right ear?
2. Is the ball close enough to defend straight back up the pitch?

The first can apply to both an inswing or outswing bowler, but it is slightly more challenging assessing inswing bowlers. If you think it would go past your right ear, then it is safe to leave. If in line with your head, you need to play.

The second applies if the ball is so wide that you can no longer defend straight, but have to defend more towards cover or extra cover. The ball, therefore, is wide enough to safely leave. If it is close enough for you to have to hit it straight, then you have to play it.

'In terms of leaving the ball, if it was missing the right-hand side of my head it's missing off. If it was missing the other side of my head it's going down leg side and I could work to leg.'
GRAHAM GOOCH

Many batters now take a middle-and-off guard to have a better understanding of where their off stump is and knowing that if the ball is beyond their eyeline, then it is wide enough to let go.

There are three main ways of leaving the ball:

1. Get your hands high above your head
2. Take your hands behind your body
3. Bring the bat across the front of your body

Hands high.

Hands behind.

The first two methods can be used when you see the ball well and make an early decision to leave the ball, not play at it. The reason batters get their hands high or behind their body is to make sure that if there is an unusually high bounce, it does not hit the bat or glove, risking giving a catch. The third method is often used when a batter has initially committed to playing a defensive shot but then decides they should leave the ball, but it is too late to lift the bat up above or behind the body. In this situation the quickest and safest option is to take the bat across in front of the body instead.

The same three methods can be used on the back foot as in these photos:

Hands high.

Hands behind.

Hands low.

The same rules apply regarding how to judge the shot, but there is an extra option for a back-foot leave. The ball can again be left, the decision made dependent on the height of its bounce. You can leave dead straight balls if you are certain they will go over the top of the stumps. This is called 'leaving on length'.

You must be certain that there is consistently high bounce in the wicket for you to adopt this method of leaving.

Ducking under a bouncer.

Swaying away from a bouncer.

Running the ball to third man – front- and back-foot

This is not a shot you will play too often when the ball is new or when there are slips and gully in place, but it is a good option when the match situation dictates rotating the strike to keep the scoreboard ticking over. It is played to balls of a good length, outside off stump, balls that would normally be left alone in longer forms of the game.

There are two main considerations for good execution:

1. The angle of the bat face on contact
2. Where you make contact with the ball

Whether playing off your front or back foot, you will need to open the bat face so it is angled towards cover, so that the ball deflects down to the third-man area. The slower the bowling, the bigger the angle you will need to create. Contact is later than you would normally play the ball defensively.

Where you may make contact alongside or in front of your front pad for a forward defensive, to get the ball to third man it helps to play the ball further back in line with your abdomen or even back leg.

New Zealand's great batsman, Kane Williamson, and England's Joe Root are two fine players of this shot off both front and back foot. These two photos show the open face of the bat and the late contact area:

Front foot.

Back foot.

Playing the yorker

The yorker is a very dangerous delivery, taking many wickets and also providing many dot balls for the bowlers. It describes a delivery aimed at the crease line, generally around the length where the batter's feet are positioned. It is extremely painful if one of these deliveries hits your toes.

Some players are more vulnerable to yorkers than others. The taller you are and the higher your backlift, the more vulnerable and susceptible you are to being dismissed by this delivery, with the ball getting under your bat and hitting the stumps. The advice on playing the yorker is quite simple: get your bat down on to the ground and ball as quickly as possible, while trying to get your feet out of the way. Hitting the ball is best achieved by trying to keep the bat as straight and wide as possible. This can often make the playing of the ball look ungainly, but that is unimportant. What matters is getting some bat on it so it does not cannon into the stumps.

It is worth taking a look at archive material of great exponents of the yorker, bowlers such as Waqar Younis, Shoaib Akhtar, Joel Garner, Curtly Ambrose, to name but a few.

In the next chapter we discuss options for attempting to score off bowlers bowling consistent yorkers.

Batting wagon wheel

Opposite is a copy of an ECB batting wagon wheel assessment sheet. This is a very useful method of assessing the current technical, tactical, physical and mental status of a batter.

It can be completed by the batter and their coach, and a comparison made between the two. The sheet identifies key strengths and areas for improvement. This will then lead to an individual development plan, discussed and formulated by both individuals, based on both short-term and long-term development goals. It can be updated on a regular basis to assess progress.

The concentric circles are numbered 1–10 (1 = weak; 10 = excellent). Each segment is shaded in to reflect the current evaluated skill level.

BATTING

CRICKETER:	DATE:
SQUAD:	COACH:

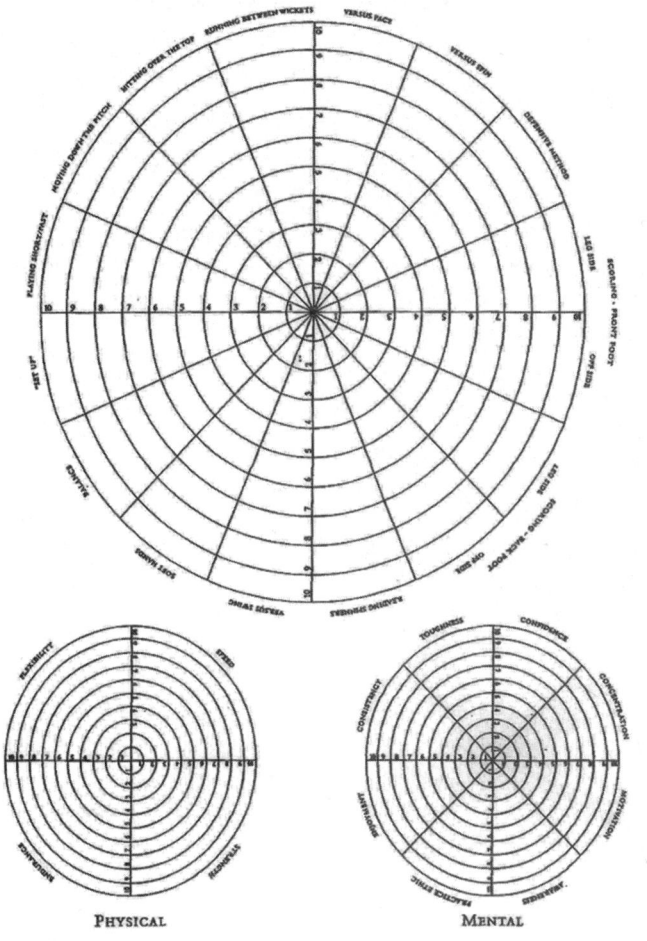

PHYSICAL

MENTAL

THREE
THE SHOTS – TACTICAL ASPECTS

> 'Get to know the conditions and how to play in different conditions. Conditions dictate how you play and what shots you can execute safely. Don't play the same way every time – you need to be adaptable.'
>
> **GRAHAM GOOCH**

Once the technical aspects of each shot are understood, it is also important to be aware of the tactical aspects of each shot, as this will determine your decision-making regarding shot selection. All of the following will influence your shot selection:

- Your own personal strengths
- How much the ball is moving in the air
- How much the ball has been moving off the pitch
- The bounce and pace of the pitch
- The field that is set
- The current match situation
- Your role within the team
- The dimensions of the ground
- The weather

We will initially attend to the first four points. If you have gone through all the shots in the previous chapter, hopefully you managed to identify the shots that come easier or more naturally to you, and shots that will need further work and development. The ones you feel currently confident in playing on a regular basis are the ones you should focus on playing in matches, and only play the others once you have mastered them. It is a similar principle to bowlers who may naturally bowl an outswinger really well but are still developing an inswinger or off-cutter. They would not use either in a match until it is a reliable alternative to their outswinging stock ball.

The importance of mindset in this area is discussed in Chapter 6.

> *'You need to be able to make quick assessments
> on the conditions and play accordingly.'*
> **MARK BUTCHER**

Front-foot drives

In the previous chapter the ideal length for a drive was identified as a half-volley or full toss. The closer the pitch of the ball is to you, the less distance the ball has to move off the seam before making contact with the bat, making it easier to hit and execute the shot safely and effectively. However, lesser movement in the air and off the pitch will provide a larger area in which you can play a drive shot to balls that are shorter than half-volley length. This is termed 'driving on the up'.

The more movement off the pitch or in the air, the greater the risk in any attacking shot, so the drive is no different. If the ball is swinging away from your bat, there are slip fielders in place and the wicket has good bounce in it, then you will need to be more precise in judging the length of a half-volley, to eliminate the chance of edging the ball into the slip cordon. That is why in the longer game format you see many opening batters leave lots of balls outside their off stump. There is still enough time in the game to allow for dot balls. The bowler will then have to bowl closer to you to make you play.

If when facing inswing bowling, the ball pitches short of half-volley length, you risk leaving a gap between your bat and pad for the ball to get through or to find the inner edge, which can cause you to play on to the stumps.

With a swinging ball you can often predict where it will be once it reaches you, making it easier to execute your shot safely. When there is seam movement it is much harder, as the lateral deviation is on pitching, rather than earlier in the air and over a longer period. Once again, if there is pronounced seam movement, the closer to a half-volley length the ball will need to be to execute the drive. Suffice to say, the same applies if the ball is turning sharply for a spinner.

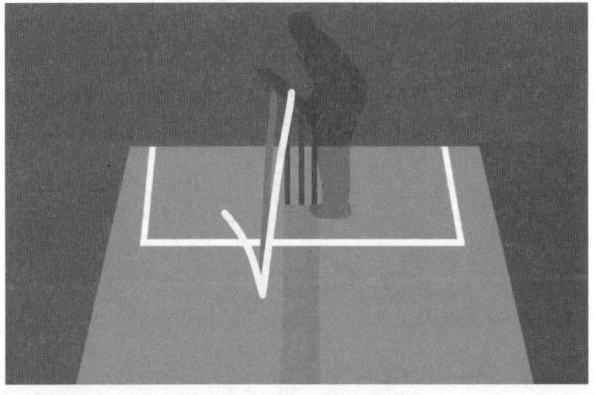

Driving a cricket ball is easier on a pitch that has good pace, with the ball coming on to the bat. This allows you to use the pace of the ball, using minimal effort and good timing to get power into your shots. If there is little swing or seam movement it also makes it easier to drive balls on the up, still keeping the ball down. On a slow wicket your area for safe contact is reduced. The closer it is to a half-volley length, the greater power you will get in the shot, with a good chance of keeping the ball down. The greatest danger on slow wickets is accidentally hitting the ball in the air. This must be taken into account when deciding your shot selection based on the length the ball pitched on.

Note for coaches

It is a good idea to regularly add playing medium-paced bowling to your sessions, challenging the batters to work with little pace on the ball. They have to be really disciplined in their judgement of length to execute a drive, and contact has to be right alongside the front foot, with the head over the ball to keep the ball down. Remember the simple relationship of the bat handle being in front of the blade to keep the ball down. If using a bowling machine, add varying amounts of swing to increase the difficulty level, and incorporate hitting over the top too.

There may be matches when you will not drive a ball at all, but it is such a good scoring option, no matter how much movement there can be for the bowlers.

Back-foot drives

When considering back-foot drives, the amount of seam movement is not as threatening because the ball has further to travel to reach the line of your body after pitching, when compared with the threat in playing front-foot shots. Playing on the back foot gives extra time to adjust and still execute the shot. Additionally, the ball usually swings less the shorter it is, and after pitching generally does not swing at all.

Tactically, your thoughts will be about the bounce of the pitch. If there is a high bounce you may consider playing a cut shot instead to get on top of the bounce, or go with the high bounce and go over the off-side field. If you commit to a back-foot drive on a high-bouncing pitch it can be difficult to find the middle of the bat and keep the ball down, and additional risks can come in the form of getting hit on the bat handle or gloves, both of which risk ballooning up a catch or getting a snick through to the keeper.

Slow pace in a pitch can also affect how you play a back-foot drive, not so much tactically but more technically, as you will need to be disciplined to play the ball late to keep the ball down. Very often on slow pitches, more pull shots are played, as the ball just sits up to be hit if bowled too short.

Cut shot and back-foot ramp

Similarly to the above, it is the bounce of the pitch that will be the predominant factor in determining your decision to execute these shots. These shots can be very effective on a high-bouncing pitch, therefore your main consideration will be if there is low or inconsistent bounce. On a low-bouncing pitch you should consider looking to play with a straight bat where possible, as it is easier to come down on the ball with a straight bat rather than a cross bat. This is essential on a wicket with inconsistent bounce. If you commit to playing a cut and the ball keeps low, you risk the bat ending up in neither a vertical nor horizontal orientation. With the bat at this approximate 45-degree angle, there is the distinct possibility that it could lead to edges on either side of the bat. 'Chop-ons' are very common on low- or inconsistently-bouncing wickets. This is a situation where the ball deflects off the inner face or inside edge of the bat and subsequently hits the stumps.

Work to leg off the back foot

Similarly to other back-foot shots, it is the pace and bounce of the pitch that will be the predominant factor in determining your decision to execute these shots. On slow wickets there is a danger of being through the shot too early, so it is critical that you retain your side-on position, combined with playing the ball as late as possible. Once again, ensure you play the ball with a vertical bat, turning the wrists on contact with the ball. Similarly, if there is outswing movement of the ball, retain your side-on position and refrain from opening up too early.

The shot also becomes challenging if there is high bounce off the wicket. If so, it is often better to be more aggressive and pull or hook with a horizontal bat. However, it is possible to ride the bounce, get your feet off the ground, and even take your bottom hand off the bat to attempt to the keep the ball down and work it into the leg side.

When facing off spin on a bouncy wicket, you may encounter a leg slip fielder. If this is the case, you often see batters leave these balls and allow it to hit their thigh pad or body. Remember to get your bat and gloves high out of the way of the ball.

Pull and hook shots

Similarly to the cut shot, it is the bounce of the pitch that will be the predominant factor in determining your decision to execute these shots. On a low-bouncing wicket it is very difficult to be consistent with your execution, and there is a high risk of bottom-edging the ball on to your stumps or getting clean bowled. You may be better off back-foot driving with a straight bat, defending or working to leg off the back foot. Equally there may be a challenge on a high-bouncing wicket, where if the ball is too high you may give a top-edge nick through to the keeper. Conversely, you may get a top edge that goes over everyone for four runs!

Coming out of your crease to hit the ball

Tactically there are additional reasons for a batter to come down the pitch that are not listed at the start of this chapter. A major benefit is to put the bowler off their length. This is mainly carried out against spin bowlers but can also be used against any accurate type of bowling. When the bowler is consistently landing the ball on a good length, on or around off stump, you have limited scoring options. By coming down the wicket you put doubt into the bowler's mind that you might do this regularly. They run up thinking about what you might do, rather than thinking what they will do. Even if you only do it once, you have added disruptive doubt into their mind, meaning they may lose their control of length and line, thus their effectiveness as a bowler.

There are a few factors to take into account when assessing the option of safely coming down the pitch. This could be a single sortie or multiple advances down the pitch. Things such as how much the ball is turning, moving off the seam or swinging, how much flight is on the ball, and the speed of the bowler need to be assessed. Is it safe to attack or safer to defend? Remember, you are using your feet to get nearer to the ball, turning it into a half-volley length or full toss. The more the ball is spinning, moving off the seam or swinging, the greater the challenge for positioning yourself on the correct line and length to safely execute the shot selected.

The position of the wicketkeeper is also a factor that has a big influence on your assessment for coming down the pitch. If the keeper is stood back, then the risk is minimal should you miss the ball while advancing down the wicket, as you probably have time to get back in. However, if the keeper is stood up, the risk in advancing down the pitch increases significantly. If you miss the ball while executing the shot, you are likely to be stumped. The risk increases greatly if the wicket is taking pronounced turn. Therefore, on such a wicket the safer option may be to sweep, either with the spin or into it. This may be a higher-percentage scoring option than using your feet to drive with a straight bat.

However, on a slow-paced wicket, coming down the wicket to drive may be the best option, as the added momentum of good footwork will enable more power to be added to the drives.

Sweep shots

The two main tactical elements to consider when assessing whether to play the sweep shot or not are:

1. How much the ball is turning
2. How much bounce is in the wicket

If there is little or no turn in the wicket, then straight-bat shots such as drives are a safer option. Using your feet and hitting over the top are also low-risk shots if executed correctly. If the bowler is bowling straight and the ball is skidding on, the biggest danger when playing the sweep is missing the ball and being out bowled or lbw. If the ball is turning a lot, playing straight-bat shots is more challenging, so the sweep is a good option. If the bowler wants to hit the stumps on a turning pitch, they will have to pitch the ball outside the line of the stumps. By playing the sweep, if you happen to miss the ball there is less chance of being given out lbw.

Which way the ball spins is not a tactical factor in terms of playing a sweep, but the field that is set will determine whether you go for a sweep to the leg side or a reverse sweep. When sweeping, play to your strengths. Go to your high success rate option firstly, before expanding sweep options later in your innings. You could also use this principle having manoeuvred fielders around through previous successful executions.

The amount of bounce in a wicket may also influence your decision to play a sweep or not, your particular choice of sweep shot should you do so, and how early in your innings you play it. Higher bounce risks a top edge and low bounce a drag on to the stumps. However, if this bounce is consistent and once you have a feel for the wicket, you should be able to execute effectively.

Ramp shots

The previous chapter highlighted how pace on the ball greatly helps with any ramp shots. Therefore, tactically, the pace of the bowler and the pace of the wicket will need to be assessed when deciding whether to play this shot. The field placing will also need evaluating. Often, a ramp is played when either fine leg or third man is up in the ring, so the ball can be lofted over their heads to the boundary. However, if either of those fielders are back on the boundary but set squarer, a fine ramp or skim is still a good option. On a slow wicket, or facing medium-pace bowling, this shot can be less effective as there is often not enough speed on the ball to get it over the fielder's head. There will be alternative higher-percentage run-scoring options to turn to.

Running the ball to third man – front and back foot

Once again, pace in the wicket and on the ball help this shot, but with third man back, the shot is still a good option to keep the strike rotating, picking up singles and twos. Even against slower bowlers and on slower pitches the ball can be deflected softly into this area either side of fielders to accumulate runs. Your main tactical considerations will be the match situation at the time and how much the ball is moving. With a moving ball and slips in place, this shot will be a higher-risk option because there is a greater chance of edging the ball to the keeper or slip cordon. If the scoring rate required at the time is not a priority, then tactically balls that you may attempt to run to third man can be left alone.

Front-foot and back-foot defence

How often you defend or leave the ball will be dependent on the game format, match situation and the amount the ball is moving. Similarly to drives, the more movement there is off the pitch or through the air, or if the pitch is slow, the safe driving pitching area reduces drastically. Therefore, you may be inclined to cautiously defend or leave more deliveries.

There is also an important psychological factor to take into consideration when the bowlers have a lot of assistance on offer. They are naturally under more pressure to take wickets, as it is expected by team-mates, captain and coach. So by surviving and accumulating runs with sensible, intelligent shot selection, a batter can turn the tables on the opposition, and redirect the course of play back into the batting side's favour. Therefore, if you can defend and leave well when conditions favour the bowlers they can become frustrated and bowl more loose balls to score from.

Similarly, if a batter is on a belter of a wicket on a sunny day, where the bounce is true and there is no seam movement and/or swing in the air, there is now an expectation to score runs. So, by accumulating runs with sensible, intelligent shot selection, a batter can drive home the advantage they have batting in those favourable conditions.

Field placings

It is vital that batters constantly check the field placings the bowlers have employed against them. When you first arrive at the wicket, your field-placing assessment will almost certainly tell you how the bowler bowls, what their game plan is and what the match situation currently is. On most occasions, there will always be a slightly more attacking field set to the new batter. These positions will be constantly changing as the match moves forward.

It is important to have good knowledge of the general fielding placements that different types of bowlers set, both for when they are attacking the batter to when they employ a more defensive field-placing option. By studying these field placings, you can plan in advance which shots may be successful against the field set for you when you are at the crease. You can also plan your options when fast run scoring is required. Remember, you should always try to set the fields you want and not bat to the fields the bowler wants.

Some typical field placements for the following bowlers are shown below, for both attacking and defensive situations. The bowlers are outswing seamers, inswing seamers, off-spinners, and leg-spinners.

Out Swing Bowling

Out Swing Bowler – Right-Handed Batter
Attacking Field

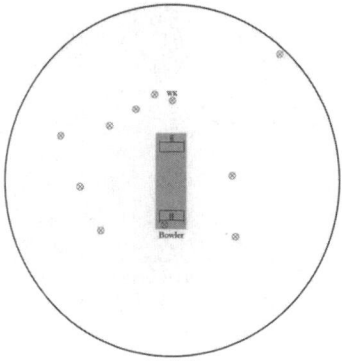

Out Swing Bowler – Right-hand Batter
Defensive Field

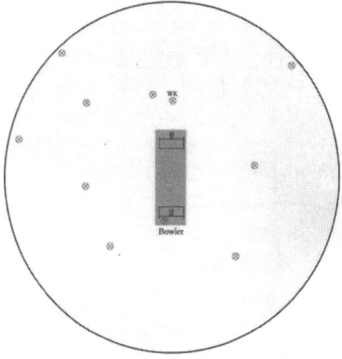

In Swing Bowling

In Swing Bowler – Right-Handed Batter
Attacking Field

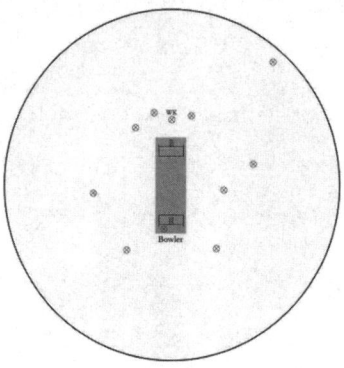

In Swing Bowler – Right-hand Batter
Defensive Field

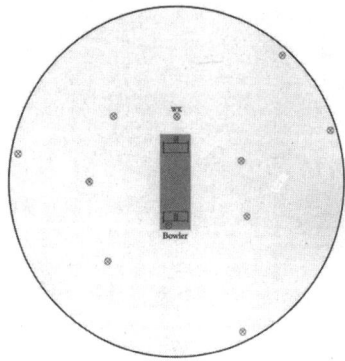

Off Spin Bowling

Off Spin Bowler – Right-Handed Batter
Attacking Field

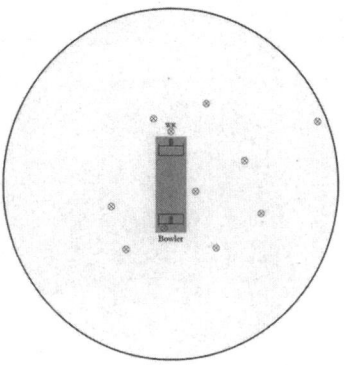

Off Spin Bowler – Right-hand Batter
Defensive Field

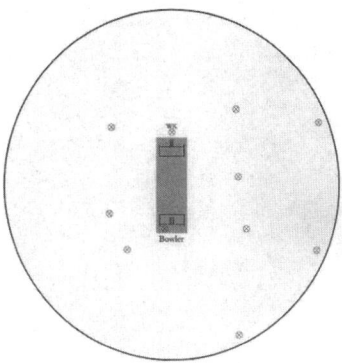

Leg Spin Bowling

Leg Spin Bowler – Right-Handed Batter
Attacking Field

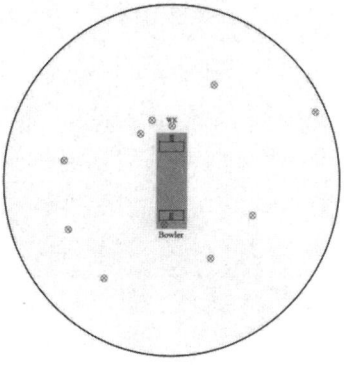

Leg Spin Bowler – Right-hand Batter
Defensive Field

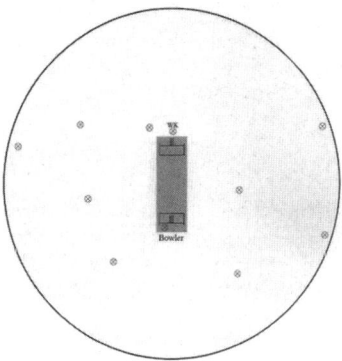

FOUR
FURTHER TACTICAL CONSIDERATIONS

> 'Alastair Cook had that priceless ability to know his own game early in his career. He scored his first Test century with just two shots – he knew how he could score runs.'
>
> GRAHAM GOOCH

In this chapter we explore some additional tactical aspects that can give you an edge when you are out in the middle batting: suggestions on what you can do pre-innings to assess conditions, to how you can correctly pace a run chase. Initially, the discussion will be about you, and what your personal batting strengths are.

Know your game

To be a consistent run scorer against different types of bowlers, pitch conditions and match situations, you need to develop an understanding of your own game and batting strengths. These will be unique to you, as no two batters are the same.

It can be very easy to make comparisons with other players, even finding yourself wishing you could do what they do. Analyse the particular skills they have that you do not and come up with a plan for adding that skill to your game. Remember, they are probably looking at you enviously, wishing they could be more like you!

For longer formats it is often the shots that you choose not to play as opposed to the ones that you do that will define your innings. The former England great, opening batsman Graham Gooch, said he only played three shots in Test match cricket, and he certainly ingrained that when he coached a young Alastair Cook. To the quick bowlers, Cook would cut and pull the short ball, work off his hip or pads, and occasionally drive through the off side or down the ground. It was a similar game plan against spin, especially when the ball was turning away from him. Added to this, of course, was sound defensive technique and accurate off stump line judgement.

Cook knew that this minimal selection of shots were his best ones, so he stuck rigidly to that game plan for 135 Test matches, never once being dropped from the team, and subsequently becoming England's greatest-ever run scorer in the process. Put simply, he knew his game and he had the mental discipline and self-belief to stick to it.

Of course, Cook also played ODI cricket for England and T20s. Here he had to expand his game beyond Test match self-imposed limitations, so your own game plan will have to be adaptable, responding to the format, match situation and the quality of the opposition.

Australian greats Allan Border and Steve Waugh became batting legends by also reducing their scoring options down to a minimal number of shots, coupled with an intense desire to succeed, a solid defence and an ability to concentrate for long periods. India's Rahul Dravid was another such batter.

The shots that brought Alastair Cook so much success may not be your own personal favourites, so think about this and try to identify your best scoring shots against different types of bowling. What are your best shots for picking up singles? What are your best shots for scoring boundaries? If you have to hit a good-length ball for six, where would you target? What is your own best/higher-percentage option? Only you can answer these questions, but if you are able to, you can build your game around that template. Undoubtedly this will come with experience and playing the game more and more, and with practice you will improve many aspects of your game, therefore possessing a long list of strengths to turn to in a match.

Pre-match and pre-innings
– reading a pitch and assessing bowlers

'For a T20 game, tactically you need to pre-plan who you feel you can take down and hit boundaries off before you've even walked to the crease. Mentally, don't panic, there is plenty of time in a T20. Give yourself a chance to get in.'
BEN DUCKETT

To give you an advantage before you even go out to face a ball, it is important that you assess the pitch pre-match. Additionally, the ground dimensions, position of wicket on the square, batter's eye view at each end, condition of surface (both wicket and outfield), and any cross-falls and gradients to the wicket and outfield can be assessed. The direction and strength of the wind should also be noted. Further help can be gained by looking at the ground on satellite photos, as this may give you helpful information before you arrive. The predominant wind direction in this country is from the south-west, so it is beneficial to assess the implications on your batting strategy if this is present on matchday. If the wind is strong, this may determine your tactics for attacking one particular boundary and not the opposite one.

Your ability to read a pitch will come with experience, so initially you will be reliant on more senior players or the coach to give some feedback in this regard. The hardness of the pitch will give you an indication on pace and bounce. The amount of grass present will indicate how much seam movement there may be. Moisture can also lead to seam and swing movement, and a very dry pitch is likely to take more turn.

A pitch that has lines and hollows of live green grass on it can be an indication that parts of it are lower than others and therefore there may be some variable bounce and pace to be aware of. Remember, live grass is green, dead grass is white. If there is a pronounced slope down the pitch, it may be greener at the lower end where the water may have collected. This could mean that the lower end of the pitch possesses more seam movement than the upper end. Some pitches can be cracked and have a crazy paving look to them. These cracks can open up as the game goes on, especially if it is a longer format game. The wider the cracks the more chance of variable bounce or sideways movement if the ball lands upon them.

Often in club cricket a pitch may not have covers, so if there has been rain leading up to the match, it will still have a lot of moisture in it and be quite soft. Therefore, the ball will sink into the surface on pitching. This will reduce its pace on to the bat and can also lead to more seam movement. How would you then look to counter that when at the wicket? Take a guard out of your crease? Look to get forward as much as possible to negate the seam movement? If the pitch is likely to be slow, should there be more time to play the short ball? So mentally you should be ready to put away the short ball, but be careful when driving because there is little pace on to the bat as well as seam movement. You may find yourself occasionally playing on used pitches, so it is worth assessing bowlers' footmarks and their implications on your batting strategy.

All of these pitch variations can influence your decisions concerning how you will combat them in a match. Areas such as where you take guard, out of your crease or deep in your crease, will need assessing. Will you look to get forward or back more than normal, or will straight or horizontal bat shots be good options early in your innings? The length to safely play a drive will need careful assessment. Conditions can also dictate how long you give yourself to 'get in' and determine the most suitable method of playing a long innings. The more consistent the pace and bounce, combined with minimal seam movement, the less time this will take and the more expansive your stroke play can be early in your innings.

Another area to assess in your pre-match inspection is the potential pace of the outfield. Inspecting the length of the grass and determining how firm the ground is will reveal this. The longer the grass and softer the ground, the slower the outfield will be. This may affect your game plan in terms of whether to drive the ball in the air or along the ground, but it will also affect running between the wickets. On a quick outfield, the ball will get to the fielders quicker, whether in the ring or on the boundary, which will affect your decisions on quick singles and taking two to the boundary riders.

These may require careful assessment, but you will get more value for shots that do pierce the inner fielders. A slower outfield will mean the ball reaches a boundary rider slower, so more twos may be possible. On extremely slow outfields, be aware of the dangers of looking for a two when hitting the ball through the infielders. The ball can slow up extremely quickly allowing the fielder to retrieve it faster than you anticipated. This can lead to ill-judged run outs. The other consideration here is to ensure you are prepared to run hard and build your innings with runs accumulated, rather than boundaries, which are going to be harder to come by.

Of course, if you bat in the middle order you will usually have time to assess the conditions from the sidelines, noting pace, seam and spin movement. Which lengths are easier to score off, and which ones are not? What the carry is like to the wicketkeeper will indicate bounce, and how far back they are indicates the pace. If you can station yourself at a sightscreen for a few deliveries you will be able to observe the swing, seam and spin movement. From here you can start to give some thought to your game plan to each bowler. Additionally, you can identify whether a bowler has any variations to their stock delivery.

Hopefully, you can also gain knowledge from batters who have been in before you, or the batter you join at the wicket. Avoid speaking to the outgoing batter as you walk past each other – they are probably not in the mood for a chat. However, once a batter is unpadded, and re-joins the team watching the game, it will be safe to approach. Bear in mind that feedback can be unhelpful. 'It's a minefield out there, the ball is doing everything!' is not really going to enthuse you with confidence, so it is best to make your own judgement and trust your instincts when out in the middle.

It is also important to note fielding positions and where there are gaps for scoring. Invariably, the field may change for you when you get to the wicket, so it is critical for you to review the field again before your first ball.

Furthermore, and most importantly, is the need to identify which hand a fielder uses for throwing. By ascertaining this you will be able to anticipate which side of their body they will have to run around to release the ball, enabling you to judge runs more effectively and safely. Also look for strength of throwing arms and general mobility. There may be fielders you will have greater success getting singles or twos to if they are on the boundary. Distance from the bat and how far fielders walk in from those initial positions will be critical factors for the judgement of singles. Batters should always be looking out for fielders that are not switched on mentally. This could be a player who has previously misfielded the ball, or a fielder who has dropped a catch. Can you apply more pressure to them? Do they want the ball to come to them?

Further information on assessing fielders, etc. can be found in Chapter 5.

Ground dimensions may affect your game plan. A long boundary may be harder to score fours and sixes on, but there will be more opportunities for twos and threes. When assessing whether or not to take on the hook or pull shot to a fast bowler who has fielders back on the leg-side boundary, the length of that boundary will affect your game plan for the short ball.

Do you still play the shot, hoping to clear the ropes, but risking that a top edge may get caught by a fielder, or do you attempt to keep it along the ground to reduce the risk of creating a catching opportunity? This could be the same for sweeps one side of the ground or the other, or if the boundaries straight are short, and square of the wicket they are long. Will you target down the ground more at this particular ground?

Certainly, a short square boundary will encourage you to hook, pull and sweep more as you will have a greater chance of reaching the boundary, and even if you mishit or top-edge it, it still might go for six. This will almost certainly not be the case with a long boundary.

All of the above will help you to develop a plan for your innings, which is termed a 'game plan'. The greater you understand your own game, and the more proficient you become at developing and executing game plans, the more runs you will score. Your overall game plan will also be influenced by the match situation but, needless to say, it is important to have a plan and have the determination to stick to it when out in the middle. Game plans need to be flexible, and you need to be adaptable whenever the match situation dictates.

> *'To build an innings you need to get used to the surface and then figure out which bowlers you can target and score off more freely.'*
> **BEN DUCKETT**

Constructing an innings and partnership building

Wherever you bat in the batting order, your overall game plan will be dictated by the match situation you face at the time. If you come in towards the end of an innings needing 50 off five overs, you simply cannot allow yourself 20 balls to get in before you go for your shots. Your job initially may be to simply get the other batter on strike as much as possible. However, if you are opening the batting in a 50-over match and the plan is for you to bat through the innings, you will have more time to achieve this.

If you have done your homework before starting your innings, you will have started to formulate a plan. Where can you pick up singles? Which fielders have strong arms? Where are the shorter boundaries? Where are the longer parts of the ground for pushing twos?

While getting yourself in, for almost all formats, it is important that you still look to score and rotate the strike. This is something that Joe Root does very well. Bowlers want to have prolonged spells at individual batters so they can determine the best way of dismissing them. There is no better way to frustrate bowlers than when batters keep pinching singles and rotating the strike. Additionally, the more frustrated a bowler becomes, the less likely they are to bowl well, culminating in more bad balls to score off. The more the conditions favour the bowlers, the greater the importance of strike rotation. This is why many teams like to pursue a left- and right-hand opening combination. Continuing to have this mix in combinations throughout the innings is extremely disruptive to the bowler's rhythm, as they have to continuously adjust their line to each batter, resulting in less consistent control of their deliveries. This strategy can also be very challenging to the fielders, who are continuously changing positions.

Note for coaches

It is advantageous to re-enact situations with scenario practice work, either in a net or middle practice. You can set the scenario or ask the players to choose one, then assess how the batters and bowlers apply themselves. Rewards can be offered to players that achieve a certain target, with feedback given to individuals or pairs. Ask the bowlers to think about their fields and the lengths and lines they will bowl to individual batters. If a net or middle practice is not available, then these can also be facilitated through a classroom-style tactical discussion. Some scenario examples are given in the drills section of this book, but any scenario can be worked on, being initiated by the current necessities required by the team.

Another good way to put a bowler under pressure is to look to score a boundary early in the over, particularly in limited-over or T20 formats. This immediately puts them under pressure to retake control of the over, rather than trying to put you under pressure by continuously bowling dot balls. If you then additionally hit three or four singles in the over it becomes a very good over for the batting team. After hitting a boundary try to get a single. If your partner then does the same it is a really big over for the batting side.

When the field is up at the start of your innings, consistently hitting a boundary early in the over will enforce a field change, potentially meaning sweepers going back to the boundary, allowing for more opportunities for low-risk singles and twos. If the field is tight, making rotating the strike difficult, you will need to hit some boundaries to force fielders back, thus creating openings for strike rotation again.

It can also help to keep track of the number of balls left in the over. Once within two balls of the over's end the most important thing (depending on the match situation) is that you are still there and the partnership keeps going into the next over. This is especially true if you have already had a good over in terms of run scoring. Do not give the momentum back to the opposition by playing a shot that is not required. Do not give them a chance of a boost – get to the next over and then go again.

Although the majority of this book talks about you as an individual batter, you never bat alone in a game, and for you to get a big score you will need to form partnerships with your team-mates. The more substantial these are the more it will help you in your own run scoring. The larger the partnership gets, the more the fielding side's heads drop and they lose focus, and the less consistent bowlers often bowl. Therefore, the bigger a partnership is, the easier it is to score runs.

To post substantial team scores and win matches, partnerships are vital in any format. Two 'in' batters are always more effective than one on their own. As mentioned earlier, strike rotation is important throughout an innings, but is particularly important early on. If you have just arrived at the wicket, try to give the batter that is already in as much of the strike as possible. Generally, the percentage chance of a fielding team taking a wicket doubles after three consecutive maidens. Try to avoid this situation whenever possible. Look out for this in matches you play in, whether it is your own side or the opposition. You can see the pressure building on the batters. After the 18-ball period, batters can become impatient. Indicators such as a big-shot play and miss occur, a bad run call is heard, a near run out happens. Frustration builds and inevitably a chance is given. Fielding sides should actually prepare themselves for this situation as it develops, by actively anticipating that a wicket-taking opportunity is imminent. To counter this, batters should also be aware of the developing situation and the dangers it can bring. Stay calm, do not panic, and have a specific game plan for meeting this challenge. Normally, if the two batters are rotating the strike well, this situation is avoided. Remember again: 'Heart in the oven, head in the freezer!'

Communication between the batters is the key. Helping out your partner with some advice on conditions and fielders when they first join you at the crease or what to look out for in a bowler's action for variations can all be crucial. If your partner is having difficulties facing a certain bowler, offer encouragement and support from the other end to keep them going and cultivate a positive mindset. Between overs you can discuss game plans for the bowlers that are on and discuss where you are looking for singles and other scoring options. It may also be advantageous for one batter to face more of the bowling than the other. For example, an off-spinner bowling more to a right-hander than to a left-handed batter in the partnership. You may also decide in this case that the right-hander will look to attempt to score more off the off-spinner than the left-hander does, as they are hitting with the spin.

These midwicket chats can range from anything technical, tactical, physical or mental, through to motivational encouragement. Very often even non-cricket-related topics can be discussed to help with players' relaxation.

Target setting is also a good way to keep a partnership going and add motivation. This may be a run target for the next few overs, or simply to make sure that you are both still at the crease in a certain number of overs' time. Instead of overs this could be a time target, or to reach a break in the innings such as drinks, lunch, tea or end of the day's play. There is no better way to build confidence in a batting dressing room than when two well-set batters come in at lunch or tea with an established partnership.

Initially, targets need to be small and achievable, so a time length of 10–15 minutes, duration of 4–5 overs or scoring 20 more runs are acceptable, rather than setting yourself to still be there in two hours' time. Of course, that may be the ultimate long-term goal, but in between set smaller targets that, once achieved, you can reward yourself for. Then set yourself another small target for the forthcoming overs or minutes. Your partnership will build and develop, making batting easier the more time passes.

In tough match situations or within a long partnership, it is important to try to switch off in between overs. Although you will still be aware of what is going on around you, it is good to have some non-cricket-related conversations to mentally relax and lighten the mood. The topic could simply be what you might be doing after the match, etc. – anything so you can mentally relax.

The mental aspects of batting are discussed in greater detail in Chapter 5.

Eventually the match situation will dictate that the scoring rate will need to increase. Again, you can discuss this as a pair. One can opt to be the aggressor, while the other opts to mainly rotate the strike, becoming the one to bat through the innings. Of course, in some situations you may both have to be the aggressors.

It is crucial that you inform your partner of any field changes while you are standing at the non-striker's end. These can change mid-over, so if you suspect they are not aware, you need to communicate this. The same applies if you spot any grip variations, or signals with the wicketkeeper. By passing this information on, you are greatly increasing the chances of developing a big partnership.

If you have just lost your partner it is vital that you are not the next batter out. You need to refocus your concentration and work hard to build the next partnership, even by being willing to come back down the gears and accept a lower scoring rate while your partner gets in and the partnership builds. Having lost your partner, and the flow of the innings changes, this can affect your mindset, so you need to readjust, refocus and continue batting.

Teams want to avoid having two new batters simultaneously at the crease as much as possible, as the scoring rate can slow as more wickets fall, and the new batters attempt to get themselves in. If conditions favour the bowling side, the more important this becomes, as it is going to be a lot harder for a new batter to survive and pick up the scoring rate than it is for the two currently out in the middle.

Run chases

Although a lot of teams like to have the scoreboard pressure of runs on the board in the first innings of the match, it can also be an advantage to bat second. There is so much you can learn from the first innings, as you will already have had a good look at how the pitch is playing, observing pace, bounce, swing, seam movement, turn, outfield speed and boundary distances.

You can also learn a lot from how the opposition batters played in that first innings. This could be a player that did really well. How did they construct their innings? Which parts of the ground did they score successfully into? Which scoring shots were the easiest to play? This can provide a good template for your own personal game plan, especially if you bat in a similar position to them in the batting order. You must remember to factor in your own personal batting strengths when formulating your batting plan.

Equally, batters who played poorly in the first innings can be used as an example of how not to play. Highlighting shots that were difficult to execute or lengths that were hard to score off should be noted. Assess whether it would be better to sweep or drive the spinners, play front or back foot to the seam bowlers. By assessing the first innings closely, you can give yourself a distinct advantage in the run chase.

Note for players

A good motivation is to pick out a player in the opposition that bats in a similar position to you or is the opposition's best player. Aim to outperform them in the match. If everyone in the team achieves this you will win more often than not.

As a general rule of thumb, never aim to finish the match in the final over. If you need 250 in 50 overs, work out the run rate as if you need to get those runs in 47 or 48 overs. This will hopefully mean that you are always ahead of the rate rather than behind, which can give you added flexibility if the team loses wickets, particularly two set batters in quick succession, giving you the safety of allowing the scoring rate to temporarily drop for a while.

Another important consideration is your tactical awareness as the scoring rate goes up. Three, four or maybe even five per over, you should consider as achievable in singles, but once the rate hits six per over or higher, you will need to be scoring at least one boundary an over. This is simply because there are bound to be a couple of dot balls bowled in the over. Once again, if the boundary can be found early in the over, the pressure is immediately put on the bowler and taken off yourself.

Note for coaches

A great drill for run chases is an escalating target practice. This can be done in a net or middle practice but is equally as good on a bowling machine. Set a field and the initial runs per over target. This can start quite low depending on age and ability, but at an amount of runs they are likely to achieve. If they achieve that then move immediately on to the next over, where the required rate goes up by one run per over. Highlight any changes to the field and then begin the new over.

Keep doing this until the target is not attained. Then discuss with the batters the possible reasons why they did not achieve the required rate and devise a plan for success next time. Keep increasing the required run rate, changing the field accordingly, so the batters have to change their tactical approach as the rate goes up. Keep ascending the run rate until the score is unobtainable. Review and highlight how they altered their game plan/scoring areas as the rate went up and the field placing changed.

If batting as a pair, ask the players to run between the wickets at match pace, and only count the run if they run it hard and correctly. If using a bowling machine, adjust the amount of swing and pitching lengths, to replicate different bowling types. You can also develop a competition between the group, recording which individual or pair achieved the highest run rate per over.

A team should always assess how many runs they could potentially score off the last ten overs of a 50-over innings, the last eight overs of a 40-over innings, and the last four overs of a T20, assuming you hypothetically have wickets in hand, with two batters well set. This will help dictate the pace you will need to score at the start of the innings and in the middle overs to set up the final chasing down of the opposition score.

Sometimes the run chase does not go to plan. Wickets may have been taken with the new ball, or there is a mid-innings collapse with several wickets falling in a short period of time. Here, your game plan will need to adjust accordingly. The most important consideration here is to take the match deep and bat out as many overs as possible, keep a positive mindset and work hard to get a partnership going. Your communication with your partner here is crucial.

If in a 50-over match the rate required is six an over off 20 overs, you may have to accept three an over for ten of those, but not losing wickets, aiming to score 90 off the final ten overs. If you have very few wickets to play with it may become 60 off the last five overs, with 30 off the last two. This is still achievable, especially if you are both well set. By still being there at that stage of the match you have given yourself a chance of victory.

Whether batting first or second, a good habit is to make sure you are aware of the number of balls left in an over, and get into the routine of asking the umpire when you feel the end of the over is near. This will give you a tactical advantage depending on the match situation. It will help to keep you focused and have a plan for the final balls of the over. You may need a boundary, or if you have scored well that over, simply make sure you are still there at the start of the next over, thus ensuring the continuation of the partnership. It is a great idea to convert the overs remaining to the number of balls remaining. This simplifies the calculation, and psychologically makes it less of a mountain to climb. So 20 off 18 balls sounds easier to achieve than 20 off three overs.

Breaks in the innings

We have already highlighted that losing your partner from a long batting partnership can also break your own flow and concentration. Another dangerous time is when the game is coming up to a scheduled break. This could be drinks, lunch, tea or end of day completion. It is vital that no matter how many runs you are on, or however big the partnership is, you and your partner mentally refocus for the first couple of overs after the break. The opposition have had an opportunity to regroup, refresh and formulate plans to dismiss you. Be prepared to counter this, ensuring that the stoppage does not break your focus and concentration. This potentially threatening period needs to be part of your discussion with your partner, thus formulating appropriate targets for the next few overs or minutes.

Motivational chats are particularly important after formal drinks breaks. Batters should remind each other of this potential and accentuate the positive mindset that their continued partnership will bring to themselves and the team.

Further to this is how you approach the last few overs before the break commences. One option is to keep playing the way you were, as this was clearly working. Certainly in a limited-overs match how you play will be dictated by the match situation at the time and you need to play accordingly. Longer formats can be approached differently. Your team-mates, captain and coach will want you and your partner there after the break to carry on batting. This situation can be practised with scenario work, where you come down the gears to make sure you are still there when the umpire calls time. If practised well, it will feel natural to do so, and it simply becomes part of your game. If you have not practised it then definitely keep batting as you were.

The psychological effect of losing a wicket just before or directly after a break should not be underestimated. If the bowling team take a wicket a few overs before a break, it may allow them a few balls or even a couple of overs to target a new batter, perhaps even taking another wicket. This gives such a lift to the opposition, particularly if a big partnership is broken. They walk off feeling much better mentally, and you as a batting unit have a 'lower' mental state than if both batters were still there and able to continue after the break. They know they have a new batter to target when play resumes. If you and your partner both see it through to the break, it will be your dressing room that will be in a better mental state to approach the next session of play.

Different tactical batting approaches dependent on format and your strengths

If you watch international cricket played now, there is a big difference between T20 and 50-over cricket, compared with a five-day Test match. The white ball does not move much in the air after the first couple of overs, and the pitches are usually very good, bordering on 'batter friendly'. This allows the batter to be very aggressive as there is little or no sideways movement even when the ball is new. Generally, shot making is easier. In Test match cricket the red ball swings more when new, and it is easier to maintain a shine on, even revealing reverse swing later in the match. Opening batters and top-order players tend to take a very different approach in this format. Shot making is harder and batters need to be more selective.

How you and your team approach T20 and 50-over cricket will have to be decided on individual strengths of the batters, how much the ball swings and how good the wickets that you play on are. Your tactics are therefore determined by the players in the team, the conditions you encounter, the ground you play at and the opposition itself. This will vary a lot in youth cricket where the physicality of players will vary dramatically.

FIVE
RUNNING BETWEEN THE WICKETS

> 'Being able to rotate the strike regularly is vitally important when building partnerships and batting in the middle overs of white ball cricket.'
>
> BEN DUCKETT

The object of the batter is to score runs, and while it would be great to hit boundaries every ball, the bowlers and fielders do their utmost to stop that happening. Consequently, apart from scoring runs through the fielding team giving the batters runs in the form of extras, the only other way to score runs is through running them. This chapter will highlight the best ways of doing this, from both a technical and tactical point of view.

It is essential that the two batters batting together do so in such a manner that they are able to take all the runs available, without endangering their wicket by run out, which would bring the partnership prematurely to an end, potentially altering the outcome of the match. If every available run is taken the score will mount steadily, without the batters having to take unnecessary risks. The fielding team can also become discouraged as they are unable to apply pressure to the batters, and the score continues to grow. Constant rotation of strike is also annoying to bowlers, who can become frustrated. This can affect the quality of their performance, meaning they bowl more bad balls for the batting side to score from. Conversely, the batting team become encouraged, and confidence grows as their individual and the team score mount.

Both the striker and non-striker have definitive roles to play in ensuring that they generate run-scoring opportunities, while performing this with the minimum of risk. Each batter should be familiar with the responsibilities inherent in the two roles, as these role obligations will be changing ball by ball if they are running between the wickets well and rotating the strike.

Rotating the strike is so important in a partnership, as not only does the scoreboard keep moving and the batters' confidence increase, but it also disrupts the bowlers' rhythm and potentially their desired field placings. Good backing up from the non-striker can also put the bowler off their concentration, balance, rhythm and timing as they approach their delivery, potentially wondering they can possibly run the batter out.

Remember, a batter should be looking to set the field they would prefer to bat to, rather than having to bat to the field the bowler wants. Being a good runner between the wickets greatly contributes to that. Furthermore, regular strike rotation will continually present the bowler with a different batter. This could be a right-hander one ball, then a left-hander next ball. It could be a tall batter, then a short batter. Each batter will have their own shot preferences, etc., so it makes the bowler's task much more challenging. They will be continually changing their line and length, field placings and potentially having to regularly switch between bowling over or around the wicket.

A few years ago, James Taylor and Will Jefferson regularly batted together for Leicestershire and Nottinghamshire, with James being 5ft 4in tall, and Will being 6ft 10in! Both require different ideal lengths from the bowler each time the strike is rotated, which is not an easy task for any bowler.

The duties of the striking batter

Before the striking batter takes their stance, they should note the location of all the fielders and identify the gaps within the fielding unit. By identifying the gaps, rather than picking out the fielders, some batters find this a much more positive way of looking at the bowler's field. The gaps are big, the fielders are small. A powerful way of seeing the benefit of this form of assessment is to view a satellite image of a cricket ground. Imagine the field placings for a particular type of bowler, and see how small the fielders are and how big the gaps are in comparison. Do not forget, you can hit over the fielders as well as along the floor past them.

Another crucial duty is to identify any poor fielders and where they are stationed. This could be a fielder who is a slow mover, does not anticipate well, slows down as they approach the ball, uses the long barrier continuously, has a weak throwing arm or is a poor ground fielder and catcher.

Additionally, it is essential that the batter ascertains whether a fielder is a right- or left-handed thrower, as this will play a massive part in your judgement of potential runs. Be even more aware of ambidextrous throwers!

Being aware of the playing environment and climatic conditions contribute to your assessment of run-taking opportunities. The height of the sun, wind direction and strength, bumpiness of the outfield, width of the cricket square, wetness of the outfield, dimensions and topography of the outfield, power of the shot, etc. all have an influence on your decision-making. For example, a poor-moving fielder with a weak throw, who is also a poor ground fielder, on a long boundary with a bumpy outfield, throwing into a strong wind, would mean that you could probably take that extra run! Conversely, a ball hit through the field when the grass is really long may not be the easy two runs it would normally be and the batters need to take this into account when deciding when to come back for a second run.

Finally, the batter should be looking out for any field changes that may have taken place, along with any bowling signals the fielding team may be employing. If the striking batter is confident at picking a spinner's delivery grips and variations, and the non-striker is not very good at picking the deliveries, the batter can advise the non-striker of what to look for in the grip/action. This can also be useful for helping play a seamer swinging the ball.

After playing the ball

Immediately after hitting, leaving or missing the ball, the striker should be alert to the possibility of taking a run. A batter should be looking for a run off every ball if possible, only deciding not to if they are absolutely sure that it is not safe to do so. Do not be happy to stand still and admire your good defensive shot – take a couple of steps down the wicket to see whether there is a quick single to be had. As well as giving you a head start if the single is on, this also shows positive intent to the opposition. If the ball is in front of the wicket, the striker must quickly decide whether there is a run available or not and call instantly. If the ball goes behind the wicket, the striking batter may not see it, so in this circumstance the non-striker makes the call. The striker should look at and listen to the non-striker's call and respond immediately.

Very often, a good strategy to keep the scoreboard ticking over is for the striking batter to execute a very gentle form of defensive shot, deflecting the ball into a gap or hitting it so gently that it does not reach a fielder operating in the inner ring. This is commonly known as 'tip and run'. This method of strike rotation needs decisive and immediate communication as it can be a risky form of running, but if mastered it will lead to frustration within the fielding team, with potentially counteractive field placing changes made. This may then open up other scoring options for the batters. This form of 'run stealing' has even greater potential when the wicketkeeper is standing back (striker's end), and if the bowler does not get back to their stumps (bowler's end) while the run is taking place.

Calls should be made loudly and clearly. There are only three calls to be made: 'YES' for a run, 'NO' for no run, 'WAIT' for when it is initially uncertain whether a safe run is possible. 'WAIT' should be viewed as 'be prepared to run'. The call of 'WAIT' must be followed by 'YES' or 'NO'. Communication is the key. Remember, the worst calls in cricket are 'YES', 'NO', 'SORRY'!

To accompany the call of 'NO', the batter can reinforce this by showing a raised palm to their batting partner. This is particularly useful in noisy conditions, such as wind or large crowds.

Finally, a batter should never use the call 'GO' when setting off for a run, as it sounds very much like 'NO'. This can very often lead to confusion and an embarrassing run out for one of the batters.

While running

If the ball is hit in front of the wicket, upon passing the non-striker, the striker should verbally indicate whether there is a possibility of further runs; for example saying, 'Looking for two,' or 'Possibly three.' The call should be loud and positive as this alone can put the fielder under pressure and force an error. If the ball is behind the wicket, the striker should listen for the same information from the non-striking batter as they pass. There is no need for the striking batter to turn round and look for the ball until they have turned after completing the run.

The batters should run the first run quickly, thus giving themselves the best opportunity for extra runs, should they exist. The striker should also take note of the fielder's fielding ability, as referenced earlier in this chapter.

The batters should never run on the playing surface of the pitch. The striker should always run on the off side of the pitch if the bowler is bowling from that side of the wicket and run on the leg side of the wicket if the bowler is bowling from that side. This ensures that the batters never collide when running, as the non-striker always stands on the opposite side to the bowler when standing at the non-striking/bowler's end.

Apart from the initial first steps to take you off the wicket, or to get you round the bowler, you should run in straight lines wherever possible to reduce the distance you have to run.

Batters should always be positive with their backing up, calling and running between the wickets. After completing any run, a batter should be looking for another one, so they should turn as quickly as possible and start the next run before looking and calling 'YES', 'NO' or 'WAIT'. Remember, communication is the key.

The duties of the non-striking batter

In this example, it is assumed that the bowler is a right-arm seam bowler, bowling over the wicket.

The first thing the non-striker can do is check the field, etc. as detailed above. Additionally, they are in a great position to check the bowler's grip and action, and any changes or variations in these areas. This information can be used for assistance in playing the bowler and can also be passed on to their batting partner at the first opportunity. Finally, the batter should be looking out for any field changes that may have taken place, along with any bowling signals the fielding team may be employing.

If the striking batter has trouble picking a spinner's delivery grips and variations, and the non-striker is very good at picking the deliveries, they can advise the striker of what to look for in the grip/action. If the batter still struggles, the non-striker can help by temporarily holding their bat in a hand corresponding to which way the ball will turn for a short while at the start of the bowler's run-up. The non-striker should then return the bat to the correct hand coincident for the side of the wicket the bowler is bowling from. This can also be used for picking the shiny side for a seamer swinging the ball.

The non-striker takes up a position on the opposite side of the stumps to the bowler. They stand near the bowler's crease line, with the bat in their left hand. This is done so that the non-striker is facing the bowler and has them in their view throughout their delivery. If the non-striker was standing on the other side of the wicket, the bat would be in their right hand. Whichever hand the non-striker is holding their bat in, their hand should be positioned at the top of the handle.

As the ball is being bowled

As the bowler approaches the stumps, the non-striker starts to move forward with the bowler. The non-striker moves past the popping crease just before the bowler releases the ball, ensuring that their bat is still grounded behind the line. The non-striker should aim to be far enough down the pitch so that their left arm is stretched out far enough to still have the bat grounded behind the popping crease. Holding the bat at the top of the handle will enable them to have a longer reach.

As soon as the ball is delivered, the non-striker can positively advance down the pitch a few paces, then either they or the striker make a decision and loudly make the appropriate call: 'YES', 'NO' or 'WAIT'. This is called 'backing up', which is crucial to good running between the wickets. The non-striker can gain quite a few yards on the striking batter, which is particularly important if the non-striker is running down to the danger end when stealing a quick single to a shot where the ball has not travelled very far, or if it was hit very close to a fielder. One thing to remember when backing up is that because the non-striker has effectively a head start over the striker, they may complete their runs quicker than the striker. The non-striker must remember this when running multiple runs and decide accordingly whether another run is safely possible.

Bad backing up.

Good backing up.

After the ball has been played

Immediately after hitting, leaving or missing the ball, the non-striker should be alert to the possibility of taking a run. If the ball goes behind the wicket, the striking batter may not see it, so in this circumstance the non-striker makes the call. The striker should look at the non-striker and listen to their call, then respond immediately.

We mentioned previously the advantages of the striking batter executing very gentle deflections of the ball into gaps, or short of fielders operating in the inner ring, commonly known as 'tip and run'.

This method of strike rotation needs decisive and immediate communication, so the non-striking batter has an essential part to play in this. Remember, the non-striker should always be backing up a few yards down the wicket so they have an immediate advantage in taking any potential single. Bearing in mind the nature of the tip and run shot, the ball will always be in the immediate vicinity of the striking batter, so any run out possibility is more likely to be taken by attempting to hit the stumps at that end. Therefore, the non-striker must be aware that they are more than likely running to the danger end, so they must be alert and take advantage of the need to back up positively.

The non-striker should also consider the shot shape that the striking batter is in after completing their shot, as this can affect the ability of the striker to set off powerfully for the run. The sweep shot is a great example of this, as the striker is likely to be still kneeling on their back leg, being in no position to move quickly for a run. This can then result in two batters standing at the striker's end, with stumps being broken and a run out taken at the bowler's (non-striker's) end.

If there is no chance of a run being taken, the non-striker should stop backing up, call 'NO' if it is their call, turn round and immediately return to the popping crease, removing any chance of a run out by grounding their bat behind the popping crease. To accompany the call of 'NO', the batter can reinforce this by showing a raised palm to the batting partner as mentioned earlier in the chapter – this is a very good habit to get into.

The non-striker is most at risk of being run out when the striking batter hits a legal delivery straight back down the pitch. There is a high possibility that the bowler will attempt to stop the ball, but if the ball accidentally strikes any part of the bowler and deflects on to the stumps (knocking off a bail), the non-striker is out if they are out of their ground (i.e. no part of the body or bat are grounded behind the popping crease). This is a most unfortunate method of dismissal but the non-striker must be aware of its potential when the ball is struck straight down the pitch. A good way of minimising the possibility of this form of run out is to try to keep the bat low or on the floor in the backing up follow-through, so that if the ball is hit straight, the non-striker has a better chance of grounding their bat over the popping crease, than if it was being carried high in the air around waist height.

How aggressively you back up will vary depending on the format of the match and the current match situation. Where all runs are vital you will take a few extra steps down the wicket (which gives you the best chance of completing a quick single), but where runs are not as important and keeping wickets intact is of greater importance, then do not back up as far. This will enable you to regain your ground easier at the bowler's end should the ball be hit back straight by your partner.

General running between the wickets

Where more than one run is taken, the batter who is running towards the ball or towards the stumps to which the ball is likely to be thrown is the batter who is most likely to make the call. If for some reason it is easier for the other batter to call, then they should do so. This can happen when an experienced player is batting with an inexperienced one, a fast runner is batting with a slow one, a fit player is partnering an injured one, or a fresh new batter is partnering a tired batter who has been batting for a lengthy period.

Batters should ensure that they run on opposite sides of the pitch as previously described, thus avoiding a collision or having to take evasive action, which could lead to one of them being run out. Once again batters are reminded not to run on the playing surface of the pitch at any time. Batters should remember that there is the possibility that when running they may be either on the outer edge of the cut strip playing surface or the lusher grass of the remaining cut square. This may be particularly challenging during or after heavy rain. If the playing surface has been protected by covers, when play resumes the strip will be dry, but the uncovered part of the square will still be wet, hence it would be advisable to bat in spikes.

In fact, footwear has a major role in the success of a batter's ability to produce good running between the wickets. It is essential that batters wear appropriate footwear for the conditions they encounter on the running surface, as they do not want to slip over or feel unstable when accelerating through their push-off, sprinting, and slowing down and turning phases. It is a cardinal sin to be run out because of inappropriate footwear.

Cumbersome, ill-fitting batting pads can be a problem for younger players, so it is essential that they are made aware of the importance of wearing the correct size pads and they are correctly worn and fastened, thus reducing potential run-out possibilities.

We discussed earlier how crucial it is for batters to assess the strengths and weaknesses of the fielding team. Some fielders, particularly some on the boundary, do not always attack the ball directly in a straight line. This correct and attacking approach is commonly known as the 'tiger line', so called because it replicates how a tiger approaches and attacks its prey. Rather than adopt the 'tiger line', some fielders run across to cover the line of the ball while still on the boundary. This means the ball takes longer to reach them, hence if a batter immediately sees a fielder doing this, there is a greater chance of taking an extra run to them.

Depending on the scenario of the match at the time, another potential area for making an attacking run is when a fielder only has one stump to aim at when throwing. If the wicketkeeper is stood back and has failed to get up to the striker's stumps, or the bowler has failed to get back to cover the stumps at the bowler's end, this creates that opportunity. Fielding positions that can create this scenario are: mid-on, mid-off, point and square leg. The batters must obviously assess the fielders stationed in these positions, but often it is a risk worth taking, as the throw must be 100 per cent accurate to hit the stump. Evaluating whether to attempt this type of single will be partly dependent on the format of the match and the match situation. You have to balance risk with reward.

If there is a possibility of a run out, while sprinting at full speed the batter concerned should ground their bat with their arm fully extended in front of them for approximately two yards before reaching the popping crease. When trying to get in, a batter should never turn their head to look behind them to see what is happening, as this slows them down and alters their running style. If a batter is really struggling to get in, the only option left is to dive for the line, trying their best to ground the bat behind the crease line. Dive low and in a straight line (not up and over in an arc) with the arm holding the bat outstretched. An arcing dive is less effective and there is also more chance of the end of the bat getting stuck in the surface rather than sliding across it. The bat should be held so that the lower intersection corner of outside edge with the toe of the bat runs along the ground. This is easy to slide across the ground, offering little cross-sectional resistance. However, the bat should never be held such that the front face faces the ground, with the complete width of the toe running into the ground. It is then not easy to slide the bat across the ground as the cross-sectional resistance is high in this orientation. There is the distinct possibility of stabbing the bat into the ground, thus removing its forward momentum and increasing the chance of being run out, dropping the bat or sustaining a wrist injury.

If the fielder attempting the run out is behind the batter, the batter is entitled to run between the fielder and the wicket. The batter does run the risk of being hit by the ball, but that may save them from a run out. However, you must run in a straight line and not change course to deliberately shield the stumps from the fielder. This is against the laws of the game, and on appeal you can be given out for obstructing the field, should the umpire deem your movement to have been deliberate.

We have highlighted previously how crucial rotating the strike is in all formats and match situations.

Having a positive mindset to running between the wickets will enable you to look for singles even off a defensive shot. If you practise it enough in training, with positive calling, you will be amazed at how often and how easy it is to steal extra runs in a match! If you execute this in a match, it shows the opposition that you mean business and are thinking about scoring rather than just occupying the crease.

All coaches will advocate running 'the first one hard' when you hit the ball to a fielder on the boundary. This is especially true if you are a young player, as all your cricket will be short, limited-over matches. It is important to put the fielder under pressure as the ball reaches them. Pressure can lead to a mistake and a fumble of the pick-up, or force them into a long barrier, either of which may give you time to come back for a second run. This sort of running also adds intensity to the partnership you are building and adds more positivity to it, adjusting your mindset. When running a two, never jog the first run and sprint the second, sprint the first run and jog the second. Better still, sprint the first and second, and look for a third!

However, once you start playing longer formats, particularly multi-day where you have a long-term target of batting throughout the innings or a whole day's play, then it is not advisable to push these fielders as hard, as you need to conserve energy. As the match evolves, there will be a time where it will be important to raise the tempo of the running between the wickets, but it is difficult to keep it up for a whole day's play. Pushing the boundary fielders adds intensity to your batting and the partnership, but if your target is to bat the full day you want an air of calm about you and the partnerships you build, giving the opposition the impression you are set in for a very long innings.

Technical aspects of running between the wickets

In simple terms, running between the wickets is basically sprinting up and down the pitch, carrying a bat, ensuring that this bat is grounded behind the popping crease at the end of each completed run. The pair of batters should do this simultaneously. A run out occurs when the ball hits the set of stumps the batter is running to, before the batter's bat is grounded behind the associated popping crease.

In addition to judging when a run is possible, the main challenges to the batters are sprinting as fast as they can, slowing down to turn, stopping, completing the run by grounding the bat behind the popping crease, accelerating out of the turn and into another sprint. This is done in full protective kit while carrying a heavy bat, these regular sustained bursts of energy taking place over a long period of time. Generally, the only rest period is at the turn around between overs and the changeover between innings.

Sprinting the run

The following text provides general guidance about sprinting. For more expansive knowledge the reader should consult literature beyond the scope of this book.

Normal sprinting is performed by firstly driving forward from a stationary position, bursting powerfully forward into a full sprint. After the drive phase the sprinter transitions into the maximum velocity phase. The stride lengths are normally short to start with in the driving phase, lengthening up into their maximum distance when in the maximum velocity stage.

A high knee-drive is essential to generate power, with the knees pumping in a forward motion, ensuring they do not cross the centre line of the body. The arms generally make a 90-degree angle between the upper arm and forearm, and powerfully pump in a forward motion, trying not to cross the centre line of the body. The left side of the body moves in the opposite way to the right.

All this is fine if running a 100m race. As mentioned earlier, running between the wickets involves sprinting while carrying a bat, then slowing down, stopping, turning, etc.

A full-size cricket pitch is 22yds long, stumps to stumps. The distance between popping creases is just over 19yds. Therefore, the whole activity of running takes place within approximately 19yds. A batter should never run up to the popping crease and tap their bat behind the line before turning and running for another run. The quickest and most efficient way is to stop short of the crease and reach out with the bat in their hand, until the toe of the bat is grounded just behind the popping crease. The lower the batter can be to the ground the better, as this will enable them to stretch out their arm and bat further to the crease. Therefore, their feet may end up stopping at least $1^{1/2}$ yds short of the crease line. By doing this the maximum traversing distance may now reduce to approximately 16yds.

Of this 16yds, approximately 2–3yds at each end will be the slowing down/stopping zone and driving/accelerating zone. Therefore, the batter will only be sprinting at full speed for a potential maximum of 12yds. When you analyse the mechanics of motion involved in sprinting runs, it is obvious that this is an extremely tiring and energy-sapping form of running. The constant acceleration and deceleration is exhausting. This is exacerbated by wearing kit and carrying a heavy bat.

The biggest challenge to the batter is carrying the bat while sprinting. Some batters carry it in one hand, while most carry it in two hands. Therefore, the sprinting motion is only really carried out efficiently with the lower half of the body (the legs), with the upper part (the arms) no longer fully pumping due to holding the bat. A shoulder roll is probably the only motion in the upper half of the body. Understanding this highlights how draining taking runs can be.

Two hand.

One hand.

Batters should ensure that they run in straight lines when running between the wickets, as this is the shortest and quickest route from A to B. Young players should be encouraged to do this as early as possible, as there is a tendency for many of them to run in a curve when turning and putting their bat down behind the popping crease.

Slowing down to complete the first run

As the batter completes the first run, they will have to slow down and eventually stop. While sprinting, they are running in a front-on position. When starting to slow down they will need to rebalance and manoeuvre into a side-on position. This is a much more efficient way of braking and sets the batter up for a powerful turning and drive position. While sprinting, the batter runs in an upright position, but when slowing down, stopping and turning, they should be lowering themselves into a low powerful turning/drive position. The stride lengths will also reduce, until the batter stops running completely.

If they are turning with the bat in their right hand, they should stop with the right foot nearest to the popping crease, with the feet parallel to the crease. If they are turning with the bat in the left hand, they should stop with the left foot nearest to the popping crease, with the feet again parallel to the crease. On both occasions the free hand can sometimes touch the floor to stabilise the batter.

The final part of this manoeuvre is to stretch out the bat and slide it grounded just behind the popping crease. Once again, the batter should hold the bat at the end of the handle, thus extending their reach length. Remember, the bat should be held so that the lower intersection corner of outside edge with the toe of the bat runs along the ground.

The location of the ball in the outfield will determine which hand the batter decides to hold the bat in as they ground it behind the line. For instance, if a right-handed batter hits a cover drive, at the end of the first run they will hold and turn with it in their left hand. At the same time, the non-striker, who is running away from the ball, will hold and turn with it in their right hand. The golden rule is to always try to have your chest facing the side of the ground where the ball is in play. If a three is run in this example, the order of hand holding the bat would be – left, right, left for the striker, and right, left, right for the non-striker.

If this principle is ignored, it is called 'turning blind'. This means that the batter makes a turn with their back to the side of the ground where the ball is. Therefore, they have lost sight of the ball and cannot be in a position to see it clearly and assess whether another run is safe to take or not. Using the previous example, transpose the order of hands holding the bat so that both batters run the three turning blind. Turning blind is to be discouraged, as it can lead to unnecessary run outs.

It is essential that batters practise swapping their hands when turning, as everyone has a natural preference. Drills can be used for this purpose, as it is not only crucial for feeling the bat in the other hand, but it also trains the body to feel and adapt to the movements, whichever way the batter turns. Most people turn quicker one way than the other. Once you are an experienced cricketer and you are a good judge of whether the second or third run is on, it is not as important to turn facing the way of the ball as if this slows you down then it increases the chance of a run out. Before touching down with your bat behind the crease you can call to your partner whether you think the next run is on and then reconfirm this once you have turned and have the ball/fielder in your sights again.

If during the running process a batter fails to ground their bat or any part of their body behind the popping crease, the umpire will call to indicate 'one short'. This should not happen, as every run given away like that could be the difference between winning or losing a match.

Turning and setting off

Once the bat has been slid and grounded behind the popping crease, the next manoeuvre is to turn and set off for the next run. While in the low, stretching position, the chest is swung round to face back up the pitch. At the same time, the feet spin around from an orientation parallel with the popping crease, to one where the toes are also pointing directly up the pitch. The knees are also primed in this position.

Bad turning.

Good turning.

As the bat is withdrawn back towards the body, the feet and legs load up to power away from this low position, raising the body up into the full-height position as the batter accelerates back to the maximum velocity position when in full sprint.

While withdrawing the bat back into the body, some batters like to throw the arm holding the bat forward, using the weight of the bat to help drive them forward. This is a technique needing a strong upper body, which can work for them. However, young batters may find this a great challenge, as they may not have the strength to control this manoeuvre, which could lead them to either drop the bat or lose balance and fall over.

If during the running between the wickets process a batter accidentally drops their bat, they should continue running without it, ensuring that if multiple runs are being taken, one foot is grounded behind the popping crease at the end of each run. If it does not add to the risk of being run out then it may be safe to pick the bat up while continuing to run, but this should never be the cause of a run out under any circumstances.

Completing the last run

When completing a single or the final run of a sequence, the batter should always ground the bat behind the popping crease. If there is no pressure of a potential run out, the batter can just run naturally behind the crease line. However, if there is a potential run out, it is crucial that the batter extends the bat out in front of them as far as possible, grounding it at least 2yds before the popping crease and ensuring that the bat stays grounded until it is past the line. This will invariably be done while sprinting at full speed but it is still vital that the batter attains a low fully stretched profile. Holding the bat at the end of the handle once again could make the difference between an out or not out decision.

Very often a batter, when completing their final run, will be confronted with the opportunity to gain extra runs through an 'overthrow'. This occurs when a throw misses the stumps and the wicketkeeper, bowler or fielder fail to cover that set of stumps or fail to gather the ball. When this occurs, loud verbal communication is vital, as the batter should immediately call to the other, informing them of the extra runs available. Some batters when completing their final run continue running past the stumps way off into the distance, either to avoid injury or possibly as a point of showing the effort they made to get in. If this occurs, it reduces the chance of running the overthrows, as they have travelled so far beyond the stumps that they are unable to get back quickly enough.

Batters should also assess the backing-up fielders patrolling the boundary. For example, if the ball is hit into the off side, the leg-side fielders should attempt to back up the incoming throws. If they are boundary fielders, they should be sprinting in from the boundary to stop any potential overthrows occurring. If they do not do this, additional overthrow runs can be captured by the watchful batter.

In severe cases a full dive is necessary to get in. Although once again this manoeuvre is carried out at full sprinting speed, it is essential that the dive is as low and as flat as possible, while again fully extending the reach of the arm.

Batting with a runner

On rare occasions a batter may sustain an injury that renders them unable to run. When this occurs, they are entitled to have a 'runner' in all formats except international cricket. A runner is only allowed if the injury was sustained during the day's play. If a batter arrives for the match carrying the existing injury, they are not allowed to have a runner. The runner must be a member of the batting team but not the 12th man, and they can only do so if they have already batted in the innings.

Basically a 'runner' runs all the runs that the incapacitated batter cannot run. They must be externally dressed identically to the injured batter, including ALL protective equipment – chest guard, arm guard, helmet, etc. (It may still be wise to wear a protective box if appropriate.)

Although this situation is not common, it is essential that all batters familiarise themselves with the procedures involved, whether as the 'injured' batter or the 'runner', as any confusion could be fatal if you happen to find the situation a reality. Batting with a runner is covered in Law 25 of 'The Laws of Cricket'.

When the injured batter is on strike

In this situation the striking batter's runner stands in the vicinity of the square leg umpire, between them and the striking batter, ensuring they have their bat grounded behind the popping crease. The runner and striker are not allowed to impede any of the opposition fielders at any time. If the runner is out of the crease and the wicketkeeper attempts a stumping of the striking batter, irrespective of whether the striker was in, the striker will be given out. This will not be given as a stumping but as a run out. Both the striker and the runner must then leave the field of play.

When the striker hits the ball and they or the non-striker call for a run, the runner sets off running as they would in a normal situation, albeit they are running on an adjacent pitch to the striking batter and non-striking running batter. All normal rules apply, and all three batters can be run out if the opportunity arises.

When the injured batter is off strike

In this situation the runner stands in the normal non-striker's position at the bowler's end. The injured batter now stands with the square leg umpire. They are not allowed to impede any of the opposition fielders at any time. After the ball is struck and the action ensues, the injured batter must stand still until they are next required to take strike or change positions for the forthcoming over. All normal rules apply. If the runner is run out during the ensuing action, both the runner and injured batter must leave the field of play.

Batting with a runner can be a huge challenge, even for the most experienced batters. Imagine the confusion and dangers inherent when young, inexperienced batters are exposed to this scenario. There is even the possibility that both batters require a runner! Furthermore, imagine if you are dealing with a right-hand/left-hand batting combination. Where do the runner and striker stand if they are rotating the strike every ball?

Being prepared with some knowledge of this potentially confusing and subsequently disastrous situation is an essential element of sustaining a match-winning individual innings or partnership. The reader is encouraged to familiarise themselves with 'The Laws of Cricket' for the full rules regarding batting, running between the wickets and batting with a runner.

SIX
THE MENTAL ASPECTS OF BATTING

'The most important mental aspect for scoring runs is concentration – it is everything if you want to score big runs and influence the match. You also need self-belief and to create a structure that works for yourself. What you put into it is always what you get out. Having the right attitude is number one. It is everything in life. Are you prepared to make sacrifices? Are you prepared to work hard?'

GRAHAM GOOCH

So far we have delved into the technical and tactical aspects of batting. Most players and coaches will tell you that batting is not just played with the bat in hand, it is what is going on between the ears that counts. In this chapter we take an investigative look at the mental aspects of batting from concentration and staying focused, to fear of failure and resilience. While continually searching to develop your technical and tactical elements of batting, the same should be true of the mental skills.

Just like these other aspects of your game, mental skills can be worked and improved on over time as well.

Concentration

'Concentration is the most important mental aspect of batting. However, you don't always get that long in training so it is hard then to drill/practise concentration. Your practice needs to measure up to what you do in a match. I used to practise on my own and get bowlers in to bowl at me. I would replicate a match and have a break between each ball just like in a real game. I would put money on the stumps, which was theirs if they got me out, and I aimed to bat through the entire session without being dismissed. Longer practice allows you to build an innings, but if you only have a short time in a net session you are more likely to work through your full repertoire of shots.'

SIR GEOFFREY BOYCOTT

The longer the format of the match, and therefore the longer the innings required from a batter, the more powerful and robust their concentration must become. The ability to focus clearly on the next ball you receive and then repeat that over and over again throughout the innings is an essential element of batting.

The secret for concentrating for long periods of time is to only have a really tight mental focus for the period that the bowler runs in and releases the ball at you. This will be somewhere between five and ten seconds depending on the length of the bowler's run-up. Full concentration will be needed immediately after the ball is hit, as there may be runs to be taken.

The period outside of this when the ball is being returned to the bowler, you need to be able to 'dial down' that mental focus and relax more, though you will still need to check for field placing changes, etc. Like any skill, you can train yourself to do that and, once mastered, it will help you avoid mental fatigue, enabling you to concentrate for much longer periods of time and therefore avoid lapses in concentration that can lead to poor decisions and execution of the shots you play. Many dismissals of batters are not through unplayable deliveries or poor technique, but usually a slight loss of mental focus that leads to a poor decision, resulting in a wicket-taking opportunity for the opposition.

> *'In long formats, mentally you need to be able to focus sharply for short periods of time over a long period of time.'*
> **MARK BUTCHER**

There are numerous techniques batters use to help them switch their concentration on and off. For switching on, a lot of batters have some body movement triggers: for example, adjust thigh pad, retake guard, etc. Even a simple trigger movement of moving back and across pre-delivery is not just a cue for the body to get ready to move, but also acts as a mental cue to focus fully on the ball. To switch off, many batters scratch their guard again or walk away from the wicket to the leg side, this being their cue to mentally relax and switch off. As the bowler gets to the top of their mark, the batter walks back, retakes guard, this being the cue to switch back on mentally.

Self-talk is another common technique associated with tight focus. As the bowler is running in, many batters can be seen whispering to themselves. The content is not necessarily that important, but it is relevant to the individual player. 'Watch the ball' is very common, as is 'play straight' or a simple 'come on' as if the player is reminding themselves to concentrate. Yours may be 'move your feet' or 'get my head to the ball' or 'you are not going to get me out'. Say whatever works for you, thus ensuring you are fully focused mentally for the next delivery. It does not even need to be verbally externalised. It can be internalised in your head without any verbalising at all.

It is very likely that you do some of the above without realising it. If you can get some video of match play and take a look at what you currently do, you could assess whether there is anything you could add or remove that will help you switch on/off.

A lot of batters mention being in the 'zone' when they have played well and put a long innings together. They found a mental state where their focus was absolute each ball, everything feeling effortless. This can come at any time in an innings. Similarly to working on your trigger movement or a cover drive, your mental cues can also be developed so that they feel very natural, potentially allowing this absolute concentration 'zone' to be achieved in any innings you play.

While batting, a batter should never be worrying about a technical aspect of their game. If you are focusing on your bat going back straight you will not be truly focused mentally and achieving any sort of 'zone' will be much more difficult. If you have practised correctly, you will feel confident about the technical aspect of your technique, thus now allowing you to simply watch the ball and trust your instincts.

Note for coaches

To help batters build this switch off/on into their practice it is worth having sessions where bowlers bowl individually to one player for six balls, allowing time for the batter to go through and practise their in-between delivery routine. Most net sessions, one bowler follows another in quick succession and a batter's routine is very different to how it is out in the middle. You may also need to bat most of the team in your practice, meaning that a batter may only bat for 10–20 minutes, much less than the time required to bat out in the middle. If possible, try to factor in some one-on-one contests into your sessions.

'Out when you are out' sessions are also a great way to develop concentration skills for batters. They know that one mistake will mean their practice is over, but if they concentrate and play well they have the opportunity to have a much longer practice. You can set a target of a certain amount of time with a reward at the end – perhaps four overs of T20 batting practice if they bat through their allotted time without being dismissed.

'You don't want anything too complicated but you need a mental process. Self-talk is one thing that can help. Simple cues like 'watch the ball', 'play straight' – you should focus on one important thing.'
GRAHAM GOOCH

Personal targets

We discussed setting short target goals in the tactical session as a way of building partnerships to achieve a longer-term goal. These targets can also be used to good effect to aid concentration and focus. Your long-term target maybe a fifty or a hundred, depending on the match format and how long is left in the innings. In a run chase the goal may be to be there at the end regardless of your own personal score.

When you have just arrived at the crease these targets seem a long way off. You need to break the task down into smaller chunks that are easier and faster to achieve. Initially this could be to simply get off the mark. Then, once achieved, set a new goal – get to ten or to still be batting in 15 minutes' time maybe. Once achieved, set the next target and so on and so on. Many batters count their runs for this reason. It helps them to stay focused and they get a sense of personal achievement once each small target is reached, which encourages them and builds confidence.

This also helps batters avoid getting to 20 or 30 runs and then making a mistake. So many players (young or old, beginners or experienced) can have this issue. They focus well for a certain length of time but always seem to get out on a similar score. If this applies to you it will help to have these small targets as personal goals, and perhaps look at periods of time rather than runs themselves if there is a particular score where you have become vulnerable to being dismissed.

If you do reach a long-term target but there is still time in the match for more runs to be scored, or the match is still to be won, it is important to take some extra time before facing the next ball, and reset a new target. It is very common for batters to get out shortly after scoring a fifty or a century simply because they achieved their goal and then failed to reset some new targets. By not resetting, they lose the sharp focus that helped them achieve the milestone in the first place.

Remember targets, run counting and time counting are a personal preference. Some batters personally do not like to know what score they are on.

It is simply finding what works for you to make sure you are focused for each ball and concentrating fully every time the bowler lets go of the ball. If you can achieve this without targets then it may not be necessary for you.

It is worth mentioning your mindset as you approach a target or milestone. Often players get out in the forties or nineties. It is not so much that they lose concentration, but the long-term target is now within sight, and internally you can put more pressure on yourself. The opposition may well start talking about it as well and you become more nervous.

Irrespective of how tense the match situation, how nervous you are or how quick the bowler, it is important that you stay relaxed and the body does not tense up, as this will affect your movement of both feet and hands. You might not get your front foot to the pitch of the ball, and the path of the bat coming through can be affected, which will affect your ability to strike the ball cleanly. Tensing of the muscles can be very common if you have had a recent run of low scores. You feel under more pressure and therefore anxious, which can tighten the muscles. It is so important to relax as much as possible. Focus on your breathing (which should be deep breaths and a slow release) and try to ensure you 'switch off' fully between deliveries. Try to exude a calm body language as much as possible, even if that is not how you are feeling inside.

As you approach a milestone you may also want to reduce your short-term targets to aid concentration. It is crucial not to play any differently for the last 10–20 runs. Your method has been successful up to this point.

It is worth moving away from your personal milestone and focusing upon the team's requirements. What does the team need at this stage of the match? The answer will nearly always be for you to keep batting as you are, just forgetting about your own milestone for a moment, which can ease the pressure when you get near it and is another way to alleviate the internal pressure.

The next ball is always the one that counts

One of the most important aspects of run scoring is being able to put errors and bad shots behind you, focusing clearly on the next ball, removing any negative thoughts of events prior to that moment. While you are out in the middle it is only the next ball that counts, and this needs your full focus and concentration.

Perhaps you have just played and missed, swinging wildly at a wide delivery, been dropped or just survived a missed stumping. Perhaps you have been hit on the head by a bouncer that knocked you to the floor. All of these experiences can affect your ego and play on your mind. Did I look silly? Did I look out of my depth? These are only fleeting thoughts though, and will pass if you allow them to. Put a positive spin on it and tell yourself that the next ball could be the best shot you have ever played regardless of the type of delivery next delivered by the bowler. You are still there in the middle and therefore you are still able to score runs and help the team.

There will be time to review your innings at the end of the match or the day's play, either by yourself or with a coach. This is the time for honest reflection and analysis. You then have time to make any adjustments prior to your next innings. The time not to do it is while you are out in the middle. You need to relax, remain focused, trust your instincts, stay calm and try to remove your ego and emotions from the situation. A caveat to this is when you think that if you do not make some sort of technical adjustment you will not survive much longer. Again, trust your instincts.

It is worth bearing in mind that you will never play an innings where every ball comes out of the middle of the bat and where you do not play and miss at some stage. Inside edges on to pads, a play and miss outside off stump, a nick through the slips for four can all happen. Sometimes batters think that they are batting so badly that they might as well get out. The higher standard you play the more moments there will be like this as the opposition gets stronger. It is simply part of the game, and if you can accept that, then you will be in a much more robust state of mind to deal with them when they happen.

If you are a young player reading this, the above point cannot be emphasised enough. Scoring runs and looking good is fantastic, the ultimate goal for each innings. However, the goal for every innings is to score runs, pure and simple. As a batter that is your job. How you get them or how good you look getting them is secondary.

'I prefer to use term 'make runs' rather than 'score runs'. To score means it goes well – everything falls into place on that day. When you make runs you will have those good days but you can also deliver when you're not at your best. You know your game well enough to make runs even when not feeling your best.'
GRAHAM GOOCH

Motivation and single-mindedness

It is desirable to develop a positive mindset where you want to play against the best players in the opposition and test yourself. It can be easy to slip into a mindset of hoping the opposition's quickest or best bowler will not be fit, as that increases the chances of making runs yourself. This may be true, but why not imagine how good it would be to face them and score runs. This is a much greater achievement and will give you far more satisfaction if you make a big score. Additionally, as you step up to each new level, the greater your chance of immediate success will be rather than taking more time for you to acclimatise. Never be afraid of taking yourself out of your comfort zone; you will not only grow as a player but also as a person, which will give you much greater self-belief.

Although often mistaken for selfishness, it can be advantageous for run scoring to have a single-minded attitude. Performing for the team and batting to the match situation are essential. A slow hundred in a run chase but lose the game is not the objective a batter should aim for. However, you do need to develop a strong feeling of pride in your own performance.

PRIDE – Personal Responsibility In Developing Excellence.

A lot of players can be negatively affected when their partner gets out or a string of wickets fall at the other end. While disappointing in terms of the team's efforts to win the match and for your team-mates not scoring, you still need to be able to focus on your own game and keep concentrating on every ball. This single-mindedness will serve you well during difficult times, match situations, and conditions, and help develop you into a player the team can rely on.

Another really positive mindset to have in terms of your own motivation is the desire to outperform the opposition's best batter, or an opposition batter that bats in a similar position to you. If they score runs use it as an extra incentive for your own performance. There is nothing wrong with wanting to be the best. That in itself is not arrogance, it is simply a state of mind where you want to keep learning, improving and developing to become the best version of yourself as a player. Arrogance is when you believe you are already the best. This ultimately leads to complacency because you believe you have nothing left to learn.

Positive mindset and enjoyment

'You have to go out there convinced you are going to be successful. Think positively, but everyone has negative thoughts. Think about the times when it's gone well. You've got to say to yourself that I except the negative thoughts – it's a normal human emotion – but then to put those to the back of your mind and have a positive mindset – that it is going to be my day today. Put that to the forefront of your mind. I've got runs against Malcolm Marshall – I can do it again.'
GRAHAM GOOCH

It is not always easy to have a positive mindset but it does help to be become adept at turning negative thoughts into positive ones. It could be that you are playing in a cup final, or the league can be won in this match, so there could be more external pressure and expectation placed upon you. You could easily turn to thoughts of failing and letting the team and supporters down, but try and flip this on its head to thoughts of how great it would be to produce a match-defining score. Visualise this in your mind. Imagine how good it would feel to perform in this match and delight your team-mates, coach and supporters. The bigger the match or match situation think, 'I could really make a name for myself here.'

Similarly, in tough match situations where conditions suit the bowlers or there has been a batting collapse, think of the positive outcome if you manage to perform well and get your team out of trouble. There may be fielders placed around you in catching positions, where you think that you cannot make a mistake or you will be out. Once again, flip this on its head and think that if there are so many attacking fielders there must also be plenty of gaps to score into.

Positive thinking does not necessarily mean aggressive thinking. It simply means to think positively about your own game, the match situation, and conditions. Visualise a positive outcome. A clear, positive mindset leads to better decision-making, coupled with better body movement so you can execute the correct shot efficiently to the next delivery. You should reward yourself internally for playing the shot correctly, and give yourself a mental pat on the back, whether it was an attacking shot, a defensive one or a good leave. If it was the right shot to that ball then you should be pleased with yourself.

Sometimes you can middle three brilliant shots straight to fielders, naturally feeling disappointed that you did not score off any of those deliveries. It is tempting to mentally beat yourself up for not having made more of those scoring opportunities. It is very common, particularly with younger players, that through frustration you then become impatient and attempt to make up for this by going for a risky shot, and subsequently give your wicket away. Instead, mentally reward yourself for having correctly executed the shots, and think positively that the next one will hit the gap when the opportunity presents itself again. Do not let feelings of frustration cloud your decision-making and positive mindset. A great phrase to remember is: 'Heart in the oven, head in the freezer!'

Turning negative thoughts into positive ones can be worked on and improved with practice, just like any other skill in the game.

Enjoyment is a major part of our coaching philosophy, and when the game gets tough or you are going through a run of low scores it is important to think back to why you started playing the game in the first place, whatever level you are currently at. As a batter this was most likely for the enjoyment you got from simply hitting the ball out of the middle of the bat and watching it fly away. It is important to take yourself back to this if you find your enjoyment waning during a period of low scores.

Go and hit some balls in a net, served up by throws, bowlers or a bowling machine. Have some fun. See how far you can hit them and just enjoy that feeling of ball striking. Keep training fun and interesting. Yes, work on areas you need to develop or where you need remedial work, but make sure you do some fun stuff as well to relax and bring a smile to your face. For some it is not just a game, it is their profession. Whatever profession you are in it is important that it is enjoyable and fun. This applies if cricket is your livelihood, or you have aspirations that it will be.

You also need to enjoy the contest and challenges the game throws at you. These can often be against friends in the opposition or players you know well. There may be some banter and chat and the situation may be difficult. Enjoy these moments, enjoy the challenges and do not have a desire for the game to always be easy. There is always much greater satisfaction and pleasure when you have had to work hard for it.

A simple equation for enjoyment: Good practice leads to improved confidence in your game = better individual performances in the middle = greater enjoyment = improved team performances = even greater enjoyment.

Great personal performances or winning matches for your team are not the only areas of the game that are enjoyable; there is also the satisfaction achieved from giving your best even if it did not work out. Finally, great enjoyment can be taken from being part of a team comprising good friends and team-mates.

Confidence

How often have you heard a batter say that they knew they were going to get runs today, they just felt good and confident about themselves with no apparent reason why. Some people just appear more confident than others, but any sort of natural confidence in their self is an illusion. It is not simply that they woke up feeling good that day. You cannot allow how you personally feel on the morning of the match to have an impact on how you visualise yourself performing during it.

In terms of batting, confidence comes from a deep understanding that you can handle the situation at hand. You can appear to be the most confident person in the world, but if you have never practised playing the short ball with the bowler coming round the wicket and firing it into your ribs and throat, you are not going to feel very confident about handling it. You may need to hit 20 off an over to win the match, but if you have never practised range hitting it will be an enormous challenge. A left-arm leg-spinner is turning it both ways and you have never worked on reading their delivery grips and actions. You will not feel confident as you have no game plan in place for this bowling or match situation.

Improved batting confidence, enabling you to walk out to the middle knowing you can genuinely handle whatever the opposition throws at you, comes from hard work in training, combined with previous match experiences. Knowing that your basic technical skills are embedded, you have developed a good understanding of your own game and have solid game plans in place will reinforce self-assurance. Confidence in your batting ability grows from the hard work you put into your training and preparation. Of course, it also comes with experience as you face different bowlers and match situations out in the middle. These can all be mentally referred to, making you feel confident in your batting ability.

Resilience

There is a lot of talk these days about resilience. This is the ability to withstand adversity. In a batting sense, resilience is the ability to deal with tough situations, a great bowling spell or grinding out runs when you are out of form and struggling to bat fluently. Probably the best example of a resilient modern player is Alastair Cook, who was never once dropped from the England Test team. He had certainly come close, with pressure applied by the media, but when he found himself in these situations he found a way to get runs or a series of scores to keep his place.

Batting resilience largely comes with experience, but it can be developed through practice, taking yourself out of your comfort zone in both practice and matches. Spend time working on aspects of your game that you find difficult and challenging, maybe match scenarios that do not suit your natural game. If you are a swashbuckling hitter, do some sessions where you need to block and defend for five overs to save a match, or net sessions where you will be given out if you hit the ball in the air. Similarly, an accumulating opening batter needs to have sessions of range hitting and scenarios where they need a high volume of runs per over. Over time you will discover you are more adaptable and capable of building more into your game, improving self-confidence continually.

If possible, ask whether you can bat out of position in a match or two. If you have always batted five, ask to open and learn to handle the new ball. It will be highly challenging initially but so rewarding in the long term. Upsetting team dynamics and balance can be an issue in this situation, so this method of development may need to be enforced naturally, for example an injury to an existing opener. If not, the proposal needs to be suggested sensitively to the other batter concerned.

True resilience is also about putting your inner pride to one side, not being concerned about what you look like. We have already discussed that batting becomes more challenging as you ascend up the levels, testing yourself against the best players. They may test you technically, physically and mentally, even asking questions about your bravery. But if you can stick it out, battle hard and come out the other side still at the crease, this builds your batting resilience and your self-confidence.

Dealing with nerves and fear of failure

Probably the most crippling mental aspect of any sport is fear of failure. Cricket is no exception. When you have placed too much importance and pressure on an outcome of a particular innings, you can often switch to a greater emphasis on not getting out rather than confidently attempting to achieve your initial target. This may be because it is a big match or you are hoping that through a good performance this could lead to selection for the club's 1st XI, the county team, the regional team or your next contract. Moreover, it could simply be that you got two low scores in the previous match and you are desperate not to fail again. All of these factors can lead to you putting more pressure on yourself, becoming more nervous than normal as you walk out to bat.

Firstly, remember that these thoughts and nerves are very natural, everyone feels them, whatever level they are at. They are not unique to you; therefore, you should not feel weak because of them. This realisation is important in coming to terms with feeling nervous or afraid of getting out. It is the same for everyone.

Next is the realisation that a part of batting is getting out. Every batter who has ever played the game has got out or has made a mistake, whether that leads to a dismissal or not. Look up any of the great players and see how many not outs they have. It will be a tiny percentage of the number of innings they play. Getting out is part of the game and your thoughts about being dismissed should not influence your decision-making. Only the match situation can do that. A batter should remember that there is a very high possibility that they will be dismissed in their innings; it is just a matter of how many runs they will score before this happens.

Batters need to have a phlegmatic outlook. Getting out is part of the game and once dismissed you cannot rewind time and have another go. You need to look forward not back and believe that the next time you bat it will be your day and you will get runs. As disappointing as getting out is, once it has happened it has happened and you do not want to overly dwell on it. There will be another match, another innings to look forward to.

Playing the match situation or focusing on the team needs can help alleviate the self-imposed pressure put on yourself when trying to impress and gain selection for a representative side, etc. A good example of this is young county players who are close to selection for the ECB Bunbury Festival, this being the regional U15 boys competition. It is the first time that the best U15 players in the country are assembled together into four regional teams. It is a big competition and very prestigious if you are selected. In lead-up matches prior to the selection announcement, it is very common for some players to discard their natural game, as they overly worry about the fear of failure and missing out on selection. Immediately after the selection has been announced, freedom returns to their natural game, whether they have been selected or not.

It is so important that any of your long-term targets are just that, they are long term. At that particular moment in time you can only focus on the next ball and setting small attainable targets. The next ball is all that matters, so clear your head, focus and watch the ball.

Nerves and fear of failure can be heightened if you have a poor record against a certain team or at a certain ground. Again, try to put a positive spin on it and think that today will be the day when you are successful. Those low scores are a thing of the past. Tell yourself, 'Today is going to be a good day, I am just going to play each ball as it comes and enjoy the challenges of batting at this ground or against these bowlers again.'

If you are an established match-winning batter, the expectation placed on you by others and yourself can lead to a heightened fear of failure. If you are a young player, perhaps having just broken into the senior 1st XI, there is less expectation on you to score from the senior players, and you probably do not feel too much pressure to either. A score is a bonus. However, once established as a major run getter for the team there is an expectation for you to play match-defining innings on a regular basis. Even the opposition may be expecting this. Where once you received verbal distractions, there is now silence. This can be unnerving, as it is different. Similarly to other external pressures, these are only self-induced thoughts that will pass. One innings is never more important than another. These are natural feelings, they are part of the game and form part of the experience of playing over a long period of time.

Nerves are very natural, and you will probably feel them whenever you walk out to bat to start an innings. It is important to accept the realisation of this and to appreciate that nerves are a good thing, as the adrenaline pumped into your body acts as a stimulant, enhancing reactions and body movements. It is the body firing up and you can channel that energy into enhancing your performance. Many like to turn this into aggression, which can be useful if facing a quick bowler, but it may not be as helpful against spin. Adrenaline should be a natural performance enhancer, not a detractor.

There are ways you can control and channel these nervous feelings. As you walk out to bat it is important to get the body moving, particularly the feet.

Many players like to start running, do some squats, groin stretching, shadow-practise a few shots and get the arms swinging. Combine this with deep controlled breaths and you will start to relax. Taking your time before you face your first ball is also important. Check the field again, even if you have already noted it. Walk off to square leg, enact some more body movements and inhale more deep breaths. You will still be fired up, but hopefully in a controlled way. Removing the tenseness from your body will enable better footwork, and the calmer mental state will encourage better decision-making.

Visualisation

Some batters visualise a lot, others not so much, but in terms of controlling nerves it can be important to the individual. As you are walking out to bat visualise yourself getting a positive stride in to your first ball, swaying out of the way of a bouncer, or striking the ball straight back over the bowler's head if it is a T20. This visualisation can help remove thoughts where you unintentionally visualise yourself getting out first ball, which is a surprisingly common thought.

Visualisation can be a very valuable training technique, whether you have been physically able to practise between matches or not. The frequency of practice sessions depends entirely on the individual. Facility accessibility, coach availability, work commitments and time availability are all factors. However, you can still visualise yourself batting, rehearsing trigger movements and shots in your mind. Imagine an opposition bowler and visualise them running in at you. Furthermore, you can add to this by shadowing these shots with a bat in your hand, standing in front of a mirror for extra realism.

There are two methods of visualisation: internal and external. Internal visualisation describes seeing the situation from inside yourself, your own mind's eye. The feelings, sounds, images and even smells can be present. External visualisation describes observing the situation from another viewing point, such as a member of the crowd for example. You see the whole situation from afar, not just from inside your own head. Both methods are equally powerful, but which one is chosen is down to individual preference. It is worth trying each method initially to discover which is more useful to you.

When used correctly, visualisation can be a powerful tool, as it leads to positive thinking and ultimately it is the mind that commands your body to move. It can even be used in the middle of an innings. For example, perhaps a bowler has been consistently hitting an area outside off stump with the ball swinging away. So far you have let them go, but you can visualise in your head the next time they pitch there, you take a positive stride into the ball and drive it through the covers. When this actually happens, you will have already gone through the mental rehearsal to execute the shot successfully. You could even imagine yourself in a situation when you are receiving verbal distractions from the opposition fielders, then visualise your favoured response and the performance benefits gained from it.

Dealing with fielders' and bowlers' verbal distractions

At every level of the game there is a certain amount of noise from the opposition. This is often simply encouragement for the bowler or another member of the team. But there will be times when it is directed at you. It tends to be worse in club cricket where umpires are often not strong enough to prevent it or to intervene. In youth cricket, coaches are present and normally step in if it oversteps the mark. At the highest level, in the professional game, there are strict regulations in place concerning what is acceptable and what is not.

It is important to remember that this chattering is only there to distract and break your concentration. It is nothing personal about you. The opposition simply want to distract you, in order that you make a mistake and give your wicket away. By breaking the 'zone' you are in, distracting you in this way can be a successful way of achieving this.

The fielders are entitled to say as much as they like between deliveries, but they are not allowed to speak a word as the bowler runs in. As this is your period for sharp focus, you should not have any verbal distractions at this time. If you do, this is outlawed in the rules of the game and you should pull away from the wicket. You should also highlight it to the umpire so they can speak with the opposition captain. This is not a sign of weakness but of strength; you are simply giving yourself the best chance of not being distracted at a time when you need to be focusing hard. It can also inspire you to a positive mindset and add more motivation, making you even more determined to perform well.

Most teams eventually quieten down once you have been in for a while. It is very hard to keep a verbal distraction tactic going for a prolonged period, as the fielders become disheartened as you establish yourself. Ultimately you can only counter any opposition verbal distractions by getting a score on the board or walking off with a stump after you have won the match for your team.

A batter verbally responding back to the fielding side is a matter of personal preference. If it motivates you to play better and enhances performance, then that works for you. But if it distracts you mentally, you should definitely not get involved. Stick to your routines and focus on the ball, ignoring all the verbal interference. Ultimately, would you prefer to win the war of words but be dismissed or not get involved and complete a match-winning innings? Sportsmen and women generally perform better when the emotions are taken out. Once again, remember: 'Heart in the oven, head in the freezer'.

SEVEN
ADVANCED BATTING SKILLS

'A vital skill is being able to rotate the strike regularly. But also having the expansive game to regularly hit boundaries at the end. So, it is important to know you have a boundary option, for me it would be a scoop, or a reverse sweep. If I'm under pressure I know I can go to one of those options for a boundary.'

BEN DUCKETT

This chapter looks at additional skills you can add to your game, as you become more experienced and move up the levels. We discuss playing spin bowling as well as pace bowling, varying stance and pre-delivery movements to open up different parts of the ground for run scoring, and a whole host of other tips and tactics that can add a further edge to your game.

The training cycle

To break down your annual training cycle we recommend the following:

End of season to November:	Rest
November to January:	Technical focus
January to March:	Continued technical focus with introduction of tactical sessions
March to April:	Tactical play becomes main focus
In season:	Match play focus with training specific to the opposition you face and technical tweaks only

If you have had a busy summer, it is important that you factor in some downtime from cricket for at least a month after the end of the season. We recommend anywhere between four and eight weeks. This not only gives the body time to rest, but also gives you a chance to mentally switch off from the game too. Enjoyment is such an important aspect of playing any sport, so a break will you give you the opportunity to come back to training fresh and focused, hopefully returning with a renewed vigour, no matter how the previous season went.

The early part of your autumn training is a good time to focus on any technical changes you want to make to your game. This could be a trigger movement, how you pick up your bat, or technical enhancements for specific shots. Next season is still a long way ahead, so you have plenty of time for any changes to become thoroughly embedded in your game before the season begins. This is important, as you do not want to be playing your first match thinking about technique. It needs to feel totally natural by then, so you are just simply focusing on the ball as the bowler runs in.

During the second part of the winter you should continue to work on the technical adjustments, but with tactical elements and game plans to various bowlers, coupled with different match scenarios added. This segment then leads into pre-season, where the tactical elements become the main focus. The season itself will mostly be focused on specific match preparation, but you still need that self-awareness to honestly assess your game, and possibly make some small technical changes if deemed absolutely necessary. The key element of practice during the season is to practise as you intend to play, to get into good habits and routines that you can take into matches. Remember, having good technique and game plans develops confidence, and so will good pre-match practice.

Game ownership

The older you get, the more experienced you become, and the more you practise the deeper your understanding of your game. As a player, it is important you take ownership of your game and development. No matter how long you have been playing or whatever level you are playing at, there will always be something new to learn, either from the players you play with or against, or from coaches within your team. Early in your career you will be relying on senior players and coaches for information, but as you develop and gain experience, you need to take more responsibility for and ownership of your own performance.

Do not be afraid to be different, but do not do it just for the sake of it, just because you see someone else doing it. Remember, everyone is different, we are all individuals, so what works for one may not work for another. There needs to be logic in anything you want to add to training or match play. Additionally, it is important that you are open to new ideas. Assess the reasoning behind them, try them, and see if they work for you. Be patient, and do not give up too early when trying something new. If you persevere it may lead to a huge advancement in your game. Ultimately, all coaches, parents and team-mates want you to improve, be successful and enjoy the game of cricket.

Good examples of players taking ownership of their game come in the form of three great international batters. At a critical point in their careers, they all stressed a realisation that their current method of batting was not working, so they needed to make changes to become more consistent run scorers. This was their decision, they personally determined the changes needed, not the coaches, although the coaches would have been involved in the subsequent remedial work.

The three players are Graham Gooch, Steve Waugh and Steve Smith. All had played international cricket but had not managed to become a regular team members due to inconsistency in their batting. With Gooch, it was a problem with planting his front foot and getting out lbw. With Waugh, it was a reliance on his off-side game and a problem with playing the short ball. With Smith, it was playing at wide balls and getting caught behind the wicket regularly. Through honest self-reflection they identified their problems, decided they wanted to do something about them and then worked methodically in correcting them. All three players went on to become the number-one ranked batsman in Test match cricket at the time and became legends of the game.

In T20 cricket, Joe Root has made some fundamental changes and worked hard on his power hitting to get back into the frame for the England T20 XI. He identified shortcomings in his game for this particular format of cricket and has given himself the best possible chance of becoming a regular member of that team.

The most important recommendation from this segment is the necessity for honest self-reflection and taking responsibility for and ownership of your own game. How good you want to be is in your own hands. Hopefully, the fact that you are reading this book indicates that you are already on this path.

'You need to realise you are your own best coach. You are responsible for your performance and your development. A coach can give you ideas and direction. From this select the right things that work for you and are suitable for you.'
GRAHAM GOOCH

Here is a comprehensive list of items that affect your success or influence your effectiveness as a batter, which may help with assessing any areas where you can gain additional percentage performance gains:

Natural ability	Eyesight	Dominant eye
Hearing	Set-up	Judging length
Reactions	Hand-eye-foot coordination	Technique
Balance/head position	Strong base	Shot selection
Playing the ball late	Weight of bat	Preparation
Organisation	Warm-up	Cool-down
Grip/glove condition	Footwear (studs?)	Batting equipment
Forgotten equipment	Borrowed equipment	Attitude
Confidence level	Perfectionist	Positive mindset
Fixed or growth mindset	Patience	Enjoyment
Relaxation levels	Mental strength	Nerves
Fear of failure	Dealing with failure	Resilience
Perseverance	Pride	Arrogance
Fear of injury	Injury	Batting helmet
Past experiences	Player experience	Batter's strengths
Batter's weaknesses	Confidence	Concentration
Control	Commitment	Distractions
Sledging	Breaks in play	Motivations
Training/work ethic	Self-responsibility	Honesty
Learning style	Coaches	Team-mates
Controllables	Uncontrollables	Physical fitness
Speed and power	Endurance	Tiredness
Physical impairments	Targets (short-term)	Targets (long-term)
Current and past form	Batting average	Match format
Batting first or second	Match situation	Batting plan
Know your role	Tactical awareness	Situational awareness
Scoreboard pressure	Type of bowling	Knowledge of lbw law
Bowlers' reputations	Gender of bowler	Level being played
The opposition	Field placings	Hitting along the floor
Hitting through the gaps	Hitting over the top	Rotating the strike
Partnerships	Assessment of bowlers	Bowlers' plans
Assessment of fielders	Ball condition/age/type	Pitch condition/gradients
Pitch assessment	Bowlers' footmarks	Outfield condition

Outfield slopes	Boundary distances	Lack of sightscreens
Available batting time	Innings time of day	Weather
Temperature	Sun protection	Sun in batter's eyes
Westerly sun height	Reduced light levels	Wind direction/strength
Position in batting order	Wickets in hand	Number of overs left
Batting declarations	Running between wickets	Calling
Communication	Role of striker	Role of non-striker
Run outs	Batting with a runner	Strength of partner
Practice/preparation	Lifestyle	Injury prevention
Sufficient sleep	Nutrition	Dehydration
Energy levels	Rest and down time	Recovery
Waiting to bat	Superstitions/routines	Development plan
Availability		

Pre-match preparation

As a young player, it can be hard to know what form your pre-match preparations should take to put you in a confident state of mind before going out to bat. Your first cricket may not allow much time between arriving and starting the match. You simply go and play. As you advance through the levels of cricket, the expectations on players change, regarding when they are expected to arrive and the content of the pre-match warm-up.

It is so important to develop an understanding of your own game, and every player will be different regarding what they like to do in their own pre-match preparation. The important question to ask yourself is: what form of pre-match preparation will put me in a confident state of mind before I go out to bat?

Again, we can go back to the reason why you started playing the game in the first place, that wonderful feeling of the ball coming out of the middle of the bat. Maybe all you need is to have a few full toss throw-downs, where you work through a few shots, making sure you are watching the ball hard, just feeling the ball coming off the middle of the bat. Perhaps 20 balls on the front foot and 20 off the back foot may be all you need.

Time available is not the only consideration for your pre-match preparation. Every ground will have different facilities. Some will have net facilities, others may not. As you move up playing levels, more grounds will have net facilities, so this will increase your pre-match preparation options, culminating in an earlier arrival time at the ground. This may extend the number of throw-downs you have, if that is your preferred method of warm-up. If the surface is good, you could move from full toss throws to overarm bounce throws.

You may also want to face some bowling in the net, to check that you are watching the ball closely, picking up length and that your early innings game plan is in place. You may know the opposition has a fast bowler, so you may want to do some short ball practice.

Ultimately, it is for you to decide what best prepares you for the day ahead, makes you feel confident about your game and puts you in a positive state of mind before going out to bat.

Being ready, both physically and mentally, for that first ball is so important, no matter which format or level of the game you are playing. It could be the best ball you are going to face. A wicket has probably just fallen and the bowler and the opposition team are on a high. There may be some extra vocals and noise. You need to ensure that on your way to the wicket you have physically warmed up with dynamics such as shot shadowing, heel clicks, jogging, squats and jumps. Mentally, you should try to be as relaxed and focused as possible. Take your time, check the field, take deep breaths, retake your guard, walk away again, repeating some dynamics if necessary. Only come back to the crease when you feel in the 'zone' or as close to it as possible, ignoring any discouraging comments coming from the opposition. Then simply focus in on that ball.

If you are waiting a considerable time to go in because of a long partnership, it is important to get up regularly to stretch your legs, maybe shadow a few shots. Take a break from watching the game for a while to ensure you stay mentally fresh. When shadowing, some players like to use two bats so that when they go out to bat, their own bat feels lighter and easier to swing.

> *'I like to have a bit of a feel-good net or a few throw-downs. The bulk of your practice should have been done in the days building up to the game.'*
> **BEN DUCKETT**

Hitting the gaps

One vital part of run scoring is hitting the gaps in the field. The more you pick out these gaps when playing attacking shots, obviously the faster you will score, and the bigger your score will be. Batters such as Kane Williamson and Joe Root are masters at this. Despite not having the power that other top international batters have, they are able to score at a quick pace simply because they hit the ball into the gaps regularly. You may well have watched matches yourself or played in some against or with batters who do not appear to be scoring quickly, but when you check their score they are already 30 not out.

The earlier you start practising 'gapping' the more proficient you will become at it. Whenever possible, when practising, ask the coach or bowler to set a field and, if possible, have these marked by cones or other markers so you can see whether your shots are in the gaps or not. You can then begin the process of identifying how you can hit the gaps more often. This could be to play the ball later or to use your wrists to open or close the face of the bat to beat the fielder.

Note for coaches

Setting fields and marking them with cones can be done for bowling, throw-downs, bowling machine work and 'sticking'. Add match scenarios for more realism and ask the player to be honest about whether they have just hit the gap or not. You can keep score and see whether the batter improves over the course of a few weeks or training cycle.

Manoeuvring the fielders

There can only be nine fielders at any one time on the cricket field, so it is a game of cat and mouse between the fielding captain, bowler and batters as to where these fielders will be positioned. As you become more proficient at hitting the gaps, you will find the field changing to stop you scoring in a certain area. Very often, an area that would provide a safe scoring option may be covered by a fielder. In this situation, your ability to use your wrists and hit gaps is important.

Here is an example: You are facing a left-arm spinner and you want to play a drive with the spin through extra cover, but there is a mid-off, a tight extra cover, and a deeper extra cover on their left shoulder. As much as you try you cannot get it through and the dot balls start building. However, there is not a fielder on the 45 on the leg side, and only a backward point square on the off side. It takes courage, but you could try a reverse sweep past the backward point fielder, or a paddle sweep into the vacant 45-degree leg-side area. Play either shot successfully and the fielding captain may well move one of the extra cover fielders to plug one of those scoring options, then making the drive past extra cover a much easier option.

Judgement of length and line, the hitting area and hitting on the up

The majority of batters find it easier to judge line than length, but the most successful ones are experts at judging length too. These players rarely get stuck on the crease, displaying no footwork, as they consistently play forward or back according to the length of the ball the bowler delivers.

Similarly to the principle of hitting the gaps, it is important to practise picking length, whether to seam or spin, as early in your development as possible. To do this it is vital that you pick up the ball as early as possible in its flight, preferably as the bowler releases the ball. You can also pick up cues from the bowler pre-delivery. For example, cues such as cocking the wrist, attacking the crease harder, dropping the front shoulder earlier, a slight delay in the release, a slight falling away in the action, or even where the bowler is looking can consciously or subconsciously give you a clue about the length of the next delivery.

To practise reading length, an area marked on the pitch can be used as in the photograph that follows. A ball short of the area should be defended, whereas a ball full of the area should be driven, and the area within the box is the batter's call. If they are in a good position, producing a good stride, they should be able to drive the ball slightly on the up.

> **Note for coaches**
> After each delivery, whether it be from a bowler, throw, stick or machine, ask the batter to point at the spot on the pitch where the ball landed. This confirms how well they are watching the ball and how accurately they are picking the length.

It is possible to drive a ball that is not a half-volley, pitching short of the boxed area as seen in the drill and photo above. This is called hitting on the up, and the technique is slightly different to driving a half-volley. Here you need to stand taller, so that you can get on top of the bounce, striking the ball in the middle of the bat. Remember the simple principle: if you want to hit the ball down, the bat handle should be in front of the blade at point of contact.

To generalise, the more pace a wicket has in it, and the more consistent the bounce, the easier it is to drive on the up. Remember to let the ball come in line with your head, playing it late, so you ensure hitting on the downswing, keeping the ball down. To reinforce this, imagine a small box beneath your head, alongside your front foot if playing forward, or your back foot if playing back. If you aim to play the ball in this area, whether attacking or defending, the greater success you will have of playing the shot successfully. The further out in front of the box, or the further to the right of the box you play, the greater the risk becomes of executing the shot incorrectly.

The boxed area is where you have the greatest chance of hitting the ball in the middle of the bat and keeping the ball down. As you get in and start seeing the ball better, the bigger this box becomes. The imaginary box becomes even bigger if you are playing on a really good wicket. There will also be innings where your feet are not moving as well as you like and you are tending to get stuck on the crease regularly. This can happen, but if you continue to focus on playing the ball in the boxed area, this will help you until you start moving your feet better.

Scoring off bad bowling

Everyone has done it, you get a thigh-high full toss, throw your head back and try to hit the ball out of the ground, only to misconnect and hit an easy catch to midwicket. It is easy when you get a delivery like this, or perhaps a half-tracker from a spinner, to lose all resemblance of technique, not attain a solid base, and forget to watch the ball on to the bat. Your eyes light up as you try to hit the ball into the next county!

It is still important to give yourself a solid base to hit from, keeping your head still on contact, with your weight forward. If you achieve this you will hit the ball in the middle of the bat, getting the result you desire. Additionally, hitting the gap is still important, so it is imperative that you score off the delivery, rather than thinking it has to go out of the ground. This way you avoid overhitting and losing your shape and balance.

Note for coaches

Coaches quite rightly spend lots of time grooving technique for hitting good deliveries or half-volleys, as this is where the bowlers most regularly bowl. It is important to intermittently set up sessions where batters work on hitting poor deliveries, so when they occur in matches they are better prepared for scoring off them safely. This can be set up as a range-hitting practice with a boundary marked out. The batter can then see whether they can regularly clear the ropes or should be focusing on hitting the gap and keeping the ball down.

Playing swing bowling

There has been lots in this book relating to playing the ball as late as possible, right under your head, to give you the best chance of hitting the ball consistently. When the ball is swinging a long way it is very important that your footwork is also as late as possible. An outswing bowler starting the ball on the stumps and then swinging towards the off side is hoping to commit your front foot to that initial line and then have you reaching for the ball. By the time it reaches you, you have less control of the shot and are less able to play with a straight bat, increasing the chances of you edging the ball. An inswing bowler wants to commit your front foot to going across the crease so that they have a chance of trapping you lbw as you have to play round your front pad.

It is therefore vital that your footwork is as late as possible so you can still arrive alongside the ball and the bat can come down straight to present the full face. Movement should be late, but quick and decisive. Getting a decent stride in alongside the ball can also help negate some of the movement of the ball.

In respect to outswing, the bowler wants to find the edge of the bat to have you caught by the wicketkeeper or the slips, so leaving the ball well is important, as is playing straight when you do have to play the ball. Depending on the amount of swing and whether there is any extra movement off the pitch, driving through the covers and square of the wicket become higher risk shots as you are effectively presenting less of the bat to the ball and it is easier for it to find the edge.

If you can leave well this will make the bowler have to start the ball straighter and often it does not swing as much, allowing runs to be collected on the leg side. A simple game plan, if the match situation allows, would be to be patient to wait for balls off your pads to score off and aim to punish anything short!

Driving an inswing bowler through the off side is less of a risk as long as your footwork has been spot on and you have played late enough. Just be careful of being on the shot too early and leaving a gap for the ball to get through or inside edging on to your stumps. Again, defend as straight as possible and do not get that front pad across the crease.

Later in this chapter we talk about limiting your game.

Playing fast bowling

*'You have to relish the battle of facing fast bowling.
Keep your head still and trust your eyes – given that
you've done the work, your eyes will take care of the rest.'*
MARK BUTCHER

When the opposition have a really quick bowler, there are often pre-match discussions taking place amongst the players, with a few nerves surfacing, especially when arriving out in the middle to face them. It is important to keep a positive mindset, and the best way to do this is to tell yourself that playing quick bowling also provides more opportunities to score. Fast bowlers can sometimes be less accurate than slower seam bowlers, so there could be more bad balls to score off. Because they possess good pace, you do not have to hit the ball as hard to score quickly. By thinking about scoring and the greater opportunities to score, you will have a more positive mindset when facing a really quick bowler.

A vitally important mindset is to understand that you have more time than you think to play the ball. Stay calm, keep a still head and watch the ball hard. Aim to pick it up as early as you can from the bowler's hand, and as you gain experience you will learn to pick up cues the bowler might give regarding the length they plan to bowl. This could be a cock of the wrist in the gather, attacking the crease harder, a facial expression, dropping of the front shoulder, or even where they are looking. You may pick these up in your peripheral vision, not actually identifying them directly. Science has proven that picking up on these cues is the only way batters can anticipate and respond to bowlers of express pace. This is very useful when bouncers are flying around!

Taking a guard deeper in the crease, or even with both feet inside the crease, can give you a fraction more time and also help with your positive mindset. If you do find yourself being rushed, you can look at using a shorter backswing, as this will enable you to get down on the ball quicker. You could also bring your top-hand grip more behind the bat handle to enable you to defend higher, while still keeping the bat angled down. Keeping a loose grip will ensure the ball drops quickly to the ground, rather than being caught by a fielder. You can also pick up singles this way.

Watching the ball intensely is an integral part of batting, no more so than when you face bouncers. It is natural to want to take your eye off the ball as soon as you see the bowler dig it in short, but you must keep watching it. If it is coming straight towards your head and you keep your eyes fully on the ball, your instincts will take over and you will get your head out of the way in time, either swaying or ducking to take evasive action. To keep a positive mindset, think about scoring first with a hook or ramp shot, then ducking or swaying if you decide those options are unsafe. Your brain is amazing, it will process that information in an instant, then your reactions and instinct kick in!

When ducking, you still need to keep your head facing forward, and get as low as possible in case the ball bounces lower than expected. Additionally, keep your hands low. Your bat should never be above your body height. This will avoid the ball striking the bat as it goes past, therefore eliminating the risk of a catching opportunity.

When swaying, it is again important to keep the head facing the ball, in case it moves and follows you. If so, you can sway further or even fall backwards to avoid being hit. Additionally, keep the hands low again, so they are well below the bounce of the ball.

Ducking.

Swaying.

It is important when you sway to keep your profile as narrow as possible and not to square up. This presents a smaller target and often you can receive blows to your right shoulder if you square up.

You only need to move enough to allow the ball to miss you. Try to keep your movements controlled, which is not always possible, remembering the ball only has to miss your head by an inch, not ten inches.

Swaying does have an advantage where it can also present a scoring opportunity. As you arch your back to get your head away from the ball it is possible to use the pace of the delivery and 'ramp' the ball over the keeper and slip fielders. When ducking, the delivery will definitely be a dot ball, unless it strikes you and you get a leg bye.

High back foot ramp shot.

Whether you decide to duck or sway or look to score with a ramp or pull shot is down to your own personal assessment of the pace and conditions, but try to put your ego to one side, and not get caught up in the emotion of the battle. There may be some verbal distractions around when a quick bowler comes on but put these to the back of your mind and play as the match situation dictates. Do not think you have to show how good you are by taking the bowler on if you do not need to.

Like playing spin on a turning track, it will get easier the more you face, and once you have got used to the pace and bounce of the wicket, you will find it easier to execute your pull and hook shots. Remember, as the ball gets older, it loses its hardness, so the same bowler may be a much easier proposition during a later spell. Equally, if the bowler has bowled a long spell, or numerous spells, they will not be as threatening as they were at the start.

As your skills improve, you will find yourself executing more attacking pull and hook shots to short balls that are aimed at your body or head. However, there will be times when the ball beats you for pace or the bounce is high and gets above your head. Unless the match format or situation dictates that you still need to take this ball on, you do have the option of pulling out of the shot, even though you have started to shape up for a pull or hook.

In this situation you have probably got your hands high to execute the shot, but instead of bringing the hands through to play, drop them low so the ball passes above the bat and therefore you do not risk a top edge as in the following sequence.

It will not be possible to maintain a side-on profile, but you will be mainly pulling out when the ball bounces too high, so it should pass above your body as it goes through to the keeper.

Facing tall bowlers, pitches with high bounce, or some that lift sharply off a length, the ball can bounce so high that it will miss the bat altogether and head towards your gloves. This could happen on either front or back foot. The natural reaction is to take your bottom hand off your bat, which is the correct thing to do; however, this often leads to the top hand being thrust towards the ball, lowering the hands, and tightening the top hand grip. If you get struck on this hand it can be painful, even potentially breaking a finger, and because your top hand and bat are now being thrust at the ball, if it strikes the glove it can carry a long way.

It is against your natural reactions, but when you face these high, lifting deliveries and take your bottom hand off the bat, try to keep your top hand grip relaxed, and keep your elbow bent so you can still keep an angle on the bat. By doing this, there is less force going into the ball as it meets your glove, therefore less chance of the ball carrying to a fielder, more chance of the ball going down towards ground, and less chance of breaking a finger!

On slow, low wickets, fast bowlers can still use the short ball. Because they have to pitch the ball so short, much closer to where they are bowling from, it can be very hard to track the ball, and it usually ends up arriving at a height you have to play at, rather than take evasive action to. Because it is easy to lose track of the ball when bouncers are bowled this short, it is natural to want to turn your head away. Try to stand tall, pick up the ball again and play accordingly.

Occasionally a fast bowler will come round the wicket to target your body with short-pitched bowling. All of the principles above apply, but technically it can help to open your stance to get your head facing towards where the ball is coming from. Remember to look for visual cues regarding the length the ball is about to be bowled. It is also important to ensure that you do not expose leg stump when the ball is pitched up. When the bowler is bowling over the wicket, if you usually take middle, or middle-and-off stump guard, think about moving to leg stump or a middle-and-leg stump guard so you can protect the leg stump.

In 100-ball or T20 cricket you will be looking to take the short balls on with cuts, pulls, hooks and ramps. Depending on the boundary dimensions you will need to consider keeping the balls down if the field is well set to protect these shots. Most top players in this format now look to play these shots along the floor and into gaps, rather than risk a mishit and getting caught on the boundary. This is particularly relevant once the power play period is over and more fielders can go on the boundary.

If you are looking to get on top of the bounce and keep the ball down, if you do mishit it you will still score off the delivery and you will not present a catching opportunity to the opposition. Due to the size of modern bats, the strength of the players, size of boundaries, power play periods, etc., most top players can clear the ropes with ease when playing these shots.

If your back-foot attacking options are one of your strengths, but a fast bowler is always bowling full at you on a good length, you can consider walking down at them, to make them dig the ball in at you. Unlike advancing at a spinner, which often requires quick feet to get to the pitch of the ball, your movement should be slower, very controlled, with your head as still as possible. By creating a strong base throughout, you can still execute a pull shot if the bowler adjusts their length and bowls short. Here you are more likely to be pulling off a front-foot base rather than a back-foot base. If they do not adjust their length, you still need to play the ball on its merits, and have a plan B. But, hopefully, a seed of distraction has been sown, by showing you are willing to do this, and it may affect the consistency of their bowling length from now on.

'Initially you should practise with a softer ball that doesn't hurt as much and encourages you to keep your eye on it. Hard ball practice can get young players turning their head and not watching the ball. You have to watch the ball – look at it hard. A softer ball will build confidence in young players. Once they feel comfortable with a soft ball the fear becomes less and watching the ball becomes second nature. Practising against the short ball should start from an early age.'
SIR GEOFFREY BOYCOTT

Playing spin bowling

'Picking length, having a game plan, having soft hands in defence and working the angles are the most important aspects of playing spin.'
JULIAN WOOD
(ECB, IPL, BIG BASH POWER HITTING COACH)

It is important to master a good array of shots both sides of the wicket, off front and back foot, so that you do not get tied down when playing spin, both in terms of boundary options and working singles. Otherwise, a good spinner will be able to put the ball consistently on a good length, stringing up the dot balls, which ultimately builds pressure on you. Younger players often find spin the hardest to play, because there is no pace to work with, therefore the batter has to hit the ball harder to generate the power to get the ball through the field.

Many young players may not yet have the upper-body strength to hit the ball over the top consistently, which greatly reduces scoring options. That is why it is important to develop the sweep and reverse sweep early in your game, so you have scoring options both sides of the wicket to good-length balls. A ball that otherwise would be defended, creating a dot ball, can now be scored off. Spin bowlers generally hate good sweepers of a ball for this reason. This can lead to frustration and more poorer balls to score off.

That last point is fundamental in playing spin. It is essential for you to find ways to prevent the bowler from landing the ball consistently on a good length. A sweep is one option, but an equally disruptive method is using your feet to get down the wicket towards the bowler.

A misconception here is that if you use your feet, you have to score after doing it. Depending on the match situation, this is definitely not always the case. The main reason is to show the bowler that you are prepared to use your feet and that they will have to adjust their length when you do, to prevent you scoring off it. Again, whether you have scored off the ball you have just come down to or not, the important thing is what the bowler delivers over the next few deliveries. By putting distraction and disruption into their rhythm, hopefully there will be a shorter delivery or two, in anticipation of you coming down the wicket. Both the sweep and using your feet are good methods of putting a spin bowler off their length, so you receive less balls on a good length and more on lengths that you can score from more safely.

Obviously, when you first decide to come down the wicket, your first thought will be to score. Either getting a ball in the slot to hit over the top, getting to the pitch and driving or working with the spin, or better still, a full toss so the ball has no chance to turn, are all benefits of good footwork. The important aspect is that you should still play the ball on its merits and have a plan B to your scoring option. If the bowler adjusts their length and the ball ends up being on a good length relevant to where you have ended up, then you should play accordingly, and play a good defensive shot effectively enough to stop the ball getting past you. This last point is crucial. You cannot leave a ball you have come down the wicket to. If the match situation dictates, see whether you can work a single. If you feel you are in trouble, the final option is to just make sure the ball hits your pad. If you have come down the pitch a long way, it is unlikely you will be given out lbw.

If you have come down the wicket a few times, another option to disrupt the bowler's length is to pretend to come down the wicket. Just before the bowler releases the ball, make a forward press as though you are coming down the wicket and hope they drop their delivery short. If they do, then instead of taking a further step down the pitch, push off backwards from your front-foot press, getting a good stride back, so you can play an attacking shot off the back foot. Once again, you will need a plan B if the ball is not as short as you had hoped it would be, or the bowler does not change their planned delivery, with the ball still landing on a good length. You will still need to play a good defensive shot to this delivery.

How often should you sweep or use your feet to spin bowling? The answer will depend a lot on your own personal abilities and the match situation, so it will vary from match to match. But the general answer is, not as often as you think. If you have sweeps in your armoury and you are good at using your feet, it can be tempting to literally play a different shot to every ball you face. However, this is rarely conducive to playing a long innings, so you need to acknowledge that your main reason for sweeping or using your feet is to put the bowler off their length. You then receive fewer balls in the danger area of a good length, and therefore more balls that you can actually score off without having to premeditate an attacking shot.

It is also important not to be predictable, so keep the bowler guessing as to when you will sweep or use your feet to come at them. Obviously, if you are playing a short version of the game or facing a high required run rate to win, you need to use these scoring methods constantly.

As discussed earlier in the chapter, picking length is very important, and this is equally true against spin bowling. The best players of spin such as Steve Smith, Joe Root and Kane Williamson do not play many balls landing on a good length. They either get right back, deep into their crease to play off the back foot, or well forward to smother the spin to drive and sweep. By using the crease well and looking to play off the back foot predominantly, it forces the bowler to go fuller so that when they do the ball is easier to attack or defend comfortably. Remember, the best way to play the spinning ball is to get as near to it or as far away from it as possible!

Looking to play off the back foot is particularly helpful if there is turn and bounce in the wicket. The bowler will want you to come forward to good-length balls, to bring both edges of the bat into play, either carrying to slip or finding its way to close catchers around the bat. Because of the high bounce and turn there is less chance of lbw, which gives you more freedom to play off the back foot. By getting deep in the crease, you give yourself more time to play the ball, forcing the bowler to pitch fuller, which makes the ball easier to play off the front foot. Playing off the back foot also opens up scoring options to work off your hip or angle the ball into the off side with a straight bat. Both options are relatively low risk.

There is a caveat to this though. Looking to play predominantly off the back foot does suit shorter players more. If you are very tall then definitely think about using your natural attributes, getting well forward to smother the spin, as well as coming down the wicket. This will force the bowler to shorten their length, therefore producing deliveries that pitch short of a good length and are less dangerous to you because you have more time to play them.

It is not easy to start against the turning ball, as there are often close catchers round the bat, and if the bowler is bowling well, finding the middle of the bat, which all players want to do early in their innings, can be very challenging. The fielders round the bat may be attempting to verbally distract you too. This is as much a mental challenge as it is technical one. To increase your confidence in these situations, you need to practise against the turning ball, having sessions where you only look to defend. This will improve your defensive play and give you confidence, knowing that you can defend safely against the turning ball. If you do not have confidence in your defensive game, it can lead to playing over-aggressively, potentially making the wrong decisions about which balls to attack.

Secondly, it is important to remember that although starting against the turning ball is challenging, it only gets easier the longer you are at the crease. The more time you spend in the middle, the better you will start reading length and assessing the amount of turn the bowler is getting, as well as picking any variations they may have. This can only be achieved with a strong defensive game. Understanding this can be a massive help when facing a challenging start to your innings.

Thirdly, if there are fielders round the bat, that also means there are more gaps behind them for scoring into. This is an important mental motivator to keep your thinking positive, ensuring that you do take scoring opportunities when they come, even if that is only working a single. Positive batting does not mean aggressive batting.

Remember also that a sweep is nearly always a safer option than a straight-bat drive on a turning wicket. You have a greater margin of error, as you are either hitting with the spin or into it. Additionally, when the ball is turning a lot, there is less chance of getting out lbw if you miss the ball. An off-spinner needs to be pitching the ball well outside off stump to hit the stumps, so therefore if you miss the sweep, the ball will strike your pad outside the line of the off stump. Equally, a leg-spinner or orthodox left-arm spinner will need to pitch the ball outside leg stump to hit the stumps. Conversely, if there is little or no turn in the wicket, a straight-bat scoring option is of lower risk and will give you the greater chance of connecting with the ball.

Another recommended shot is one over midwicket to an off-spinner, this taking the form of either a slog sweep or a pick-up shot. There should not be many match situations where an off-spinner can bowl to you with just one fielder out deep on the leg side. If the ball is turning, then through your shot play, deep backward square should be out as well as deep midwicket. If the ball is not turning, then deep square leg in front plus long-on or a wide long-on are the field placings. With the opposition captain having to have two fielders out deep, this means there are gaps elsewhere or fewer catchers around the bat.

We have already discussed that if the ball is turning a long way, with normal to high bounce, it is difficult for an off-spinner to get an lbw if you are playing forward, as the ball needs to pitch outside off stump to be hitting the stumps. To enhance this tactically, many batters take an off-stump guard when there is significant turn in the wicket, to help them get further outside the line when playing forward, making the ball easier to hit with the spin through the leg side.

There are two additional areas that further enhance your game against spin, by greatly increasing your scoring rate, and giving you immense confidence in how you approach playing spin in any format, particularly when the conditions are in the bowler's favour. The first is having scoring options hitting against the spin, either driving an off-spinner through the off side, or working and driving a left-arm spinner through the leg side. The second is having the ability to read the bowler's action and grip and pick up any variations they have to this stock delivery.

There is an old adage that says you should always play with the spin of the ball when it is turning, and this is generally sound advice as it does give you a greater chance of hitting the ball, particularly if you did not judge the length quite correctly. However, the field is often well set on the side of the ground where you are trying to work the ball, so runs can be harder to come by. Dot balls can build up. A drive through the covers is risky to an off-spinner turning the ball prodigiously, where if you miss it, it can get between bat and pad and hit the stumps. Likewise, looking to hit a leg-spinner through midwicket risks the ball taking the leading edge.

However, it is possible to play both of these shots regardless of how much the ball is turning, but it relies on you judging the length of the ball exactly. The ball needs to be very full, a long half-volley. This length may have been created by you coming down the wicket. Remember that box beneath your head discussed earlier in the chapter? On a turning wicket, and trying to hit against the spin, the box is very small, so you need to be precise and be able to adjust to a defensive shot if the ball is fractionally off the ideal length. If you do judge the length correctly, the risk goes down dramatically, as the ball you are now driving is turning into where the bat is coming from, so you are in effect presenting the full face of the bat to the ball. It is also a good option if there is high bounce in the wicket, as higher bounce equals greater risk for a sweep shot.

If you can master hitting against the spin as well as hitting with it, you make it extremely difficult for the fielding captains, as they need to cover both sides of the pitch.

Subsequently, the part of the pitch they want to protect, with you now hitting with the spin of the ball again, becomes easier to score into as the gaps between the fielders are larger now. Add to this an occasional sweep and you become a very hard batter to keep tied down. Hitting against the spin is a particularly useful tactic if the spinner bowls very quickly, not giving you much time to get down the wicket or underneath them to hit over the top.

Some batters find reading spinners or any bowler variations difficult. For others it is easier. Do not be discouraged if you cannot, or never manage it. There are many professional batters who cannot spot the difference between a leg break or a googly, but obviously if you can start to 'pick' or 'read' what a spin bowler is about to deliver it can greatly help. Instead of trying to read the ball in the air, or worse still off the pitch, you can ascertain from the action or grip exactly what is about to be bowled. This makes batting a lot easier. Leg-spinners who have a googly often get away with the short balls because the batter does not know which way the ball is going, therefore it is harder to set yourself to attack the ball in a certain area. However, if you can learn to tell the difference then it becomes a four ball every time.

There is no better way to learn how to spot spin bowlers' variations than to face them in practice, picking up cues from the bowler's action and watching closely how they are gripping the ball. You can also do this in matches from the non-striker's end, which will give you clues as to what to look out for when you are on strike. As a guide, here are some photos of examples of different deliveries you may face from spin bowlers:

Leg spinner.

Top spinner.

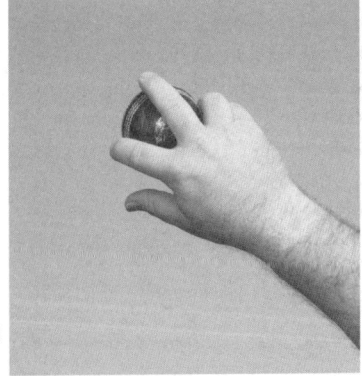

Googly.

Flipper.

Off spinner.

Undercut.

Arm ball.

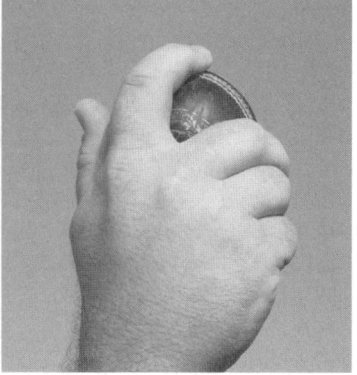
Doosra.

As well as different grips, also look out for changes in head position, approach to the crease, as well as the height of the arm on delivery. If you are very observant, you may spot signals between the bowler and wicketkeeper, which may help you and your partner anticipate the turn of the ball.

Lastly in this section on playing spin, it is worth discussing playing a leg-spinner bowling round the wicket, or a left-arm orthodox spinner bowling over the wicket into the rough created outside your leg stump. This tactic is normally used to dry up run scoring or take wickets, because if they land the ball regularly in the rough it will turn a lot more than from the untouched part of the wicket. The bounce is usually a lot more erratic too. It is usually used in formats where there is more leeway on leg-side wides and where a longer game creates larger areas of rough.

There are certainly ways to combat this line of attack. Scoring when the ball lands in the rough area is harder than the untouched areas, so watching the ball closely and reading length is important. When playing back it will help to cover your stumps by getting your back foot into off stump. If the ball bounces low and you miss it, it will hit your pad rather than the stumps, and with the ball pitching outside leg you cannot be out lbw. On the back foot, you should have time if the ball misses the rough to play an attacking shot for boundaries and singles.

With the erratic bounce of the ball, sweeping out of the rough becomes difficult, and it is highly likely that the opposition will have a 45 or short fine leg in place for a top-edged sweep. However, that probably means there is not a short third man, so there is an option to go in the other direction with a reverse sweep, but once again the bounce could be erratic.

As well as different grips, also look out for changes in head position, approach to the crease, as well as the height of the arm on delivery. If you are very observant, you may spot signals between the bowler and wicketkeeper, which may help you and your partner anticipate the turn of the ball.

Lastly in this section on playing spin, it is worth discussing playing a leg-spinner bowling round the wicket, or a left-arm orthodox spinner bowling over the wicket into the rough created outside your leg stump. This tactic is normally used to dry up run scoring or take wickets, because if they land the ball regularly in the rough it will turn a lot more than from the untouched part of the wicket. The bounce is usually a lot more erratic too. It is usually used in formats where there is more leeway on leg-side wides and where a longer game creates larger areas of rough.

There are certainly ways to combat this line of attack. Scoring when the ball lands in the rough area is harder than the untouched areas, so watching the ball closely and reading length is important. When playing back it will help to cover your stumps by getting your back foot into off stump. If the ball bounces low and you miss it, it will hit your pad rather than the stumps, and with the ball pitching outside leg you cannot be out lbw. On the back foot, you should have time if the ball misses the rough to play an attacking shot for boundaries and singles.

With the erratic bounce of the ball, sweeping out of the rough becomes difficult, and it is highly likely that the opposition will have a 45 or short fine leg in place for a top-edged sweep. However, that probably means there is not a short third man, so there is an option to go in the other direction with a reverse sweep, but once again the bounce could be erratic.

With the wider angle, it is also advised to open your stance more, to line your head up with where the ball is being delivered from, to enable you to use your feet more easily. A great tactic is to try to get to the ball on the full toss. The most dangerous rough is usually quite full, so if the bowler is aiming at that, this will increase your chances of getting to the ball before it pitches.

If runs are not really your priority at this stage of the match, then playing as few deliveries as possible with the bat is a genuine tactic, on the back foot covering your stumps with both pads and on the front foot getting a good knee-bend in to deflect the ball away. When defending like this get the hands high or behind your body to reduce the chance of the ball ricocheting off pad or body on to the bat. This tactic is valid, because you cannot be given out lbw.

Front foot leaves.

Back foot leaves.

Hands low back foot leaves.

Lastly, to reduce the risk of getting bowled round your legs, some batters prefer to take a leg-stump guard. This also helps get your head closer to the line of where the ball is being bowled from.

Conditions favouring bowlers – ugly runs and attack the best form of defence

When conditions are predominantly in the bowlers' favour, it is unlikely that you will find the ball hitting the middle of the bat too regularly. It may be moving off the seam, turning square or perhaps bouncing indifferently. You may be getting hit on the pads, gloves or body regularly, and playing and missing quite often. It is natural to start feeling self-conscious about how you are looking at the crease. We all want to look a good player as often as possible, but sometimes this simply is not possible, and as a batter we still need to score as many runs as we possible can for the team. It is time to roll up the sleeves, get stuck in and grind out a score. Similarly to playing very quick bowling, the ego needs to be parked for a while, and mentally there needs to be an acceptance that this innings will not be as fluent or as aesthetically pleasing as you would want. But you can still score runs and the bottom line is, that is your job.

On difficult wickets it may not be as many runs – 35 might be a highly valuable return in the context of the match – and just remember that the scorebook never says how you scored them, just how many you got. Put the emphasis on what the team needs. They really do not care what you look like at all if you get a valuable score for the team. What they do care about is what result is recorded in the scorebook at the end of the match! Once again remember, it only gets easier the longer you are there. That is important to keep a positive mindset.

> *'When conditions aren't favourable, think about the team. If it's a green seamer – then an important fifty is vital for the team.'*
> **GRAHAM GOOCH**

Depending on what your natural instincts are, and your strengths as a player on difficult wickets, attack can often be the best form of defence. If you feel that no matter how well you defend, there will be a ball that will definitely get you out soon, then it is important that you take advantage of every scoring opportunity and apply some pressure of your own back on to the bowler. As long as this is calculated aggression, you can put a bowler off their length, meaning that there are fewer balls on the length where wickets have been taken, and more are now on lengths you can score off.

Perhaps you could use your feet to get closer to the pitch no matter how quickly the bowler is bowling, or take a guard outside leg stump to create width to hit through or over the off side, or simply look to drive at width rather than leave the ball. Your decision will be based on the difficulties encountered in the pitch, but still attempt to influence the innings in your team's favour.

T20 batting – 360 scoring and power hitting

There is a time in all formats of the game when you need to hit boundaries, more so in the shorter forms of the game and when you are playing on great batting wickets. With 100-ball or T20 cricket you will be looking to hit a boundary most balls, working backwards from six down to one, in terms of how many you score off that ball.

On a good batting wicket, a single is a win for the bowler. In all limited-overs cricket there are restrictions placed on how many fielders can be placed on the boundary, with five being the maximum. This means that there will be parts of the boundary unprotected. With boundary hitting the priority, the ability to hit the ball to or over the boundary, all round the ground, is a vital skill to have, and the better you become at it, the more runs you will score in these formats, or when you need to increase the scoring rate at certain times in longer formats.

> *'Mentally, don't panic, there is still plenty of time in a T20.*
> *Give yourself a chance to get in.'*
> **BEN DUCKETT**

We have already discussed the technical aspects of shots that you can play to access different parts of the ground, but there are additional things you can do in your stance or pre-delivery movement to help you hit into certain areas. Simply, where you take your stance can help you access different parts of the ground.

In the photo above, the batter has taken a guard just outside leg stump. This would mean that a ball bowled on off stump or in the 'channel' now becomes a ball with enough width on it to be able to free the arms and hit through the off side. Backward point and extra cover are the two most likely fielders to be in the ring on the off side, and these are the areas to target. Of course, the bowler can see you take this guard, so can readjust their line accordingly, so it can be useful to mix this up by sometimes stepping across from this guard to around off stump, so that they bowl more towards your body, and you then open up the leg side instead.

Alternatively, take your usual guard, then step towards the leg side as the bowler releases, to create the width to hit through the off side. Try to time this movement early enough so you can still get a good base and a still head, but late enough for the bowler to be unable to make the adjustment to their line. You can also dummy to go across your stumps, moving early so the bowler sees you and then stepping back to your normal stance. The aim here is to get the bowler to target the area you initially moved to, and the stepping back to your original stance creates the width. This can also be done in reverse to create leg-side scoring opportunities, or simply by taking a guard on off stump.

The most important aspect of any movement taken pre-delivery, or just on delivery, is that they are controlled so your head remains as still as possible. A common movement adopted by many batters as a power position, and one where many parts of the ground can be accessed is this one:

Here the batsman has his back foot on off stump and has cleared his front leg, which opens up the hips and allows a powerful swing of the bat. If the bowler bowls it in the slot, full and straight, it is an extremely powerful position to hit the ball back over the bowler's head, even if the bat does not come down dead straight.

Due to the path of the bat coming down slightly more from gully line, it is also a very good way to create a curved path of the bat and hit the same ball over the off side and play 'in to out'.

Further, you also have a great arc to hit through the leg side – particularly over midwicket.

With this position, you can take your back leg deep into the crease, which can create a length to hit over the top if the bowler is trying to get the ball full and under your bat.

If a bowler is having success with their yorkers, a starting position deep in your crease can help to create a better hitting length, or to squeeze the ball through backward point.

> *'For T20 cricket it is important to create access to the ball and open up scoring options by creating angles. A lot of players are hand dominant because that's all they know. You need a touch game, skill game and power game.'*
> **JULIAN WOOD**

Earlier in the book we referred a lot to keeping your shape, to allow the bat path to remain straight, giving yourself the best chance of making a clean connection with the ball. By not actually trying to hit the ball hard you could achieve this. But there will be times when you need to clear the boundary, or on grounds with big boundaries, beat the boundary riders. Maximising power is vital. Certainly, in international T20 cricket, power hitters are dominating the format and even such a brilliant player as Joe Root cannot make the England team on a regular basis.

A high backswing is vital to maximise power. The further the bat has to travel before connecting with the ball, the more force is generated. This may mean that when you want to maximise power, you start your backswing earlier than normal to give it time to get down on to the ball.

Cocking the wrists also gives extra momentum in the swing and allows for a higher bat swing.

Here you can see the bat is pointing to the sky in the batter's set-up.

Moreover, engaging the hips into a front-on position as the ball is about to be struck will add body to the movement, so it is not just the arms and wrists engaged, which will add further power.

Try to imagine someone holding your body and arms back as though holding an elastic band at full stretch and then they let go. Visualise that same force created in your shots. Through all of this, try to keep as strong a base and still a head as possible. You can of course add further momentum by moving your feet towards where the ball is coming from. By allowing the bat to complete a full arc, with a full follow-through, it enables the full body weight to contribute power to the shot too. Remember not to overhit and lose your shape.

'Players and coaches need to know how to create force through the body to create bat speed on impact. The key factors are storing energy all the way through the movements – any weakness in the chain will severely limit the chances of hitting the ball hard. Your character as a player also dictates whether you want to/can hit the ball hard. You need an efficient timing of movement with the bowler creating momentum to come to you and you making a positive motion to him. You need rhythm to create momentum. A player's swing is defined by his body type, so you need to coach players differently. The way different body parts work together to produce the bat swing. When batting in T20 matches you need good hand-eye coordination and power.'

JULIAN WOOD

A further important skill relating to T20 cricket is the ability to read the field to give you a good idea of where the bowler is going to bowl. This is particularly important at the end of an innings when you will be wanting to target boundaries. If the bowler has three or four fielders back on the leg side and only one on the off side, then it is likely that the bowler is going to look at short balls angled into you, mixing this up with straight slower balls. A flip on this would be four back on the off side where the bowler will most likely be attempting wide yorkers. You can then think about how you will position yourself in your set-up or with a pre-delivery movement to counter this and open up parts of the boundary that are not protected.

'In the short form of the game, being able to think calmly is a very important mental skill as well as being able to bat aggressively.'

MARK BUTCHER

Reading the swing and picking slower balls

Similarly to reading spinners' deliveries, it is advantageous if you can read the grips of seamers to identify which way they are trying to swing the ball, whether it is cross-seam, producing no swing but possibly variation of bounce on pitching, or it is going to be a slower ball, of which there are many varieties.

As the bowler runs in, try to see which side the shiny side of the ball is as they are gripping it. You may not be able to do this at first, but with practice you will, and if you watch intently you will learn to spot any grip changes that are made as they are running in.

Watching from the non-striker's end, where you are closer to the bowler, provides an opportunity to see what to look out for when you are next on strike. Does the bowler do something different at the top of their mark? Do they do something different when they place the ball into their hand? Do they alter their grip during their run-up or delivery stride?

Below are some photos of different grips to look out for various variations:

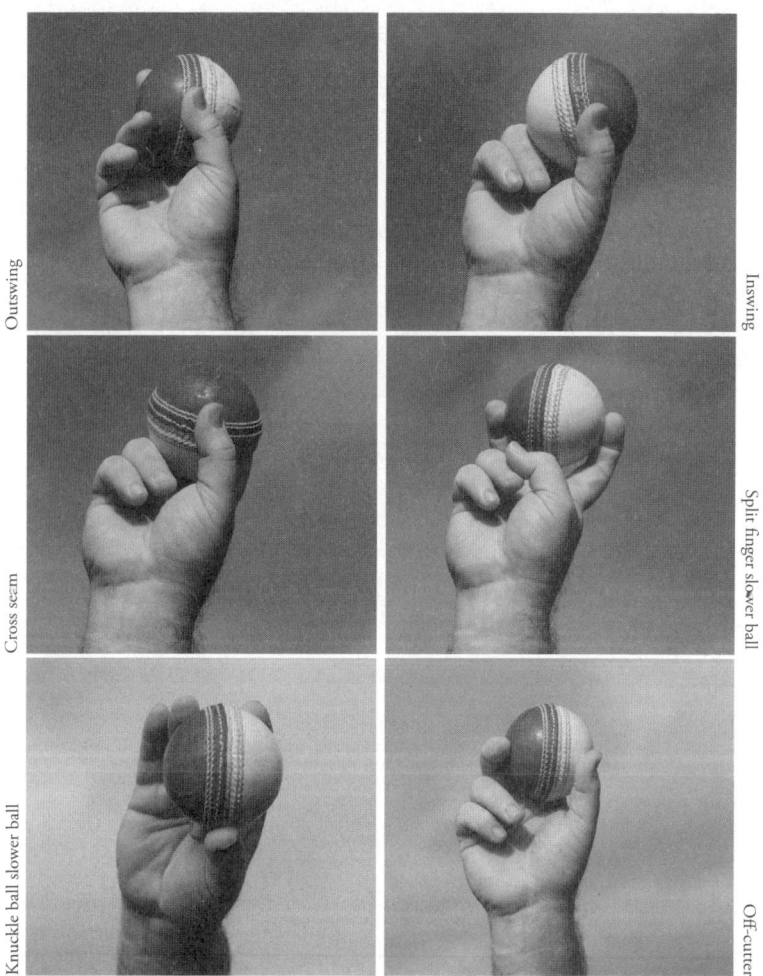

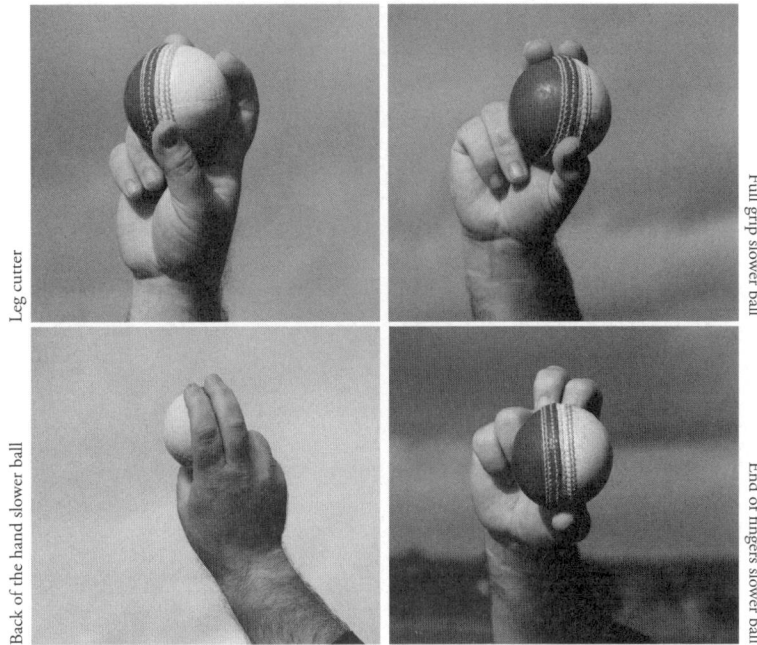

Grips for spin bowling are also included here, so that a comprehensive selection of deliveries are seen together:

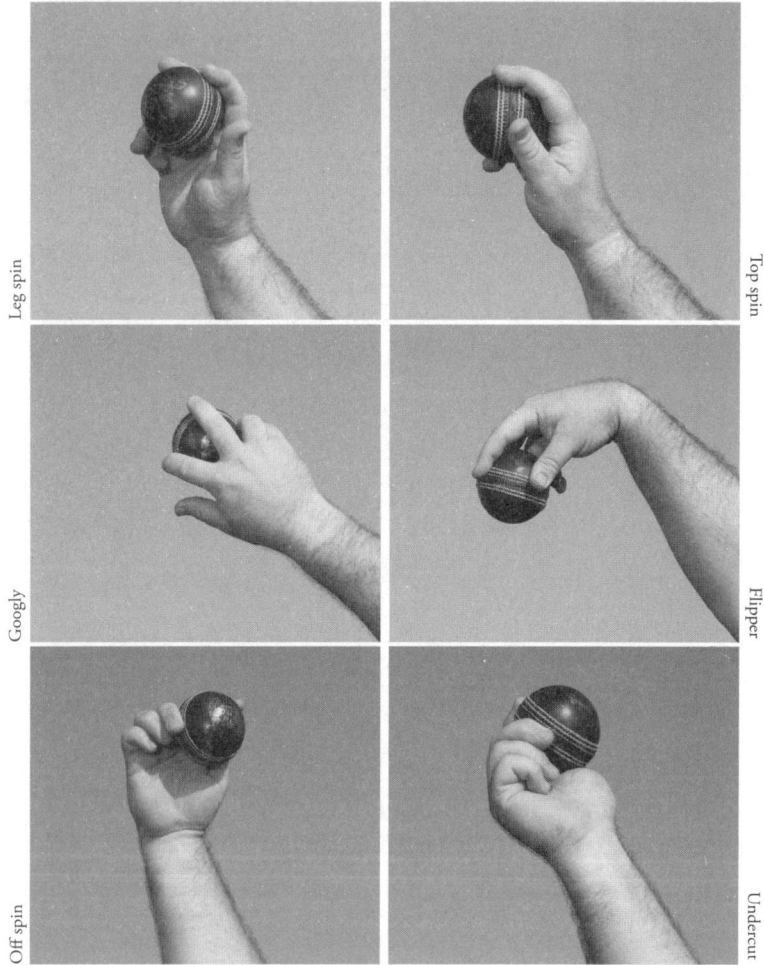

Arm ball

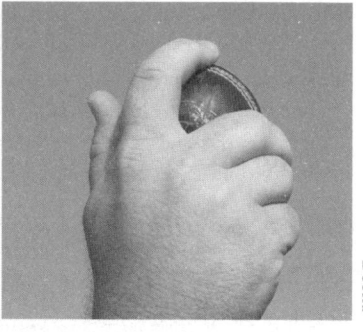
Doosra

If a ball is reverse swinging, it will be swinging in the opposite direction to the orthodox method above; that is, a ball held for an outswinger will swing in to you, and vice versa for the inswinger. Once a ball starts to reverse swing it is often harder to play than conventional swing as it tends to swing later in the air, giving you less time to adjust. It is therefore even more important that you play and move late. The bowler is looking for you to commit early to the initial line of the ball, so you are out of position by the time the ball reaches you. In other words, you commit your front foot across the stumps to a ball delivered on a line outside off stump, but then it swings in to be hitting the stumps by the time the ball reaches you. Playing as late and as straight as possible is vital if the ball is reverse swinging a long way.

Limiting your game and opening the batting

In shorter formats it is clear that you need a good range of shots to score at a decent pace, rotate the strike and score boundaries. But in longer formats, there is often less pressure on run scoring for large portions of the match. You do not need as many shots to score runs and can stick very much to your strengths and super strengths. Therefore, it can be the shots you remove from your game that contribute to your success as this reduces the chances of being dismissed. The longer you are out in the middle, the more runs you can make.

The great England opening batsman, Alastair Cook, is a great example of this. His game plan rarely went beyond his three main scoring shots: a work off his legs, front and back foot, cutting and pulling, with an occasional drive.

Even the drive he cut out completely during a series in South Africa, where he had often been getting out caught by the wicketkeeper.

Current Aussie great Steve Smith is another who went from a dashing lower order batter who bowled leg spin to the leading batsman in world cricket by limiting the shots he went for outside off stump. He became a fantastic leaver of the ball, and scores heavily on the leg side.

> **Note for coaches**
> Can you identify the shots in your game that are your bankers – shots that you rarely miss? Can you play an innings where you only play these shots? Try it in training, as it is a great way to build mental discipline.

This is a particularly important skill for opening batters in red ball cricket. The bowlers are fresh, meaning they usually bowl fewer bad balls and they have a brand-new ball to hand, which usually swings more. It has a pronounced seam that can lead to movement off the pitch as there is more bounce from a brand-new ball, which means edges are more likely to carry to slip fielders. As discussed earlier, all these factors make the conditions more favourable to bowlers and therefore the greater need for opening batters, in particular, to have good shot selection, a good defence, leave the ball well and limit their scoring shot options. The field is usually more attackingly set, which means more gaps and therefore a lesser need for attacking shot capability to score runs.

With conditions favouring new-ball bowlers there is, of course, a chance that you will get a good ball and be dismissed early as an opening batter. It is therefore vital that if you get through the period of the new ball and 'make a start' that you cash in, bat a long time and get a substantial score.

'The most important part of opening the batting in red ball cricket is being able to bat for long periods of time. As an opening batsman you're going to get more low scores than high scores. For me, I'm not happy with 50 and out as an opener. You've done all the hard work there. I judge myself on big hundreds because they will win your team games.'
BEN DUCKETT

Changing pitch conditions in multi-day cricket

If you are playing multi-day cricket, it is important to have an awareness that the pitch conditions can change between the first innings and second innings you bat. Commonly, although not always, the wicket will turn more as the game goes on, so you may well be facing more spin in the second innings, and more balls that turn, making it more challenging to play. Therefore, in the first innings, using your feet and hitting straight predominantly may have been the best option, but in the second innings, perhaps sweeps will come more into your thinking. Similarly, the pace of the wicket may have slowed, or the ball is not bouncing as high as it was in the first innings. This may determine that you bat out of your crease in the second innings, as you want to get further forward to negate an lbw.

It is advantageous to watch closely how the ball is reacting during the opposition's innings preceding your own, as this can give some clues about how you should go about your innings. If someone has batted well for the opposition, how did they go about it? Which shots were most successful, etc? Adaptability between and during innings and, of course, matches is an important part of sustained run-getting.

Walking and dealing with a bad umpiring decision

Most professional cricketers do not walk if they get a fine nick on the ball. They let the umpire make the decision. This is within the rules of the game and is not cheating. The coach or captain of your team may have a team policy on walking, but usually it is simply down to player preference.

Most professional batters do not walk because they feel that decisions that go in their favour are balanced out when they are given out to balls they have not edged, or perhaps it was an lbw where they nicked the ball on to the pad first. If they always walk and take the rough decisions as well there is no balance. In some instances, they are also playing for their careers, and if the opposition are not walking is it fair on their own team-mates if they walk?

If you decide that you are not going to walk, letting the umpire make the decision, you have to be mentally courageous, as it is inevitable that you will get a verbal backlash from the opposition. If you are happy to deal with that, putting any distractions out of your mind, focusing on the next ball, then that is your call. You are within your rights to let the umpire make the decision and you are not cheating, but there is still the 'spirit of cricket' to think about. If you do not walk, do not be a hypocrite if an opposition batter does the same.

There will be times when you get a poor decision and are given out caught behind or lbw when you know it is not out. It is frustrating and disappointing, but it is important that, whatever level you are playing at, the disappointment only manifests itself in the changing room, ideally away from your team-mates. In terms of it being a team game and giving your team-mates the best chance of success when they go out to bat, it is very distracting if you spend 15 minutes with them moaning about your bad luck. If you need to let off some steam, do this somewhere else. Remember, if you are not a walker, any poor decisions will balance out during the course of the season. You have to take the rough with the smooth. As DRS and Hawkeye have proved, umpiring is very difficult, so do have some empathy with the umpires.

Batting in different countries

The general cricket wickets of the nine Test-playing nations around the world all have different characteristics. Temperature, rainfall, humidity, geographical location, soil type, pitch preparation, etc., all have an influence on how a wicket will play. Types of and the age of the ball used also have an influence on play, as does general wear and tear of the pitch during play. In response to this, a batter will face different technical, tactical, physical and mental challenges depending on where they are playing. They could be batting on a very fast, bouncy pitch, or a slow, low-bouncing one with great spin. The list below gives a very general indication of how wickets play in these countries.

UK and New Zealand

Wickets here are generally fairly similar, with more grass on them than other countries. There is less pace and bounce, as the wickets are not as hard as some countries, but the ball swings and seams around much more. There is also less spin here. The countries are similar, both in climate and geographical conditions, but an English summer can almost go through three seasons, so the wickets can change during that period. In England the Readers and Dukes balls tend to swing more. In New Zealand, Kookaburra balls are used.

India, Pakistan, Sri Lanka and Bangladesh

There is hardly any live grass on these wickets, if any at all. There is less bounce and not much pace, but the wickets are hard and quite skiddy for opening bowlers. The ball spins much more here than any of the other countries, with bounce for the spinners. The wickets are dry and dusty, so the ball deteriorates fairly quickly. Also, the wickets themselves produce cracks and crumble, encouraging spin bowling. The ball can reverse swing regularly here. India use SG balls, while Pakistan, Sri Lanka and Bangladesh use Kookaburra.

West Indies

Because the temperatures here are generally hot all year, the wickets are usually very hard, quick, with very good bounce and carry. There is little or no grass on them. The ball does not seam or swing very much at all. There is very little turn for the spinners, but there is bounce. There was a period when the wickets here were prepared to be very slow and low-bouncing, but they are once again fast and bouncy. Dukes balls are used here regularly.

South Africa

Because the temperatures here are generally hot all year, the wickets are usually hard, quick, with very good bounce and carry. There is little live grass on the wickets, but the ball does seam around, less than in England but more than Australia. It does swing around while the ball is fairly new. The ball does not spin that much normally but does bounce. Kookaburra balls are used, which generally do not swing as much as the balls used in the UK.

Australia

Once again, the temperatures here are generally hot all year, so the wickets are very hard, quick, with very good bounce and carry. There is little live grass on the wickets, but the ball does not seam or swing around too much. The ball does spin a bit and does bounce. Kookaburra balls are used here too, which generally do not swing as much as the balls used in the UK.

Each of these countries' wickets display different challenges for the batter to contend with, but hopefully the contents of this book will allow batters to meet those challenges confidently and with great success.

EIGHT
LOOKING AFTER YOURSELF

'A high level of fitness is so important. Look at all the best players in the world nowadays – they are also the fittest. Whether that is being fit enough to bat for two days or being able to sprint a two in the 18th over of a T20 when you're 80 not out.'

BEN DUCKETT

Pre-match preparation

'Ideally, on the morning of a matchday I like to have a run around (football) and a stretch. Then have a short net, take a few short slip catches, some visualisation out on the pitch and then chill in the dressing room.'

MARK BUTCHER

The most important aspect of any pre-match preparation is to feel physically and mentally prepared for the task ahead, commencing the match feeling confident about your batting. Similar to a wicketkeeper looking to feel the ball coming cleanly into the gloves, to feel confident about your game as a batter you need to watch the ball, assess length and line, react, move your feet appropriately, sustain a stable base, execute the correct shot, and ultimately feel the ball coming off the middle of the bat.

How much preparation you can do before the start of play will depend on the level you are currently playing and when teams arrive before play is due to start. You may also be relying on your parents to get you to the match on time!

Primarily, depending on the player's age and ability, pre-match preparation is the player's responsibility, although you need an understanding of how the coach and captain can help facilitate that. Pre-match is not the time for hardcore fitness routines and drills, as you do not want to be physically tired going into the day's play. It is about good time management, knowing what you need to do, and how long for, to give you the best opportunity to enter your innings in a confident state of mind.

Ideally, most batters like to have throw-downs before a game, usually pairing up with another batter, giving each other equal time having a hit. This process is usually carried out in the nets or up against a throw-down net temporarily erected for this purpose. The amount of time you give yourself for this element of preparation will be dependent on the individual, as there is no set directive on this. Some players need only a few hits, while others may require a lot more. Some have a focus on technique, while others focus on feeling the ball out of the middle of the bat. Some may ask their partner to feed the ball for a certain shot, while others may prefer to hit totally different shots. Some prefer full toss feeds, while others prefer to have the ball fed to them bouncing, on a line and length more likely to occur in a match. Some batters even like to feed drop feeds to themselves, while others like to take time to watch the opposition bowlers warming up. Finally, some like fairly fast feeds, while others like slow feeds, replicating both seam and slow bowling. Facing slow feeds is great for getting the feel of waiting for the ball or playing it late.

Some examples of shots batters like to play in a batting pairs warm-up are:

- Front-foot work – drives, sweeps, front-foot defence
- Back-foot work – pulls, cuts, back-foot defence

Usually, this process will take place at the same time that the bowlers are carrying out their own pre-match bowling warm-ups. The batting and bowling units will normally separate to undertake their own warm-ups. The bowlers are almost certainly doing this at the side of the square, using a wicketkeeper, or coach with a mitt on, acting as the wicketkeeper.

At some grounds a net or a cage on the square will be available for batters to have practice against bowlers. Some batters like to net against bowlers prior to a match or day's play as ultimately it is bowlers they will face during the match itself. However, the playing surface must be good enough to be similar to conditions likely to be faced in the match for this type of preparation to be worthwhile. If it is not a good batting surface, batting can be difficult, which can have a detrimental effect on the batter's confidence going into the match ahead if the net session does not go well.

Time is another factor – there is not always enough time to fit in a net session prior to the start of play or batters only get a short time in the net and do not face many deliveries. However, some players do enjoy 'dog-stick' warm-ups with a partner, so once again it comes down to the individual's preferences for putting themselves in a confident state of mind, where they are also energising themselves physically, getting their feet moving and feeling the ball coming off the middle of the bat.

It is essential that these hitting sessions are carried out in a safe way, ensuring that players (feeders and batters) and spectators are not in danger of being hit by the ball, etc. For replicating match play and to encourage the correct execution of shots it is recommended that appropriate batting protection be worn at all times.

As discussed earlier, a lot of batters like to do some visualisation work out on the wicket prior to the match starting. This is often with bat in hand and visualising taking guard, facing the bowlers they will play against and the shots they will play.

While waiting to go into bat there are a few things a batter can do to prepare for their upcoming innings. Some very simple methods are highlighted below.

Some batters enjoy doing some footwork warm-ups, using either sports ladders or skipping ropes. These activities are great for getting the feet moving quickly and activating the motor system of the player. Some intermittently do a few press-ups or squeeze a tennis ball, etc. Once again, the focus is on the individual and what works for them.

Additionally, another simple warm-up exercise is to do 'bat-tap keepie uppies'. This involves the continuous hitting upwards of a cricket ball, tennis ball, squash ball, golf ball, marble, etc. off the face of the bat held in a horizontal plane. The ball is continuously hit to a height of approximately six to eight inches off the middle sweet spot of the bat. As the player becomes more skilful at this, they can alternately revolve the bat between the middle of the bat and the outside/inside edges, trying to ensure complete control of the ball. They could progress to just hitting the ball with the two edges of the bat. This simple drill is great for improving hand-eye coordination. Why not try it with two tennis balls at once, or even turn the bat around backwards!

Another suggestion for helping the eyes to focus, particularly while waiting to bat and whether reading, looking at your phone or watching the match, turn away and focus on an object that is approximately 22yds away from you for a while. This helps focus your eyes on the distance that the bowler will be bowling at you from, if you are playing on a full-size pitch.

Some batters prefer to sit in a corner listening to music through their headphones, and others sit and watch the match, gaining information about the pitch, bowlers, etc. Everyone is different, so it is important that the batter discovers what works best for them regarding the mental and physical preparation for batting.

A warm-up is an essential part of your pre-match preparations, and some pre-match drills are indicated in the next chapter.

Fitness

'Fitness is very important. The fitter you are, the easier it is to concentrate.'
MARK BUTCHER

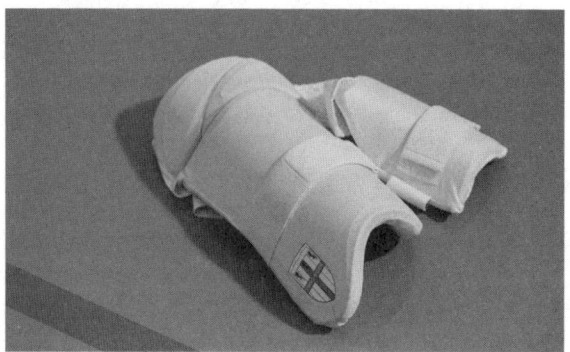

The following text provides a general outline on the subject of fitness. For more expansive knowledge the reader should consult further literature.

The challenges of batting surround the length of time you are at the wicket and the types of physical and mental demands put upon you. Batting consists of lots of sprinting and agility over a prolonged period when running between the wickets, speed when running, power when hitting the ball, strength when upholding your technique, and concentrating for long periods of time.

To bat for long periods and to maintain a high level of performance throughout an innings you need to have great levels of stamina and endurance. Additionally, batters also have to field for the duration of the opposition innings, and potentially may also be bowlers. Remember that a high level of physical fitness will also aid concentration and the ability to maintain a sharp focus throughout your whole innings.

High fitness levels also reduce the chance of injury. Without a strong, fit physique, eventually over a prolonged period of a day's play, your technique will start to disintegrate. Finally, you will also need to have good levels of agility and flexibility. A good level of all-round fitness is essential to be a successful batter.

Remember that cricket is a game generally played in sunny warm/hot temperatures, so being as fit as possible is essential, when being faced with the challenges of playing in these conditions.

Do not focus on one area more than another; they are all equally important. Focus excessively on lifting weights to build strength and power and you will bulk up too much to move quickly, which will be detrimental to your energy levels for a full day's play.

Playing multiple sports is a great way to improve your overall fitness and is also important for developing your hand-eye-foot coordination and reaction times. Games like squash, badminton and tennis are perfect for this. Basketball is a great sport for sprinting combined with endurance, as it is really punishing playing four 15-minute quarters with very little rest during play.

A strong core is very important to complement the upper and lower body power positions required, in addition to the general range of movement required to be a batter. Great core stability, coupled with a strong lower back are essential elements for a batter. Weights can be used to add upper-body strength but rowing and swimming are also great alternatives. They are excellent ways to enhance the leanness of your upper body, also providing a high-intensity cardio workout.

For stamina there is nothing better than getting miles in your legs. Unless you have knee, back or ankle issues, then running is the best way to build your stamina and endurance. You could use a slow, long-distance run as the initial part of your workout routine prior to commencing your weights. Make sure you do a long stretch after your run as this will help your flexibility. It is also important to keep stretching in breaks between sets when doing your weights routine. Cycling and swimming are also a great way to improve your stamina and endurance.

To improve balance and agility it is important to do exercises that get you moving in multiple directions. Ladders and cone work are the most common, and any drills that involve speed of movement will help you. Try to do some that also replicate front- and back-foot movements when batting. There are some great examples you can use in the next chapter.

Depending on the format of the game played – 20 overs, 50 overs, two-day, three-day, four-day, five-day – each match will offer different physical challenges to the batter. For instance, a T20 innings will be full of power hitting and continuous levels of high-intensity running between the wickets throughout the duration of the innings. There will be little or no opportunity for resting during the innings.

Sprint shuttles are a highly effective way of increasing speed and power, particularly important for running between the wickets. Try this, replicating a match situation, sprinting three runs. Carry this out on a full cricket pitch, running the full length, turning at each end. Repeat this, ensuring that you practise turning, facing both the off side and the on side. By doing this you will be competent at turning in either direction when the need arises during a match, ensuring that you do not favour one particular turning movement, which could mean you often turn 'blind'. It is wise to practise this while carrying your bat, again replicating match conditions. Why not try it in full pads and other protective equipment, etc.

In contrast, if you have progressed to a level of multi-day cricket, the intensity of play will be less, but it will take place over a much longer period. If you are an opener, your aim is to bat all day, which could be more than 100 overs. There will be times of intensity, but generally the pace is less frenetic. There are also drinks breaks every hour, and a lunch and tea interval available for a period of rest and refuelling, both on a nutritional and rehydrating theme.

A good training drill that can be used for group or individual sessions is called 'run a hundred'. It is great for increasing a batter's endurance and is similar to the bleep or yo-yo tests. The test should be carried out on a full-size pitch and can be done indoors or outdoors, with the batters carrying their bat. It can be carried out wearing minimal training clothing or with players fully padded up. For added realism, balls can be throw in, to replicate where it has been hit, and players can be eliminated if they turn blind. The test procedure is shown below.

BATTING RUNS: 100

14	Time	18	Time	13	Time	16	Time	18	Time	21	Time
3	0	2	0	1	0	1	0	3	0	3	0
2	25	2	15	2	25	4	10	3	20	1	25
1	40	1	30	1	40	2	35	2	45	4	35
2	50	3	40	3	50	1	1:00	3	60	2	1:10
3	1:15	1	1:10	1	1:15	2	1:10	1	1:10	3	1:30
1	1:40	4	1:20	1	1:25	1	1:30	1	1:20	3	1:55
1	1:55	3	1:50	2	1:40	3	1:45	2	1:40	2	2:20
1	2:10	2	2:15	2	2:00	2	2:10	3	2:00	3	2:40

Reading from the left, column one shows that 14 runs will be run in the first period, which is approximately 2min 10sec long. At the start of the stopwatch, the players run a three, which has to be completed in 25 seconds. They may finish in 15 seconds, so get ten seconds rest. At 25 seconds they then run a two, which has to be completed by 40 seconds, and so on. At the end of the first set, the players have one minute to recover, then the second set of runs commences, running the last two runs at 2min 15sec. A total of 18 runs are completed in this period, meaning the players have run 32 runs so far. Players always have one minute to recover at the end of each set. They ultimately aim to complete the 100 runs.

Nutrition

The following text provides a general outline on the subject of nutrition. For more expansive knowledge the reader should consult further literature.

Cricket is a sport that involves bursts of intense energy over a long duration. This principle applies to batting. To ensure a batter has sufficient energy stores available to meet the demands of their role, it is essential that they have a basic knowledge of the importance of eating food that will deliver energy throughout the day's play.

The food sources needed can be divided into the following categories: carbohydrates, proteins, fats, vitamins and fibre.

Carbohydrates

Carbohydrates can be divided into two forms: starches (complex carbohydrates), and sugars (simple carbohydrates).

During bursts of intense activity, it is carbohydrates that provide the essential energy source. They should form the major part of a batter's diet, approximately 50–60 per cent. They are stored in the muscles as glycogen, which is depleted rapidly during exercise, so it is essential that stores are kept topped up. Lack of glycogen in the muscles results in fatigue.

Good sources of complex carbohydrates are potatoes, pasta, rice, bread, porridge, cereals, baked beans, nuts, fresh fruit, dried fruit, etc. These carbohydrates are great at releasing glycogen to the muscles over a long period of time.

Good sources of simple carbohydrates are sugars, confectionery, jams, ice cream, etc. These carbohydrates are great at releasing glycogen to the muscles via a quick energy burst.

It is important to remember how long it takes glycogen to be produced for each type of carbohydrate.

Proteins

Protein should only form approximately 10–15 per cent of a batter's energy intake and is found in meats, fish, eggs, yoghurts, milk, cheese, dairy products, nuts, beans, protein shakes, etc.

Fats

A batter should try to regulate their dietary fat content to no more than 35 per cent of their total energy intake. Fat is extremely high in energy but is not very suitable for the time durations of a cricket match. Foods that are high in fat are biscuits, chocolate, butter, mayonnaise, eggs, cheese, fried foods, etc.

Vitamins

Most vitamins are found in a balanced diet, but many can be found in vitamin supplements and drinks. Vitamin D can also be found in natural sunlight, in addition to natural food sources.

Fibre

While fibre is not an energy source, it is essential for digestive health and regular bowel movements, and controls blood sugar levels. Foods high in fibre are wholegrain breakfast cereals, whole wheat pasta, wholegrain bread, fruit, vegetables, peas, beans, nuts, potatoes with skin, etc.

The best way of sustaining the relevant energy levels is to eat small regular meals, ensuring that glycogen levels are replenished fully. Digestion of food takes approximately two to three hours, so timing this intake is very important. There is a good reason why it is said that breakfast is the most important meal of the day.

After a match or practice session it is important to replenish your energy stores. This not only replaces the energy sources used up but also helps in the body's recovery. Eating a high carbohydrate meal within two hours of exercise is essential, as this is the most receptive time for storing glycogen.

Hydration

The following text provides a general outline on the subject of hydration. For more expansive knowledge the reader should consult further literature.

It is critically important that a batter guards against the effects of dehydration. Carrying a bat, and wearing gloves, pads and a helmet means that a batter is highly susceptible to dehydration, regardless of the temperature of the playing environment.

We have previously discussed the frequencies of intensities inherent in the various match formats, so it is essential that a player remains fully hydrated, as water plays a critical role in regulating body temperature.

Water and minerals are lost through sweating, so it is essential these are replaced. Crucially, for every 1kg loss in body weight through sweating, this equates to a one litre loss in body fluid. Performance is impaired if dehydration is 2 per cent of body weight, and if it reaches 5 per cent, this means that the body's capacity for work reduces by 30 per cent. Players can easily lose two to five litres of fluid during a match. Dehydration will produce deterioration in coordination and decision-making, and an increase in fatigue.

Dehydration can also cause decreased sweat rates, decreased heat dissipation, increased core temperatures, increased blood pressure, and the increased rate of depleting glycogen stores. To avoid this, it is essential that players drink on a regular basis throughout training and matchdays. A good rule of thumb is to endeavour to drink every 20 to 40 minutes.

Coaches and players should ensure plenty of fluids are available before, during and after activity. If you become thirsty, you are already dehydrated, so the key is to avoid this by regular fluid intakes. A great way of checking for dehydration is to check the colour of your urine. If it is yellow, you are already dehydrated. If it is clear (i.e. looking like water), you are rehydrated.

Batters should avoid alcohol and caffeinated drinks at least 24 hours before a match, as these fluids act as diuretics, thus promoting dehydration. Excessive alcohol consumption after a match is detrimental to the body's recovery system and can impair the following day's performance.

Batting in the heat

Because cricket is a summer sport, a batter will regularly be playing and training in hot temperatures and on sunny days. We have previously mentioned the importance of avoiding dehydration, so this has even greater importance on these occasions. In addition to this, batters can take certain measures to avoid the effects of these intense conditions.

Most batters nowadays wear helmets, so while this will protect most of their head from the effects of the sun, it gets extremely hot in a helmet, thus exacerbating the effect of high temperatures. Batters aged 18 or under are required to wear helmets at all times, but for older batters who prefer not to wear a helmet, it is recommended that either a cap or sun hat are worn to protect them from over-exposure to the sun.

A batter also wears gloves, batting pads, a box and thigh guards, so this also adds to their body core temperature. Some additionally wear a chest protector, arm guard and inner gloves, thus exacerbating the effects of the heat. A batter should be encouraged to remove their helmet and gloves regularly at appropriate intervals, to allow the free movement of fresh cooling air. If possible, it is advantageous to change gloves during a long innings, as very often the gloves can become wet with sweat, making it harder to grip the bat effectively.

The application of a high-protection sunscreen or barrier screen is essential. Taking a cold shower between sessions of play is a great way to cool down after a long period in the sun. When waiting to bat, batters should endeavour to stay in the shade and keep cool as much as possible.

Symptoms of heat stress can be identified as follows: loss of coordination, feeling cold, dizziness, confusion and pale complexion. If a player ever displays these symptoms, they should be removed from the field of play immediately, and appropriate medical attention sought.

Sleep

The following text provides a general outline on the subject of sleep. For more expansive knowledge the reader should consult further literature.

In addition to nutrition and hydration, another important element of a batter's preparation is having enough sleep. Sleep is the body's natural way of recovering from the day's exertions. It is essential for our health and well-being, particularly in the sporting environment, and it is recommended that a minimum of eight hours' sleep is required. If this can be achieved, a batter enhances their chances of performing well with the bat. There are a several ways this can be achieved, some of which are recommended below:

- Have a warm bath or shower directly before getting into bed
- Refrain from using mobile phones at least 30 minutes before getting into bed

- Refrain from watching TV in bed
- Keep your bedroom cool and well ventilated
- Sleep in fresh bed linen as often as is practically possible
- Take a milk or vitamin-fortified drink before going to sleep
- Avoid chocolate or cheese directly before bed
- Avoid a big meal late at night

The use of scented candles in a bedroom prior to turning in can promote a more peaceful sleep, as can relaxing music or listening to natural sound mood recordings, such as birds singing or waves washing on a beach.

It is not just the duration of sleep that is important, there are different cycles of sleep that ensure you wake fully refreshed and ready for the day ahead. The reader is encouraged to look for further information on this subject, as this is beyond the scope of this book.

Batting equipment

Buying the right equipment and looking after it is important, and below is a list of the essentials that you will need:
- Bat
- Helmet
- Batting pads
- Batting gloves
- Protective box
- Thigh pads
- Arm guard
- Chest guard
- Batting spikes/rubber-soled boots
- Cap/sun hat

What you can afford will obviously influence your decision on the quality of these items, unless you are fortunate enough to be a sponsored player.

> *'Buy the best gloves you can afford and a bat*
> *that you can swing comfortably with one hand.'*
> **MARK BUTCHER**

The bat

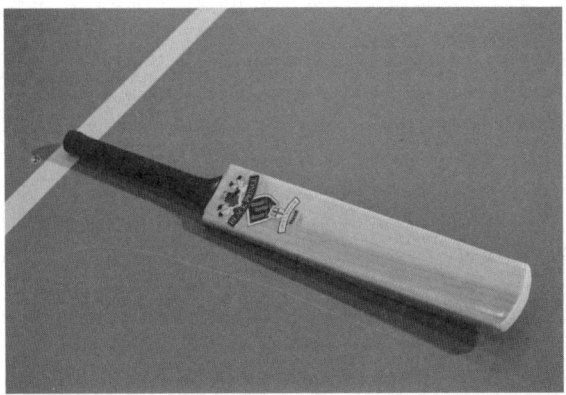

The cricket bat is the most individual and treasured item of kit a batter possesses. It is also the most expensive. Therefore, it is essential that the batter selects the best one for them, and once purchased it should be looked after and maintained in such a way that its performance and lifespan are maximised.

Selecting a bat is a very personal and individual choice. Some batters like a light bat, others a heavy one. Some prefer a high 'middle', others a lower one, where the middle is nearer to the toe, which can be advantageous on wickets that keep low. A short handle is preferred by some, while others favour a long handle. Some batters even stick with the same bat manufacturer throughout their playing days, but others continually change.

The 'pick-up' is a very important factor in the selection process. A batter lifts the bat in an imaginary backlift, and instantly they like the feel of it, going through a few air shots and liking it even more. Another batter may pick up the very same bat and it feels horrible to them. A bat may feel like it is floating up on its own for one batter, but the balance just feels right for another. Sometimes a heavy bat can have a great pick-up, depending on how it feels in the individual's hands. A light bat can also have a poor pick-up.

It is essential that you get to feel and pick up a bat when selecting one. Many people purchase their bats on the internet nowadays, selecting the weight they desire, specifying a short handle, etc. This is not ideal, as bats of any weight can have totally different balance and pick-up characteristics. If possible, a batter should try to purchase a bat from a bespoke professional bat maker, who can take into account all the personal requirements of the individual when making the bat. These bat makers also offer a great after-sales service in bat maintenance and repair and can very often bring a broken bat back to life, no matter how terminal the damage may appear.

It is worth noting that many professional cricketers may have been using the same bat maker throughout their careers, as the maker will know exactly what feel/pick-up the player requires. Even though a player may move through different bat sponsors and manufacturers, they may still have their bats made by the same bat maker, who then just applies the relevant bat manufacturer's stickers to the bat!

Many junior players like to select heavy bats because they see their professional adult heroes using one. However, younger players have not yet developed the strength to wield these heavy bats, so therefore some shots become very difficult for them to control and hit correctly. They often struggle playing off the back foot but can whack the ball through the leg side off the front foot. Hitting a cover drive can also be a problem, where top-hand control is again vital.

In these situations, it is always better to have a lighter bat at a young age, so that a large repertoire of shots can be learned and executed correctly. This will enable them to become a 360-degree batter, off both front and back foot, at a much earlier age. A good way to check a bat is not too heavy is to see whether a player can hold the bat in the top hand only, horizontal to the ground (as if waiting for the bowler running in to bowl) for ten seconds without feeling discomfort. If this is a struggle or cannot be completed at all then the bat is too heavy.

Through various reasons, mainly cost, many parents buy their children bats that are too big for them, knowing that they will eventually grow into them. If possible, this reasoning should be ignored, as it is much better if the young player can learn the correct control and hitting technique that a lighter/correctly fitted bat gives them.

Nearly all adult bats throughout the world are made of English willow. Junior starter bats designed to be used with a soft ball are mainly made using Kashmir willow from Pakistan. A third type of willow is commonly used, this being European willow, which is used predominantly for size 5–6 bats, introducing junior players to hard ball cricket.

In addition to the 'feel' of the bat, the batter should inspect the grain in the wood on the face of the bat. Ideally there should be between six and ten grains running vertically and parallel down the blade. If the bat has eight to ten grains it will potentially be a better bat but will not last as long. If a bat has six to eight grains it will last longer but will take longer to 'knock in'. If the grains do not stay straight all the way down to the toe of the bat, but twist off to one side, there is a good chance that the bat will break prematurely.

'Knocking in' is a phrase used to describe an element of the bat manufacturing/preparation process. Most modern bats come 'pre-knocked in' by the bat maker. This is done mechanically on a machine at the workshop, where the fibres in the wood are knitted back down after the bat blade has been pressed. This process is carried out to the full width of the blade from the splice of the handle, down to the toe of the bat. The edges of the bat are normally 'boned', involving rubbing them with a hard piece of rounded wood. Although bats come pre-pressed, it is advisable to add a further two hours of manual knocking in using a custom-made mallet. An alternative to this method of knocking in can be carried out using the swinging of a cricket ball in a sock. The 'pressing' element of the process is carried out before the knocking in and involves soaking the bat with water, then pressing it under increasing loads.

Modern bats also come with a protective plastic cover glued to the blade. To enhance its longevity, as part of the routine maintenance it is recommended that this is replaced at the end of every season. After a light sanding, the face and edges of the bat should be re-oiled at the same time, with the new cover not glued on for a further four weeks after oiling. The application of bat-reinforcing tape is recommended down both sides of the blade to protect the vulnerable edges. It is also advisable to oil the back of the bat at the start and end of each season.

Another vital element of bat care is to ensure that the rubber grip is in good condition and not worn out. If it is, it is very difficult to grip the bat firmly, thus making execution of the shots more difficult, increasing the chances of being dismissed. Grips should be replaced at the end of every season or when holes start to appear. If they do wear it is a good sign that you are scoring lots of runs! Replacement can either be done by the bat maker or by the batter by using a custom-made bat gripping cone. There are many videos on the internet showing how this is done. When fitted, the bottom of the grip should be firmly taped to the splice of the bat, and any excess length at the top be cut away, leaving the grip flush with the end of the handle. This removes any chance of accidental 'nick' sounds coming from the grip, whether it is too long or folded over.

Some batters like to put more than one grip on their bat, particularly those with big hands. Others find that multiple grips give their bat a better pick-up or feel. It is quite common for batters to put multiple grips on the bottom-hand area only, as this additional thickness prevents the batter holding the handle too tight in their bottom hand, thus promoting the more technically advantageous and stronger top-handed grip. Modern bats can have dual handles, where the handle is thicker at the bottom than it is at the top, for the reason just explained.

Finally, it is prudent to have a toe guard fitted to the bat, as these protect the toe from damage and the ingress of water. Toe guards are usually glued on after the toe has been sealed and varnished.

Bats should never be left near radiators or fires, as this will dry them out, contributing to premature breaking. They should be stored in a dry room at normal room temperature and stored within their own protective bat cover at all times.

CRICKET BAT SIZE CHART

Bat Size	Batsman Age	Batsman Height	Bat Length	Bat Width	Bat Weight
Junior 1	4-5 years	below 4ft 3in	25 1/4in	3 1/2in	1lb 11oz – 1lb 13oz
Junior 2	6-7 years	4ft – 4ft 6in	27 1/2in	3 1/2in	1lb 12oz – 1lb 15oz
Junior 3	8-9 years	4ft 6in – 4ft 9in	28 1/2in	3 3/4in	1lb 13oz – 2lb 1oz
Junior 4	9-11 years	4ft 9in – 5ft	29 3/4in	3 3/4in	2lb 1oz – 2lb 3oz
Junior 5	10-12 years	5ft – 5ft 3in	30 3/4in	4in	2lb 2oz – 2lb 4oz
Junior 6	11-13 years	5ft 2in – 5ft 5in	31 3/4in	4in	2lb 3oz – 2lb 5oz
Harrow	12-15 years	5ft 5in – 5ft 8in	32 3/4in	4 1/6in	2lb 5oz – 2lb 7oz
Light Short Handle	15+ and Adults	5ft 7in – 6ft 2in	33 1/2in	4 1/4in (max)	2 lb 5oz – 2lb 9oz
Medium Short Handle	15+ and Adults	5ft 9in – 6ft 2in	33 1/2in	4 1/4in (max)	2lb 8oz – 3lb
Heavy Short Handle	15+ and Adults	5ft 9in – 6ft 2in	33 1/2in	4 /14in (max)	2lb 12oz – 3lb 4oz
Long Handle	Adults	6ft 2in and above	34 3/8in	4 1/4in (max)	above 3lb

Helmet

Helmets are to be worn by every player aged 18 or below, and it is advisable that all batters should wear this essential piece of protective equipment wherever possible. Helmets come in a variety of colours, finishes and materials, and their sizes range from small junior up to large senior. Their construction uses the latest advances in ABS plastics, fibreglass, carbon fibre, steel, titanium, high-density foams and air-flow systems.

Since the sad death of Australian international Phil Hughes in 2014, many manufacturers have developed stem guards, which provide protection to the once-vulnerable area at the base of the head and neck.

A batting helmet should be safe, strong, durable, comfortable and feel light when it is on the batter's head. All helmets should comply with British Standard BS7928:2013. For further information see the guidance issued by the ECB (England and Wales Cricket Board) and the PCA (Professional Cricketers' Association).

The metal grill is an essential item, protecting the facial and throat areas. It is crucial that the grill is adjusted so that the gap between the top of the grill and the underside of the helmet peak is smaller than the size of the cricket ball, ensuring that the ball never passes through to impact the face of the wearer. The batter should always be looking through this gap when wearing the helmet. A common fault with junior players is that they wear the helmet in a way that their eyes look through the grill bars themselves, and not through the gap between underside of the peak and top of the grill. Wearing the helmet like this impedes clear vision of the ball and exposes the throat and chin area to the ball slightly more!

The helmet should sit on the head comfortably and securely, the tightness of this fit governed by the helmet chin strap, inner sponge system or rotating adjuster. There should be no movement, either side to side, or front to back. The chin strap and its rubber locator should sit ON the chin, not UNDER it!

Regular checking of the tightness of the screws attaching the grill to the helmet is critical to the safety and effectiveness of the helmet should a heavy impact be made, as the structural integrity of the helmet can only be ensured if these two elements are 100 per cent secured.

If the helmet receives a hard impact, it should be inspected immediately, and potentially replaced, even if there is no obvious sign of cracking or similar damage.

Batting in a helmet makes the batter become hot very quickly, so it is essential that the helmet is removed as often as possible to allow the head to receive the free movement of fresh cooling air. The ideal time for this is in between overs. For ease of removal and saving time it is much easier for the batter to do this with their top hand, as they can do it without taking their glove off, because there is no protection on that thumb, hence they can tuck their thumb inside the chin strap, while the fingers grip the top of the metal grill. This may be harder for younger players to do as their hands are smaller.

After a long or intense innings, where the helmet gets wet with sweat, most batters leave their helmet and other equipment in the sun to dry out. Helmets should not be left near radiators, etc., as the intense heat can damage its integrity.

Batting pads

Batting pads must have a combination of lightness and strength. They need to be light to provide the minimum amount of restriction when running, yet be strong and durable enough to withstand heavy impacts from the cricket ball should it hit them, therefore fully protecting the batter's legs from the slightest bit of pain.

Pads come in right- and left-hand versions, so they must be purchased correctly for the individual batter.

It is essential that a batter wears the correct size of pads. Too big, and they will have trouble running in them; too small, and there will not be enough protection for their legs, and the knee protection can be too low. In addition to the restriction and protection issues mentioned, ill-fitting pads will be a mental distraction to the batter, something that is best eliminated. Pads can be purchased for small juniors or large adults.

Modern pads usually come with a knee-locator gap in the knee roll protection padding. When the batter has their knee in this location, the bottom of the pad should push comfortably on to the top of the foot, with the associated side protection terminating near the sole of the foot.

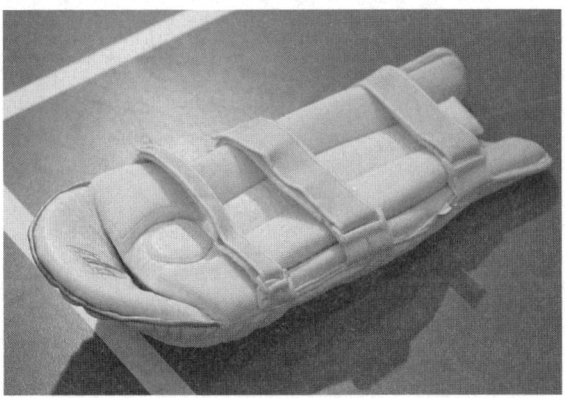

A common fault for young players comes when they do up the Velcro straps on each pad. In pulling them tight, there is often a long length of strap sticking out past the buckle and beyond the Velcro strip. This can hinder movement when running and can also be potentially dangerous as the ball could flick one of the sticking out straps, causing the umpire to accidentally give the batter out if there is an appeal! With this in mind, it is prudent to fold and attach the strap to the Velcro strip as indicated in the following photo: the end of the strap is aligned with the end of the Velcro strip and pressed down into the receiving strip. The centre section of strap is then folded and pinched, before pressing the shortened lengths of Velcro into the receiving pad. The excess length of strap now sits proud of the back of the pad, not sticking out past the pad.

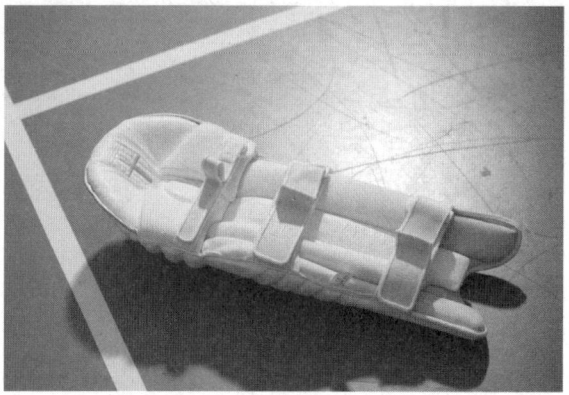

Prior to wearing brand-new pads for the first time, a good idea is to Velcro each strap up tightly (without wearing them) for a few days, so that the pads lose their stiffness, and then form around the legs much better when being worn normally.

It is also a good idea to clean your pads regularly with soap and water. Not only does it look good, but it removes ball impact marks, which to the more discerning eyes of the opposition could highlight some flaws in your technique, whether playing front- or back-foot shots! Pads should not be left near radiators, etc., as the intense heat can crack them, thus damaging their integrity.

Batting gloves

Batting gloves come in both right-hand and left-hand versions, so it is vital that a batter wears the correct pair coincident with their batting stance. If a batter is right-handed, the thumb on their left hand will have no protection, while the thumb on their right hand will. This combination is reversed for left-hand gloves. The reason the top-hand thumb has no protection is because it is hidden behind the handle of the bat, and additionally rests in a hidden position between both hands.

Batting gloves should fit comfortably and be appropriately sized for the individual using them. A good pair of gloves will provide almost 100 per cent protection to both hands.

Gloves often get very damp with sweat, so it is a great idea to let them dry naturally in the sun and fresh air after use. Never put them on a radiator to dry, as the excess heat will cause the leather to crack. Many batters prefer to wear a pair of cotton inners inside their batting gloves as these protect the gloves from soaking up the sweat from the batter's hands, the sweat being soaked up by the inners instead. Many batters also prefer the feel of a pair of inners in their batting gloves.

It is well worth buying the most expensive pair of gloves you can afford, as generally these will offer the best protection and the best grip of the bat.

As with batting pads, gloves should be cleaned regularly to improve longevity. In an ideal world a batter's top-hand glove should always wear out before their bottom-hand glove. This indicates that they are top-hand dominant, which is ideal from a technical point of view, as it would indicate that the batter is probably equally adept at hitting both sides of the wicket. If their bottom-hand glove wears out first, this indicates that they are bottom-hand dominant, which could possibly indicate that they hit a lot more balls into the leg side. Hand dominance will also be evident on their bat grip too, with the grip being worn out more by one hand than the other.

With a high volume of use with plenty of sweating then drying, the palm of the glove can develop and shiny texture. When this happens, the glove becomes less effective at gripping the handle properly and the bat can twist in the hand more as the bat makes contact of the ball. This will affect power and placement of shots. Once the sheen appears, a new pair should be sourced. A proper grip of the bat handle is vital for effective and consistent run scoring. Where possible (and affordable) a batter should have two or three pairs of gloves, which they can rotate throughout an innings.

Protective box

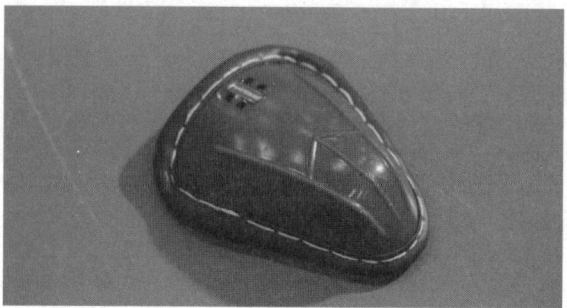

It is essential that all batters wear an abdominal protector, otherwise known as a box. It is a strong piece of plastic designed to protect the groin/pelvic region from impact from the cricket ball. Abdominal protectors are worn by both male and female players and are specifically designed differently for both sexes.

A common mistake regarding the wearing of this protection comes through accidentally wearing unsuitable underwear to locate and support the box. Ideally the batter should wear briefs or a purpose-built athletic support. Anything else allows the box to fall away, down into the batter's whites, thus becoming a mental distraction, and physically putting the player at risk.

The box should be washed regularly for hygiene purposes.

Note for coaches

With external equipment it is easy to check whether a player is wearing the necessary protective equipment, but this is not possible for boxes. For young players it is worth a verbal confirmation that they are wearing a box before they bat.

Thigh pads

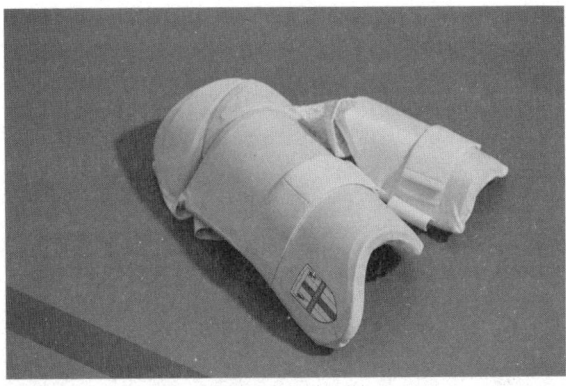

Nowadays, thigh pads are commonplace, and another essential item of cricket protection. They are a combination of heavy-duty foam with hard plastic shells, attached to the body using linen Velcro straps. Most commonly they come as a 'combi' pair, protecting both inner and outer thighs.

Thigh pads not only provide protection but are essential for gaining confidence at working the ball off the hips and thighs, thus keeping great shape and technique, something that is easy to lose if you are worrying about getting hit by the ball in this most tender of areas. We would encourage young players to have this equipment as soon as possible as it will encourage them to get in line.

Although the thigh pads come custom made and joined to each other, it is essential they are fitted in the correct position in relation to each thigh, as locating slightly in the wrong position can be very painful. The batting stance is generally a side-on position, so when executing many shots it is the side of the thighs that are most vulnerable, hence the largest pad (outer thigh pad) on the front leg should be located to the left side of the thigh, and the smaller pad (inner thigh pad) on the right leg should also be positioned more to the left side of that thigh. Reverse the above if the batter is left-handed. As with batting pads and gloves, there are specific thigh pads for right- and left-handed batters. A common mistake is to position the pads on the front of the thighs, an area that is not hit too often by the ball, leaving the potentially more vulnerable area exposed.

Never buy thigh pads that are too small. As long as they do not have an adverse effect on your movement, it may be worth buying the largest set you are comfortable with. Thigh pads generally come pre-shaped, so are usually very comfortable to wear, and additionally have an integral front hip protector on the front thigh pad.

Arm guard

Arm guards come in an ambidextrous form, sized for both junior and adult batters, offering protection to the forearm of the batter's top hand. They are made of high-quality closed cell foam and should be light and strong, and are attached via Velcro straps, or contained within an elasticated sleeve. Arm guards are particularly useful against the threat of short, fast bowling, aimed at the body and head.

The arm guard should be fitted so that it protects the outer left side of the batter's left forearm, if they are a right-handed batter. This arrangement is reversed for a left-handed batter. A smaller guard can also be worn on the bottom hand arm, where occasionally the ball can strike the arm.

In addition to the physical protection offered, as is the case with thigh pads and chest guards, an arm guard can be a great confidence booster, helping a batter to have a more solid technique against threatening fast bowling.

Chest guard

Chest guards come in an ambidextrous form, sized for both junior and adult batters, offering protection to the left ribcage of a right-handed batter. This arrangement is reversed for a left-handed batter. They are made of high-quality closed cell foam, and should be light and strong, and are attached via Velcro straps. Chest guards are particularly useful against the threat of short, fast bowling, aimed at the body and head.

In addition to the physical protection offered, as is the case with thigh pads and arm guards, a chest guard can be a great confidence booster, helping a batter to have a more solid technique against threatening fast bowling as it encourages the players to get in line and not back away from the stumps.

Batting spikes and rubber-soled boots

It is essential that the batter has comfortable footwear when batting, as their intention is to bat as long as possible, which will inevitably involve lots of running. If their footwear is the wrong size or inappropriately fitted, this will create additional physical problems, while also producing mental distractions. Additionally, if laces are not done up securely, this could contribute to the physical and mental challenges highlighted, as well as potentially contributing to the fall of the wicket of the batter in some way.

It is advised that you carry some spare spikes in your kit bag to replace any that wear down or come out. A full set of spikes on your footwear is crucial, ensuring that you can hold solid bases when preparing to execute a shot, push off powerfully when setting off for a run, or when slowing down to make a turn when running multiple runs. It would be criminal if a batter was run out because they slipped due to inadequate footwear, or lack of a complete set of studs in their boots. Additionally, a full set of studs guarantees that your weight is evenly distributed into the ground, reducing the chance of sore feet, caused when a stud or two are missing. Regular tightening of the studs with the spanner supplied ensures that they will not fall out while you are batting.

When to wear spikes or rubber-soled batting boots is a matter of personal choice for the batter. Obviously, if the pitch is wet it is essential that spikes are worn, as these give the grip that rubber-soled batting boots will not. Some batters still prefer to wear spikes on hard, dry pitches, while others prefer to wear rubber-soled pimpled batting boots in that environment.

Some boot manufacturers supply a compromise alternative known as a 'half-spiked' or '50/50' boot. This option has spikes around the toes/balls of the feet, with a pimpled surface to the rear half of the feet around the heel area.

It is not unknown for a batter to have studs inserted into a normal pair of trainers, preferring to have the comfort of the generally lighter feel these trainers give. The studs need to be fixed in professionally as there is the potential for this type of modification to have adverse effects on the soles of the batter's feet. However, this type of trainer offers minimal protection to an accurate yorker homing in on the feet! Purpose-built leather cricket boots, whether studded or pimpled rubber-soled, offer more protection to the feet due to their more robust and stronger construction. Some players even have plastic protection inserts added into the toe area of their boots to give more protection from the impact of the ball.

Finally, a good pair of lambswool socks will provide great comfort and cushioning when batting and fielding, and they also have better breathing/sweating qualities than man-made synthetic socks.

It is also a good idea to clean your boots regularly and maintain them well as with other items of equipment. Boots should not be left near radiators, etc., as the intense heat can crack the leather, thus damaging their integrity.

Cap and sun hat

Both caps and sun hats should be of an appropriate size, suitable to the age/size of the batter. They should be correctly adjusted so that they fit snugly on the head, ensuring they are neither too tight, which can cause discomforting headaches, or too loose, where they could fall off and hit the stumps, or blow over your eyes as the bowler bowls the ball, thus potentially ending your time at the crease!

Remember, it is essential that all the batter's protective equipment and clothing are in good condition and fit correctly, as any distraction can adversely affect their concentration and subsequent performance.

NINE
TRAINING METHODS AND DRILLS

> 'Practise the shots you want to perform in games
> over and over again before taking them into a match.'
>
> BEN DUCKETT

This chapter provides a comprehensive list of drills and practices broken down into the following categories:

- Technical development
- Tactical development
- Batting games
- Hand-eye-foot coordination
- Training on your own
- Pre-match
- Waiting to bat
- Introduction to video analysis
- Drill and practice safety awareness
- Useful coaching quotes to remember

Where appropriate, we list the equipment needed and describe how the drill works, with text and photos additionally offering ideas for progression. We also hope that you will be inspired to adapt the drills specifically for your target audience, and even start producing your own.

Cricket training in the UK is unusual, as there is a distinct difference between the surfaces a batter will train on during the indoor winter training programme and the playing surface a batter will play on during the outdoor summer playing season.

During the indoor winter period, October to March, the indoor surface is hard, fast and bouncy, due to the construction of indoor sports hall floors. The ball comes on to the bat well, so there is the potential for batters to reduce their amount of footwork, etc., play through the line of the ball, and generally be quite free-scoring. There are also many indoor winter leagues, so batters adopt a method of batting suitable for playing on these surfaces.

However, when it comes to the outdoor training and playing season, April to September, the playing surfaces are now the opposite. Netting and playing on natural grass pitches means that the surface is softer, slower and with less bounce and carry. The ball does not come on to the bat as well, so a batter's timing can be thrown out massively. This is seen in the number of chipped-up catches, leading edges, hitting across the line and failure to wait to play the ball late, etc.

Basically, batters practise for six months on hard, fast, bouncy surfaces, preparing themselves for six months of playing on slow, low pitches. International and county-level wickets are generally nearer to the performance of indoor training facilities than a wicket prepared for a local school or village team for example. Generally, the closest a batter will get to their winter training surface is during a long, hot, dry spell of weather during the hottest summer months, when the wickets are harder.

With this in mind, it may be worth considering slowing down the speed of bowling machines as winter training finishes, so a batter's timing is tested and enhanced as the outdoor season approaches, encouraging them to wait for the ball again.

The ECB differentiates a player's coaching development methods into three distinct areas. Each type of coaching method has its own separate characteristics and is appropriate to the age, ability and experience of the individual player. There are certain elements that are cross-referenced in all three methods, but ultimately there is a clear progression through the three-practice-type continuum. The continuum is:

FIXED – VARIABLE – GAMES-BASED LEARNING

Descriptions and characteristics of the practice methods are listed below.

Fixed practice

This is a batting practice activity that requires the batter to repeatedly hit the same shot to a consistent, accurate form of static or moving ball feed. This method enables the batter to maximise their number of hits, and is most suitable when introducing new shots or when a batter is experiencing a breakdown in their technique and success with a particular shot. Batters can immediately improve their technique and confidence. This form of practice can be otherwise described as 'grooving' their shots, or 'gaining muscle memory'.

Examples of this, indicating the progression are:
- Hitting off a batting tee
- Drop feed
- Full toss feed
- Bobble feed
- Throw-down feed
- Bowling machine feed

Variable practice

This is a batting practice activity that requires the batter to hit the ball differently from one ball to the next, randomly playing different shots to consecutive balls, with no repetition of shots. Variable practice attempts to replicate the random decision-making, shot selection and execution associated with batting. It is a good form of practice for developing match-specific technical skills, but can be challenging initially, leading to a temporary drop in decision-making, shot selection, execution and confidence while the batter adapts to this progression in practice.

A good example of variable practice is a batter facing some bowlers in the nets without any scenario or conditioned games being incorporated, or facing a coach or fellow batter delivering the ball via a sidearm (dog-stick).

Games-based learning

This final form of practice is usually carried out setting up conditioned scenario games, aimed at replicating various random situations that regularly occur when batting in a real match. For example, this could be facing real bowlers, chasing down 25 runs to win off four overs with two wickets remaining, or playing out for a draw for four overs with no wickets in hand. These scenarios could be set up on a full outdoor ground with a full team of fielders, indoors in a sports hall, or even in nets with cone fielders and the coach umpiring and adjudicating the course of play. This form of practice is as close as you can achieve to match play when training.

Games-based learning practice sessions give the coach a great opportunity to assess all of the individual batter's skills development. When challenging scenarios are set, the batter's decision-making skills and self-awareness under pressure are revealed, thus enabling further development. It is a great way to stretch good players and improve a player's performance under pressure.

Any form of practice should have a purpose at its heart, so whether a batter is practising in a fixed, variable or games-based learning session, the coach should consider the batter (person) themselves, their specific batting needs, and the form of practice most suitable to achieve those needs.

Technical development

The following drills should be selected on their suitability for the batter, based on their current ability to execute the shot successfully. The type of ball, speed and method of delivery should also be appropriate to the batter. Whenever possible the batter should be pushed to another level of progression to progress their development.

While forms of progression are suggested, this is by no means an exhaustive list, so the reader is encouraged to design their own drills and methods of advancement.

Hitting off a batting tee

When players start out or you really want to isolate a specific part of a shot (such as getting the front foot closer to the line of the ball), then a moving ball can be more challenging for the player and they are better off playing a stationary ball raised off the ground by a batting tee.

Minimum equipment needed:
 1 ball (soft ball recommended)
 1 batting tee

Additional equipment:
 Cones for providing target areas
 1 stump to practise back-foot shots
 Mats/discs/chalk to mark where foot position should be

Description:
Place a batting tee on the floor near the player standing in their stance on the crease so that they will need to make a comfortable stride forward towards the side of the tee to bring the bat through to make contact with the ball. Mats/chalk/rubber discs/hoops, etc. can be placed on the floor to highlight to the player where they should place their front foot. Cones can also be used to give the player an area to hit through.

Parts of this drill can be isolated. To encourage a player to land with the heel first, they can start in this position instead of in their stance:

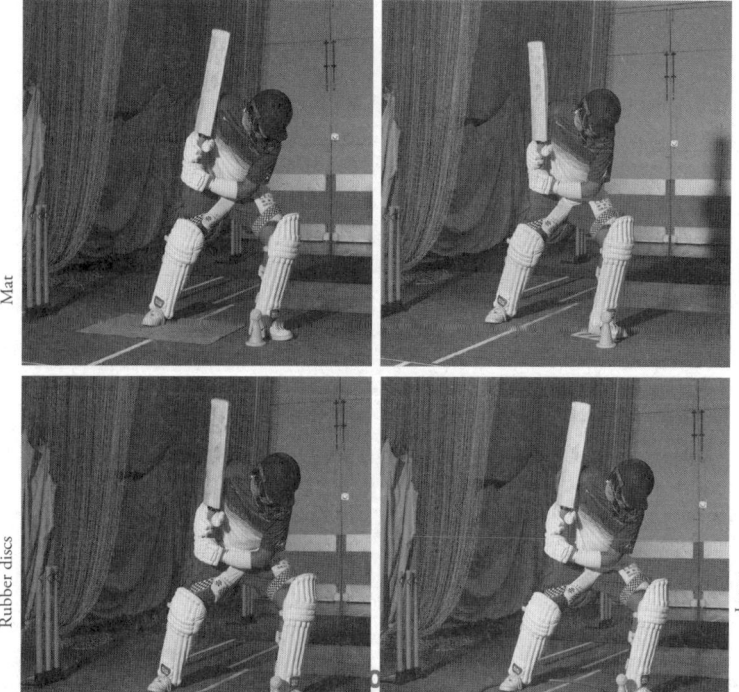

Here the player is starting from a position of front contact with the bat raised to play the shot. From here the whole foot lands, the front knee bends and the bat comes through to make contact with the ball.

In the stance position or midway position you can check the grip of the bat and if a coned target is in place this will indicate whether the bat is coming through straight or whether the bat face is opening or closing on ball contact.

If a player really struggles with getting their front foot alongside the ball to drive (very common in young players), place a mat down and ask the player to start from the final position with the forward movement having already been completed:

Here the player starts with their front foot on a mat alongside the batting tee with the head forward, front shoulder dipped and the bat raised to come through to play the ball.

To work on back-foot shots, the batting tee can be placed on top of a stump as in this photo:

Drives, cuts, pulls and hooks can all be practised this way. A plastic stump is recommended if you have one available. Mats can still be used to highlight where the back foot (and front foot) need to be. Cones can still be used to provide a target to hit through.

Progression:

Introduce some competition – how many balls out of ten can the player hit through a coned target?

Make the coned target smaller.

Ask the player to play the shot with top or bottom hand only.

Move the batting tee further away so the batter has to use their feet to get to the pitch of the ball, similar to coming down the wicket to a spinner.

Introduce drop feeds so the player has to react to small vagaries of the drop and the bounce of the ball.

Reverse chaining

In the drill above we have touched on a process called reverse chaining, where the player starts the drill in the final position just before the bat comes through to play the shot. This is particularly useful for encouraging a batter to have the correct footwork. It is very common for young players to move their front foot forward, but not across to the pitch of the ball on the front and back foot. On the front foot this can only be worked on when hitting off tees or drop feeds, unless you are a very accurate thrower of a cricket ball. On the back foot there is slightly more leeway to do this with throws, similarly when using a bowling machine. The photo sequence below shows the regression of a back-foot off drive from the final position to starting from a stance position:

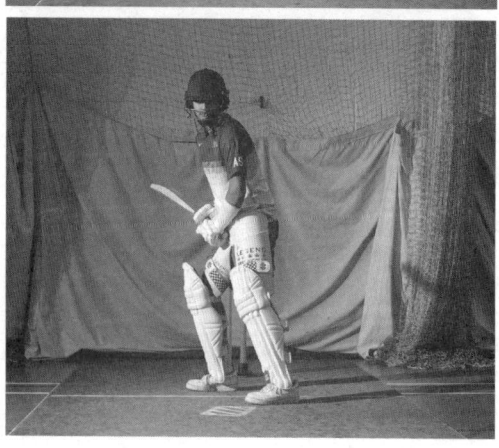

In the first photo all of the footwork has been completed and the bat simply needs to come through to hit the ball off the tee.

In the second photo the back foot has gone back and across as the start position, but the player will need to slide the front foot and bring the bat through to complete the shot.

In the third photo the player is starting from the stance position, and now needs to complete all footwork and take the bat back before playing the shot.

Note for coaches

To get good timing and rhythm in a batter's shots, it is important to encourage them to play the ball with the bat as the foot lands and the head comes forward. This brings the body weight into the shot and improves timing and power without actually trying to hit the ball any harder. The front foot batting tee drill with the player starting on their heel is a really good one to develop getting body weight into the ball. It is also a good drill to coach players out of landing on the ball of their foot when coming forward, as this is usually a very unbalanced position and also much harder to get the body weight into the ball.

The feeds

As a coach, how well you feed the ball is vital for decent practice for the batter. The more accurately you can feed the ball to a player to work on a specific shot or part of their technique, the more value the player will derive from the session. Just like a player works on their game, as a coach you need to work on your feeds. There are five types of feed:
1. Drop feed
2. Bobble feed
3. Full toss feed
4. Throw-down feeds
5. Sidearm feed

We have already talked about drop feeds as a progression from hitting off a tee, and of course if you have no tee then this is the best alternative. The player will have to make small adjustments each time to get their foot into the right place. Using a tennis ball is a good feed method to practise a sweep shot, where you can have the player set up in the end position (reverse chaining), then bringing the bat through to execute the shot. Make sure you get clear of the path of the bat!

A bobble feed adds a higher level of difficulty compared to a drop feed but is still relatively easy to deliver accurately. Again, a bobble feed is most effective with a soft ball (tennis or Incrediball) and it should be fed underarm so that it bounces at least twice before reaching the batter. Because of the slow nature of the feed this is a fantastic way to make the batter wait for the ball and play late. If you have a player that plants their foot early, not stepping and hitting at the same time, this is a good way to redirect their timing.

A full toss feed can be used for any shot in the book and, as discussed later in this chapter, is what many players do pre-match to work through their range of shots and feel the middle of the bat on the ball. As a coach it is relatively straightforward to be accurate and the players can exaggerate the correct technique when playing the ball.

A throw-down feed is as its name suggests, an overarm throw from the coach. Here the level of difficulty in getting the throw accurate increases, so the level of difficulty also goes up for the batter. Even if you are practising a straight drive, the batter will have more decisions to make as occasionally you will throw wide and they will have to cover drive, or you will hit a length and they should be defending. As a coach you can choose to hold cross-seam so the ball goes straight or you can go seam up and replicate seam bowling. Therefore, with an overarm feed you can start to replicate more match play.

To make it harder for the batter you can come closer to give them less time to play the ball. You can also add a small run before you throw to give them the feel of a bowler running in. This gives scope for tactical sessions as well as technical when you are giving throw-downs. You can also throw spin instead of seam and come wider on the crease, go round the wicket, etc. to mimic different situations and bowling types throughout a match.

The closest feed you will get to replicating a bowler's delivery is with a sidearm stick, as they can feed the ball much quicker than you can throw it. A sidearm is just like a tennis ball feeder that dog walkers use, except this is designed for bowling and throwing cricket balls.

Using a sidearm effectively can take time to master but they are great for player development so it is worth investing the time to improve your skills with it. As with throws, you can swing the ball both ways, bowl slower balls, bowl spin, change how close/far away you are on delivery, change the angles and add a run-up to further mimic a bowling action.

Hitting through targets

Setting targets to hit through when doing any of the above feeds is a good way to increase the level of difficulty for the player, teaching them how to adjust body position and bat face to hit different areas as well as the very important art of hitting the gaps. The more times a batter can hit a gap – the quicker they will score runs.

You can simply set one target to hit through with two cones or stumps (or any other markers you can think of), or you can set multiple targets so the player has to adjust each time to hit a different area. These areas can be nominated by the coach or you could have multiple balls of different colours, where certain coloured balls have to go through the matching cone colour. This becomes very easy to turn into a competition to ramp up the pressure on the player and increase enjoyment. For example, every time the player gets the ball through a target they get a point; each time they miss, the coach gets a point; first to ten wins.

Fine

Square

In the images opposite, the player has to hit through three different areas from a sweep shot from a full toss feed from the coach. Assuming the feed from the coach is reasonably consistent, the player will have to get their front foot and body in slightly different positions each time to each target. The coach can nominate which target to hit or use different coloured balls, as well as make a contest out of it.

Cones can be set up so there is a bigger target, with a smaller one in between. Here a player is rewarded for getting the ball into the bigger target with a point, but can be given bonus points for hitting the smaller target (ultimate placement of the ball).

Target cones can be set at mid-on and mid-off, set in the traditional V, and the player can work on using their feet to spin to get to the pitch and drive through or over mid-on and mid-off. Again, different coloured balls can be used, or the coach can nominate which target to hit through. Further, the coach can nominate which balls to hit in the air, and a variety of feeds or a bowling machine can be used.

Six-ball challenge

This is a great drill for working technique in a range of shots as well as developing a 360-degree game as the batter has to play the same ball with six different shots and that can incorporate six different scoring areas. This can be done with any type of feed (if accurate) but is particularly effective with bowling machines or a Merlyn bowling machine, which ensures a more consistent delivery.

Equipment:
    6 balls
    Cones to mark scoring areas
    Whiteboard or paper to mark the six shots so the batter memorises them
    Bowling machines (most effective for consistent delivery)

Description:
Write the six shots you want the player to work at on a sheet of paper or whiteboard. In this example below the batter is facing off spin from a Merlyn machine:
    1: Defence (not getting out)
    2: Work a single leg side

3: Work a single off side
4: Orthodox sweep
5: Slog sweep
6: Use feet to hit straight down the ground

The player is then fed balls on the same line and length and has to adjust body position, feet position and/or bat face on contact to play the six different shots. If a player struggles with a particular shot, this can then be isolated and worked on before going back to the challenge. The shots that you choose to work on should be relevant to the player and their current skill level.

Progression:

Shots can be changed to ones that are more challenging. In the example above this could be driving into the spin over or through extra cover.

Cones can be used to provide targets that the shots should be hit through, or to represent fielders so the player can see if they are hitting the gaps.

A competition can be created to ramp up the pressure on the batter. For example, a point to the player when executed correctly, with double points for hitting through a nominated target. A point is scored by the coach for a batter's failed attempt, with a double point for the coach for a dismissal.

A narrow bat can be used by the batter.

Boundary followed by single

Again, this drill is really effective on a machine where the feed can be consistent but can be done with good hand feeding (any variety). It is a great drill for working on boundary hitting, but also encouraging the player to hit singles once the field is back.

Equipment:
6 balls
1 cone
Bowling machine if available

Description:
The coach places a cone where he wants the player to hit the ball. The ball is

fed on to the same line and length each time and the first ball fed needs to be hit to the boundary. This can be in the air or along the ground as agreed with the batter. The batter then needs to hit the next ball for a single through the same area, imagining that the fielder has gone back to the boundary. This is then repeated several times to work on those two shots.

A good example would be driving through or over cover off a good length, and then next ball the batter has to work a single into the cover region. They are therefore working on their power game one ball and their touch game the next. Similarly, it could be hitting over mid-on one ball and next ball using feet to get to the pitch to drive through mid-on to long-on.

Progression:

Vary the boundary/single area every two balls so the player has to continue to adapt between scoring areas.

Set a field and introduce a competition, such as score 12 runs off two overs.

Batter uses a narrow bat.

Range hitting

Range hitting is a term used for hitting over boundaries – six-hitting. Most players love this practice! It is best done on a bowling machine where the feed is consistent and the coach is protected from the ball hit towards them.

Equipment:

Boundary markers (cones, flags or rope)
Bowling machine
Additional cones or mannequins to represent fielders

Description:

Using the flags, mark a boundary out at a distance relative to the player(s) you are working with. Then set up cones or mannequins to represent the boundary fielders. Discuss a bowling type and length to be worked on with the batter, such as good length, no swing for straight sixes. Feed six balls, keeping track of how many runs are scored, then discuss with a player any technical adjustments required, and repeat.

Progression:

Vary the line, length, swing to keep asking questions of the batter as to what they need to do with each adjustment to still be able to have a strong percentage chance of hitting a six.

If you have multiple batters, they can do the fielding instead of cones/mannequins. If they successfully complete a catch, they get to bat next.

Have a contest between multiple batters of who scores most runs.

Add running twos to deep fielders to mix up the six-hitting. The fielder gets to bat if a run out is achieved.

Close fielders drill

To develop the technique required for making sure the ball does not carry to close fielders, this is a good drill to work the batter on playing the ball late, creating an angle of the bat to keep the ball down and playing with soft hands.

Equipment:
1 tennis ball or other high-bouncing ball
Cones to mark the close fielders

Description:

The coach sets cones to represent close catchers round the bat – short leg, silly point, slip, etc. They then feed the ball (under or overarm) to the batter, who must defend the ball without it carrying to the close fielders.

Progression:

Batter uses narrow bat.

Ball is thrown quicker, giving the player less time to react.

Introduce some competition. For example, one point for every successful defensive shot. Four points removed for every dismissal. How many points can be scored in three minutes of batting.

Bowling machines can be used.

Markers for foot positioning

Earlier in this chapter we talked about using markers to highlight the correct place for the batter to place their feet to correctly execute the shot you are working on. These need to be flat for safety and durable so they do not fall apart as the player lands on them. Rubber is best so that it does not shift when the foot lands.

These mats are fantastic as a visual guide for the batter, as they can see after every ball whether they got their foot in the correct position. On surfaces that can be drawn on, chalk can be used instead of a mat.

Often as a coach you will want to mark the general direction the feet should be going rather than the exact spot to allow for some discretion from the player as to where their foot should be. With chalk this can be done with an arrow or with cones to show the direction of the footwork. The photo below is for a cover drive:

Short and narrow bat work

To place a higher level of difficulty on the batter we talked earlier about using short bats or narrow bats. If you are familiar with these, they will look something like this:

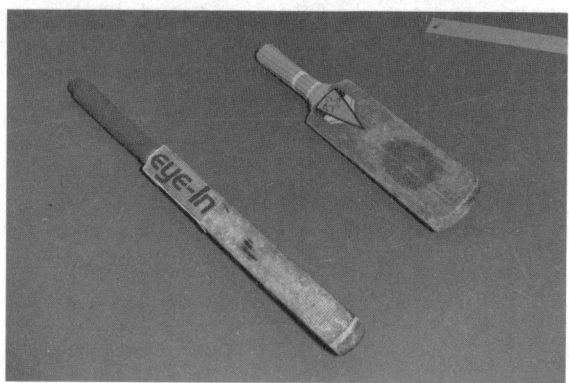

A short bat is similar to those that coaches use to hit catches but with a normal length handle. These are particularly useful for players to practise front-foot drives as it encourages the batter to exaggerate the front-foot knee-bend to get lower into the ball. This improves transference of weight into the ball and prevents the player from coming up as they drive, which is a common fault in many players. To add further difficulty, ask the player to use their top hand only as well.

A narrow bat is perfect for increasing the level of difficulty on a batter when executing any shot. They have less surface area to make contact with the ball and effectively only have the middle of the bat to make contact. Immediately this makes them watch the ball harder and for longer and to focus hard on exact technical execution to make contact with the ball. Cross-bat shots are naturally harder with this bat but all shots can be practised (and perfected) using a narrow bat. Because a narrow bat is naturally lighter than a normal bat it also drills into the player to wait longer for the ball as well. After a prolonged session with a narrow bat, the batter should find it a lot easier returning to a normal bat.

Bouncer and short-ball practice

One area that can often be overlooked is ensuring your players practise enough against bouncers. This is often due to safety and because the players themselves prefer to work on other things!

In the photo above the batter is in their normal stance and the coach has a walk-in before underarming the ball (soft or hard ball can be used) at the batter. The walk-in adds some realism for the batter and allows them to fit in trigger movements and find rhythm. Throwing from low also adds realism as it replicates more precisely where the ball would be coming from if delivered by a bowler.

To increase the level of difficulty the coach can throw faster or come closer. Further, they can throw some balls as a low full toss where the batter should be coming forward to play the ball. This then adds some decision-making and ensures the batter is not over premeditating where the ball will be delivered.

If you need to work on the batter's ability to evade bouncers, then with soft balls you can take their bat away so they have to evade (rather than play) the delivery. Some players find this easier to do chest-on to start with, as in the photos below, so they only have to move their head side to side to avoid the ball. This encourages them to keep their head facing the ball and not turn away.

From here, progress to side-on and encourage the batter to only move the amount required to evade the ball, while keeping their head forward, watching the ball as long as possible.

Coaches who have mastered the sidearm may be able to deliver consistent bouncers with it and can mix up length on occasion as well. Another option is for the coach to use a tennis racket and a tennis ball as shown below:

This allows the coach to hit at great pace, but also reduce the risk of injury to the player.

Bowling machines can also be used for bouncer practice and Bola produce a lighter machine ball that is less painful if a player misses it and the ball strikes the body.

Top-hand and bottom-hand practices

Throughout this chapter we have also talked about asking the batter to play their shots one-handed. This is a very useful tool if a player needs to emphasise either hand more in their shots. Usually, this is the top hand for drives and defence, bottom hand for cuts, sweeps and pulls, but it is always useful to get the player to play all shots with either hand before returning to two hands to highlight the importance of the correct grip for shot execution and the hands working together.

A good example of where this is a useful thing to do is if you have a player who squares up on contact when driving through the off side and the bat arc is towards midwicket rather than going where they want to hit the ball. Working both top- and bottom-hand grip only, it is easier for the player to focus on keeping the bat going through the line of the ball and highlight any grip adjustments needed.

To make it easier for the player they can take the bat up with both hands but only come down with one. Feeds can be used, and for higher-end players this can also be done using a machine.

Heavy ball work

A relatively new coaching tool designed specifically for developing power hitting is the heavy ball.

These are usually fed underarm and require the batter to keep a consistent path of the bat to make good connection with the ball. With continued use it develops strength in the muscles throughout the body that are used when hitting the ball hard. It also checks to see whether the batter has a strong grip of the bat. If not, the heavy ball means the wrists will collapse – reducing the effectiveness of the shot – or that the bat may slip from the batter's grasp on contact.

Any attacking shot where power rather than touch is required can be practised with these balls, and cones can be used as targets to hit through. As the ball does not travel a long distance once struck, it is also an effective tool to use in open practice with a limited number of balls.

With the introduction of a greater number of short-format limited-overs competitions, it is essential that the modern batter has some options for clearing the rope with some power hitting. Range hitting is an essential element of training nowadays, so the heavy ball is a common piece of training equipment. They are essential because they allow the batter to hit a ball and keep their technique, while hitting a greater load. A coach can also still assess technique, such as a strong base and efficient and powerful hip rotation.

Progression:
The batter hits one-handed if appropriate and safe.
　The batter proceeds to a heavier ball.

Front-foot shots using a batting tee

Equipment:
　Tennis balls
　Batting tees
Description:
Batting tees can be used for practising numerous shots, a few are shown here:

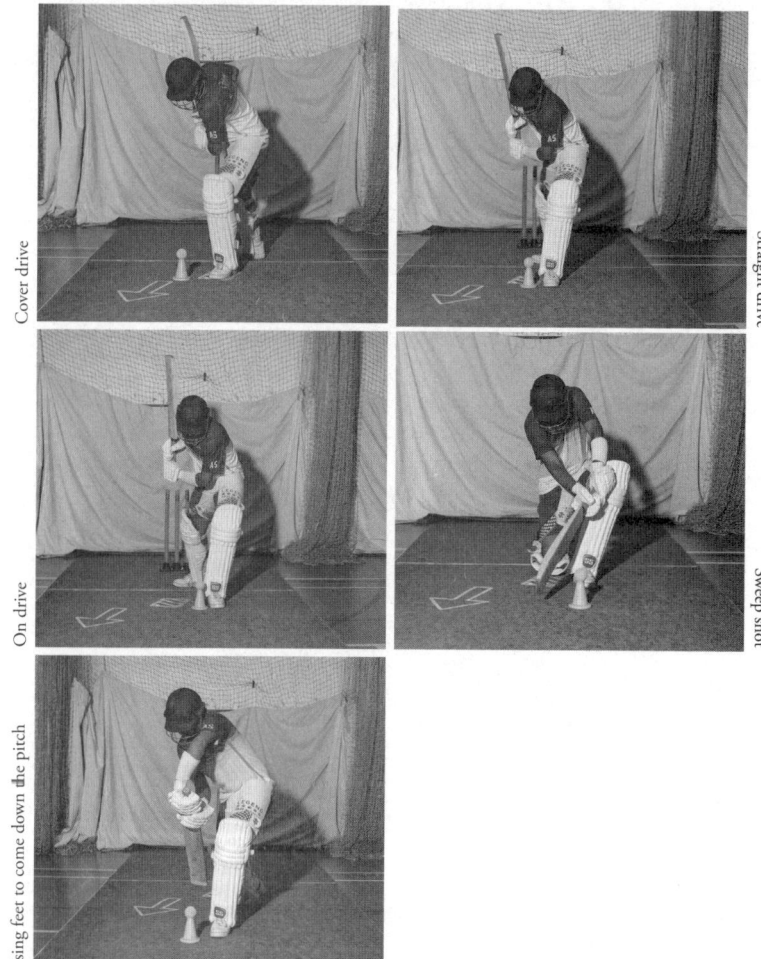

Progression:

Line up numerous batting tees/balls in a straight line, approximately 0.5m apart. The batter then works their way along the line, having to reposition each time to hit the next ball correctly.

This could be done repeating the same shot or a different shot each time.

Progress to other forms of ball feed.

Back-foot pull shot using a batting tee

Equipment:
Tennis ball
Batting tee
Plastic stump in base

Description:

Place a batting tee on top of the plastic stump. Stand the batter an appropriate distance away to execute the shot correctly.

Progression:

Progress to underarm full toss feed and bounce throw feed.

Front-foot shot – positioning of front foot

Equipment:
  Chalk
  Rubber discs
  Rubber mat
  Hoop
  Ball

Description:
To encourage the batter to create a suitable front-foot stride length and place their front foot towards the line of the ball, it is helpful to steer them to this position by using visual markers, which they either step past, on to, or out of.

Some examples are shown below:

After hitting the ball the batter should be encouraged to stay in a solid balanced position for two seconds. This can be reinforced by making it part of a game, where the batter scores a point if they succeed and the coach scores a point if they do not.

Progression:
Batter hits the ball through coned scoring area, etc.
　Use of thin bat, etc.

Back-foot shot – positioning of back foot

Equipment:
　Chalk
　Rubber discs
　Rubber mat
　Hoop
　Ball

Description:
To encourage the batter to create a suitable front-foot stride length and place their front foot towards the line of the ball, it is helpful to steer them to this position by using visual markers, which they either step past, on to, or out of.

　Some examples are shown below and overpage.

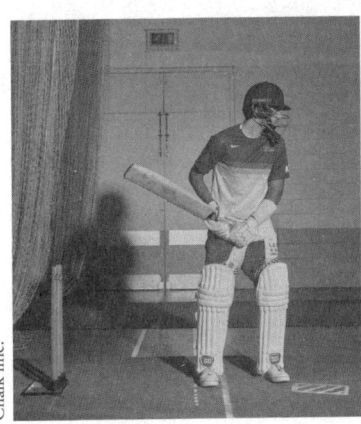

Chalk line.
Chalk line.

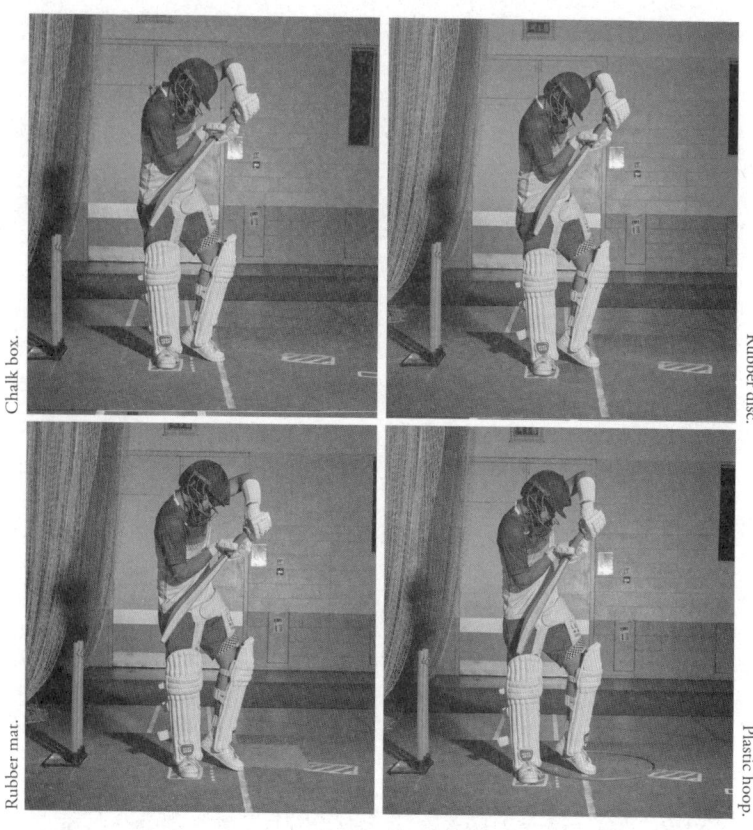

After hitting the ball the batter should be encouraged to stay in a solid balanced position for two seconds. This can be reinforced by making it part of a game, where the batter scores a point if they succeed and the coach scores a point if they do not.

Progression:
Batter hits the ball through coned scoring area, etc.
   Use of thin bat, etc.

Forward defence – soft hands game

Equipment:
Cones
Discs
Tennis ball

Description:

To encourage the batter to hit the ball with soft hands, the drill shown below is excellent. A semi-circle of cones/discs are placed on the floor in front of and around the batter, approximately 2m away from them. The ball is fed, and the batter must softly defend the ball without letting the first bounce of the ball land outside the marked semi-circle.

If the ball lands inside the semi-circle, the batter scores one point. If it lands outside, the coach scores one point.

Progression:

After hitting the ball, the batter should be encouraged to stay in a solid balanced position for two seconds. This can be reinforced by making it part of the game, where the batter scores a point if they succeed and the coach scores a point if they do not.

When the base is unstable, stumpings could be introduced, with points going to the batter or coach accordingly.

Live catching fielders (wearing helmet and box) could be introduced if a soft ball is used, and batters are instructed explicitly not to play attacking shots.

Batters could use thin bats.

Back-foot defence – soft hands game

Equipment:
Cones
Discs
Tennis ball

Description:
To encourage the batter to hit the ball with soft hands, the drill shown below is excellent. A semi-circle of cones/discs are placed on the floor in front of and around the batter, approximately 2m away from them. The ball is fed, and the batter must softly defend the ball without letting the first bounce of the ball land outside the marked semi-circle.

If the ball lands inside the semi-circle, the batter scores one point. If it lands outside, the coach scores one point.

Progression:
After hitting the ball, the batter should be encouraged to stay in a solid balanced position for two seconds. This can be reinforced by making it part of the game, where the batter scores a point if they succeed and the coach scores a point if they do not.

When the base is unstable, stumpings could be introduced, with points going to the batter or coach accordingly.

Live catching fielders (wearing helmet and box) could be introduced if a soft ball is used, and batters are instructed explicitly not to play attacking shots.

Batters could use thin bats.

Numbered tennis ball game

Equipment:
Numbered tennis balls

Description:
To enhance a batter's 'watching the ball' skill, the drill shown below is simple but very effective, and can be used when practising any shot, or part of a random shot selection session.

A clearly numbered tennis ball is fed to the batter, who immediately after hitting the ball calls out the number identified on it. This encourages the batter to watch the ball intensely and right on to the bat. The ball can be fed either by hand, tennis ball bowling machine or tennis racket.

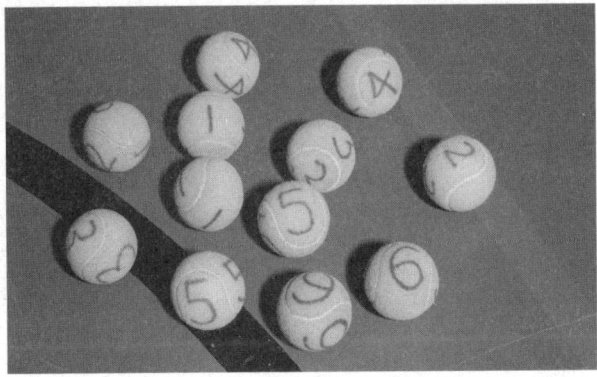

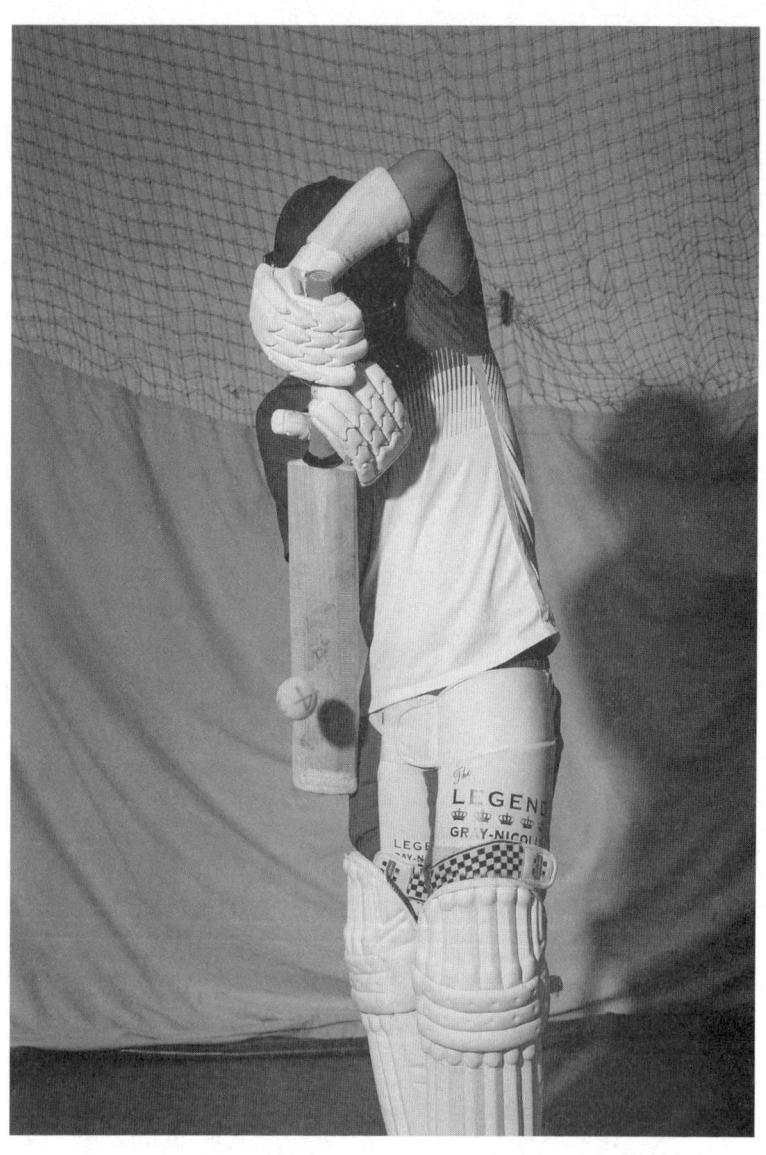

A scoring game can be introduced where the batter scores a point for correct number identification, but the coach scores a point if they do not.

Progression:
After hitting the ball, the batter should be encouraged to stay in a solid balanced position for two seconds. This can be reinforced by making it part of the game, where the batter scores a point if they succeed and the coach scores a point if they do not.

Batters could use thin bats.

Top-hand-only hits

Equipment:
Tennis balls
Plastic stumps

Description:
A common way to enhance a batter's top-hand strength is for them to hit balls or play shadow shots holding the bat in their top hand only. It is essential that the batter keeps the same grip as they would for a normal two-handed shot and does not change it due to the bat being harder to control in one hand. For example, the batter adopts a base associated with a cover drive and lifts the bat to the top of its backswing (a ball is not required). The downswing is commenced, continuing through to the full check drive follow-through. This can be done continuously without stopping for ten strokes. The batter's aim is for complete control of the bat throughout the shadow shot. To check on the line of swing, this can be done over a line in a sports hall, joints in patio slabs, etc. Additionally, the batter's downswing to follow-through could be aligned to pass between a set of plastic stumps, where the middle stump has been removed.

The batter can then drop feed a tennis ball to themselves, releasing it from their bottom hand, driving it with their top hand only.

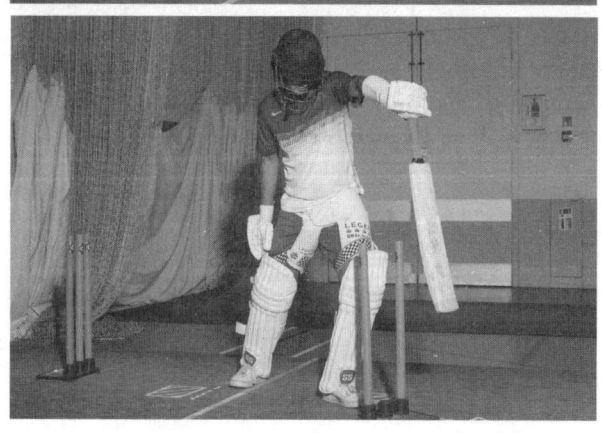

Progression:

The batter doubles the number of shadow hits.

The batter steps into the shadow hit from their stance position and repeats this when drop feeding the ball.

A coach bobble feeds a ball towards the batter, who steps into the drive and hits the ball.

The batter could use a thin bat, but that is much lighter, so the strengthening of the top hand shot is lost at the expense of watching and focusing on the ball more.

A scoring game can be introduced where the batter scores a point for hitting the ball through a targeted coned area, etc.

Use this drill for any shot, either front- or back-foot.

Bottom-hand-only hits

Equipment:
Tennis balls
Plastic stumps

Description:
A common way to enhance a batter's feel for the shape and grip of their bottom hand is to hit balls or play shadow shots holding the bat in their bottom hand only. It is essential that the batter keeps the same grip as they would for a normal two-handed shot and does not change it due to the bat being harder to control in one hand. For example, the batter adopts a base associated with a cover drive and lifts the bat to the top of its backswing (a ball is not required). The downswing is commenced, continuing through to the full check drive follow-through. This can be done continuously without stopping for ten strokes. The batter's aim is for complete control of the bat throughout the shadow shot. To check on the line of swing, this can be done over a line in a sports hall, joints in patio slabs, etc. Additionally, the batter's downswing to follow-through could be aligned to pass between a set of plastic stumps, where the middle stump has been removed.

The batter can then drop feed a tennis ball to themselves, releasing it from their top hand, driving it with their bottom hand only.

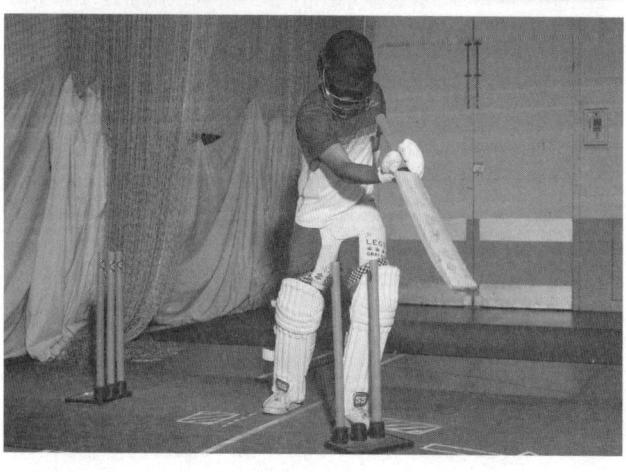

Progression:
The batter doubles the number of shadow hits.

The batter steps into the shadow hit from their stance position and repeats this when drop feeding the ball.

A coach bobble feeds a ball towards the batter, who steps into the drive and hits the ball.

The batter could use a thin bat, but that is much lighter, so the feel of the bottom-hand shot is lost at the expense of watching and focusing on the ball more.

A scoring game can be introduced where the batter scores a point for hitting the ball through a targeted coned area, etc.

Use this drill for any shot, either front- or back-foot.

Judging length drill (front foot)

Equipment:
Balls
Rubber discs

Description:
It is essential that a batter can read the length of any ball bowled at them and make the relevant foot movement suitable to position them for the appropriate shot. Rubber discs are laid out in a straight line across the pitch, at a distance from the batter that any ball landing past it means it is an over-pitched length (can be driven), and any ball landing just short of it means it is a good length (can be defended). The coach feeds the ball, randomly throwing it both short of and in front of the line. The batter attempts to play the ball correctly for the length of ball thrown, playing a combination of front-foot drives or front-foot defence.

Progression:

Introduce a game where the batter scores a point if they play the correct shot for the length bowled, and the coach scores a point if the batter does not. Points can be added for shots hit along the ground, or given to the coach if hit in the air.

This drill can be done with machine feeds or with sidearm feeds, and the rubber mats can be replaced by chalk lines. This stretches good players more as quicker decision-making is required due to the increased speed of delivery.

Judging length drill (random)

Equipment:
  Balls
  Rubber discs

Description:

We have discussed how critical it is for the batter to pick the length of any ball bowled at them and make the relevant foot movement suitable to position them for the appropriate shot. Rubber discs are laid out in a straight line across the pitch, at a distance from the batter that any ball just landing past the line means it is a front-foot shot, and any ball landing short of it means it is a back-foot shot. The coach feeds the ball, randomly throwing it both short of and in front of the line. The batter attempts to play the ball correctly for the length of ball thrown, playing a combination of front-foot and back-foot shots.

Progression:

Introduce a game where the batter scores a point if they play the correct shot for the length bowled, and the coach scores a point if the batter does not. Points can be added for shots hit along the ground, or given to the coach if hit in the air.

Machine or sidearm feeds to be utilised with chalk lines instead of rubber discs.

Judging line drill (random)

Equipment:

Plastic set of stumps base (no stumps required)

Description:

We have discussed how critical it is for the batter to pick the length of any ball bowled at them and make the relevant foot movement suitable to position them for the appropriate shot. This also applies to the line of the ball. A batter has to make a combined assessment of both length and line immediately the ball is bowled, and subsequently make the appropriate movements to ensure that both their feet and head are in the best position to execute the shot successfully. It is crucial that the batter knows exactly where their off stump is, both in their stance after any trigger they may have, and as they hit or leave the ball.

A set of stumps base is placed next to the normal set of stumps, positioned on the off side of the stumps. The normal set of stumps are numbered as follows: leg stump 1, middle stump 2, off stump 3. The base's stump location castings are numbered, continuing as 4, 5 and 6.

The ball is appropriately fed to the batter, who plays the ball normally, whether it is a front- or back-foot shot, defensively or attacking, along the ground or in the air. The coach asks the batter which stump number the ball was on when it was struck, observing that themselves, while also looking at the position of the front foot for a front-foot shot, and the back foot for a back-foot shot. If the batter has set a solid base, it should be easy to check whether their feet are in an appropriate position to play the shot safely.

The coach confirms to the batter whether their assessment of contact line was correct, and also where their foot was in relation to this. The coach and batter then have physical evidence of the correlation between the foot, head, hands and ball, and an assessment can be made. This can then be used to develop the batter's quality of line assessment and subsequent footwork, coupled with balance and regularity of hitting.

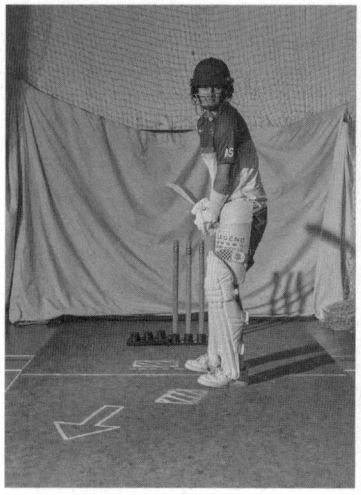

For most front-foot shots, a batter should look for a number differential of 1.5 to 2 between ball contact stump number and foot position number (measured at the toes). That is, for a ball hit from stump 5, front toes should be on stump number 3.0 to 3.5 approximately.

Progression:
Introduce a game where the batter scores two points if they judge the line of the ball and get their feet in the correct position. The coach picks up the remaining points if the batter does not score two. Points can be added for shots hit along the ground or given to the coach if hit in the air.

After hitting the ball, the batter should be encouraged to stay in a solid balanced position for two seconds. This can be reinforced by making it part of the game, where the batter scores a point if they succeed and the coach scores a point if they do not.

Batters could use thin bats.

360-degree gapping game (front and back foot)

Equipment:
Balls
8 coloured cones (4 different colours)

Description:
We have discussed how critical it is for the batter to pick the length and line of the ball bowled and respond with relevant foot movement suitable to position them for the appropriate shot. Another vital facet for the batter is the ability to hit the ball into gaps in the field, off both front and back foot, off side and leg side (360 degrees).

Four pairs of cones are set up, colours matching, approximately 3m apart, two pairs on the off side, two pairs on the leg side. They can be placed anywhere on either side of the wicket.

The coach feeds the ball so that the batter plays everything on the front foot. The ball is delivered accurately straight at middle stump. The batter is to try to work the ball into the gaps between the four pairs of cones. This can be done in a clockwise direction to start with. For instance, pairs of cones could be placed to either side of mid-on, point, square leg, and mid-off. The batter could have one attempt at each gap in turn or start on one and not move to the next until they have successfully hit through the gap. The coach could randomly call different colours to go through, etc. The combinations are almost endless.

The coach could then change line, either feeding the ball outside off stump or around leg stump. The batter must find a way of manipulating the ball into the gaps as before. This game is then adapted to suit back-foot shots only.

Progression:

Introduce more variations into the gapping sequence. A batter cannot go through a completed gap until all the others have been hit through for instance. If they do not get through a gap in three balls they go back to the start.

Record how many hits it takes to consecutively complete one circuit.

Rotate in an anti-clockwise direction.

Coach removes certain shots from the batter's repertoire.

Introduce random-length feeds, so the batter has to decide between front- and back-foot play.

Batter nominates the target gaps.

Introduce running between the wickets for realism.

Batters could use thin bats.

Moving down the wicket and hitting over the top

Equipment:

Tennis balls (for safety)

Description:

This is a great drill for increasing a batter's confidence in coming down the pitch to hit over the top.

Ideally it should take place in a roofed net, as this saves time in collecting the balls. However, hitting in a net without a roof can be rewarding for the batter, as they get to see how far they have hit the ball. The ball can be delivered in various forms, from drop feeds to full throw feeds, and bowling machines using machine balls can be used for more experienced and able players.

The coach should stand approximately 2m away from the batter when utilising a drop feed, the batter hitting the ball on its second bounce.

Progression:

Nominate hitting areas for the batter to hit to.

Alternate hitting areas.

Introduce a points-scoring game for good technique in getting to the ball and producing a stable base as the ball is struck.

After hitting the ball, the batter should be encouraged to stay in a solid balanced position for two seconds. This can be reinforced by making it part of the game, where the batter scores a point if they succeed, and the coach scores a point if they do not.

Points scored to the coach if the batter is stumped, etc.

A coned range-hitting boundary could be marked out to see how many sixes the batter hits in an over.

Batters could use thin bats.

Shots could be played top hand only.

Playing short, fast bowling

Equipment:
Tennis balls
Tennis racket

Description:

The coach stands at the bowler's end and serves the tennis ball with the tennis racket, serving short and fast at the batter. The speed should be appropriate for the batter on strike, but should be fast enough to test them. A range of shots could be played, including leaves, avoiding bouncers, etc.

Progression:

Introduce a points-scoring game for good technique in playing or avoiding the ball. The batter scores points if they play, leave or avoid the ball well; the coach scores points if they do not, they play and miss or get out in some way.

Coach could serve the ball as fast as they can or reduce the serving distance.

They could also serve the ball randomly on any length (yorker, full, short, etc.) so it is more realistic for the batter.

Use numbered balls, the batter trying to identify the number.

Batters could use thin bats.

Shots could be played top hand only.

Playing swing bowling

Equipment:

Rubber swing ball or similar

Description:

The coach stands at the bowler's end and throws the swing ball at the batter, ensuring it lands predominantly on a good length. The ball is to be thrown replicating both inswing and away swing. This is great practice for playing the swinging ball, with emphasis on playing the ball late and close to the body. A range of shots can be played, including leaves. A tennis ball half covered in tape makes a great replacement if you do not have a bespoke swing ball.

Progression:
Introduce a points-scoring game for good technique in playing the swing ball. The batter scores points if they play the ball late, keeping it on the floor; the coach scores points if they do not, they play and miss or get out in some way.

The coach could serve the ball as fast or as slow as they can or reduce the throwing distance.

Batters could use thin bats.

Shots could be played top hand only.

Playing the cut shot

Equipment:
1 cone

Description:
The batter stands in their stance and the coach places a cone approximately 4m in front of them, slightly to the leg side of the pitch centre line. The coach feeds the ball at pace, short and wide of the batter on a line suitable for the cut shot. Normal back and across footwork is assumed. The batter is instructed to sprint towards the cone the very instant they hit the ball, as if they are completing a run. They touch the cone with their bat and return to the crease. The shot is repeated many times, either thrown or with a bowling machine.

The purpose of this drill is to increase the power of the shot utilising the forward motion of the batter's body weight at the point of contact. This is simply achieved by asking the player to sprint for the single the instant they hit the ball. The player actually does this slightly before the ball arrives, hence engaging forward body momentum into the shot. While standing on their back foot, their front foot is off the ground but moving forwards down the pitch. The batter should feel better control and increased power.

Progression:
Introduce a points-scoring game for good technique and power when playing the shot. The batter scores points if they hit the ball below a height marker, the coach scores if they do not.

The coach could feed the ball faster or slower to encourage faster reactions, or waiting for the ball. Batters could use thin bats.

Running between the wickets

Equipment:
   8 cones (4 red, 4 white)

Description:
The pitch is set out in accordance with the relevant age-group dimensions. A pair of white cones is set across the full width of the popping crease at both ends. A pair of red cones is positioned approximately 1.5m away from the white ones, parallel to them down the pitch at both ends. The batter is instructed to run a two. They run, and at the completion of the first run, they stop at the red cone and stretch their bat over the white cone line. They then complete the second run, ensuring they start to slide their bat in from the red cones until it passes the white cones.

Progression:

The batter could be instructed to run more than a two.

If participating in pairs the non-striker should back up correctly before starting the running process. The stretching/turning distance could be lengthened to encourage a low turning technique.

A points-scoring game could be incorporated, players being penalised for not backing up, not stopping and turning correctly, or turning blind.

Coach could roll a ball out in a certain direction and call for a certain number of runs to be taken, while checking that the batter does not turn blind at the completion of each run.

The striking batter could hit a tennis ball fed by the coach for realism and run a certain number of runs.

Players should wear full kit when practising this drill for realism.

Reaction ball work

Equipment:
　1 reaction ball
　Hard flat surface

Description:
The coach stands a safe distance from the batter and underarm throws the reaction ball at the batter, ensuring it lands predominantly on a good length. Upon pitching, the ball is likely to deviate a lot, so this is good practice at playing the spinning ball, turning and bouncing off a worn pitch. The batter may play a range of shots, both attacking and defending, front foot or back foot, but successfully reacting to the unpredictability of the ball is their main objective.

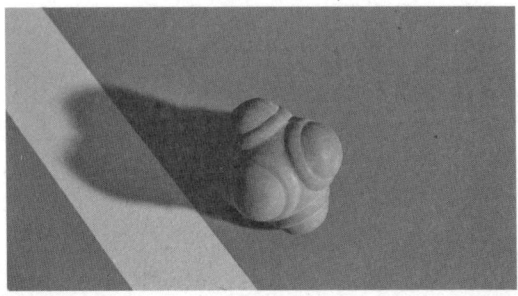

Progression:
Introduce a points-scoring game for good technique in playing the unpredictable reaction ball. The batter scores points if they play the ball late, keeping it on the floor, or successfully leave the ball, the coach scores points if they do not, they play and miss or get out in some way.

Coach could serve the ball as fast or as slow as they can or reduce the throwing distance.

Introduce cones as close-in catching fielders.

Batters could use thin bats.

Shots could be played top hand only.

Debris on the pitch

Equipment:
Tennis ball
Cricket ball
Rubber discs
Cones
Towel
Shower mat
Katchet board

Description:
Similarly to the reaction ball drill, this drill is about reactions. Debris items are randomly scattered on the pitch in front of the batter. The coach stands a safe distance from the batter and overarm throws the tennis ball, attempting to land it on an item of debris. Upon pitching the ball is likely to deviate if it hits an item but may not deviate if it misses them completely. Once again, this is good practice at playing the spinning ball, inconsistently turning and bouncing off a worn pitch. Successfully reacting to the unpredictability of the ball is the batter's main objective.

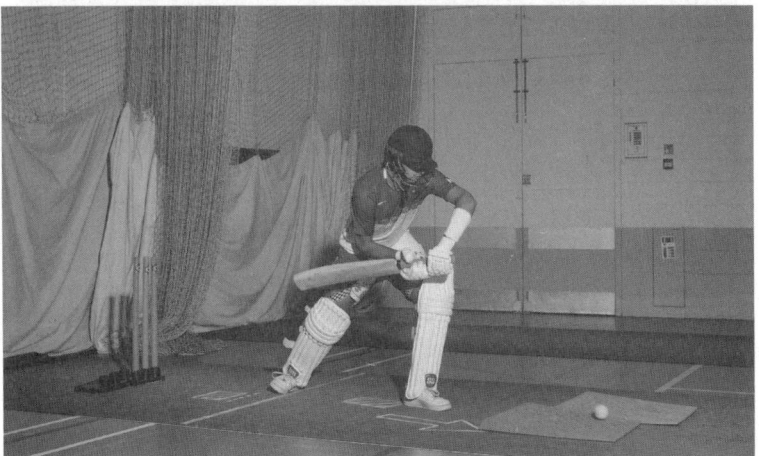

Progression:
Introduce a points-scoring game for good technique in playing the unpredictable wicket. The batter scores points if they play the ball late, keeping it on the floor, or successfully leave the ball; the coach scores points if they do not, they play and miss or get out in some way.

Introduce a points-scoring game for good technique in producing a stable base as the ball is struck. After hitting the ball, the batter should be encouraged to stay in a solid balanced position for two seconds.

Coach could serve the ball faster or slower or reduce the throwing distance.

Introduce cones as close-in catching fielders.

Use a real cricket ball.

Batters could use thin bats.

Shots could be played top hand only.

Core strength wobble cushion

Equipment:
1 wobble cushion

Description:
A wobble cushion is a great way of enhancing a batter's balance and core strength. They can be placed under a player's front or back foot, as they practise shots using drop, full toss, or bounce feeds. The player will have to try to stabilise themselves as much as possible if they want to succeed in hitting the ball cleanly, while attempting to hold their balance.

Progression:
Place a cushion under both feet. Step on to one as opposed to starting on it.

Bungee resistance restraint rope

Equipment:
Bungee resistance restraint rope

Description:
Another way of enhancing a batter's balance and core strength is to use a bungee resistant restraint rope, which is attached around the player's waist. They can be used for either shadowing shot practice or in feeding drills. It is an equally effective method for both front- and back-foot shots. For front-foot shots the coach stands behind the batter, applying the resistance as they move forward, and for back-foot shots the coach stands in front of the player, applying resistance as they move backwards. The player will have to try to stabilise themselves as much as possible if they want to succeed in hitting the ball cleanly, while attempting to hold their balance against the resistance force.

Progression:
The coach applies a higher level of resistance.

It is also used regularly for coming down the wicket exercises.

Place a cushion under both feet. Step on to one as opposed to starting on it.

Squash ball in bottom-hand batting glove

Equipment:
1 squash ball

Description:
We have previously highlighted the importance of not gripping the bat too tightly with the bottom hand. Many players strangle the handle by having the full area of the palm and all the fingers and the thumb tightly squeezing it. To encourage the batter to have a looser grip and make better shapes with the thumb and first two fingers of the bottom hand, a squash ball is inserted into the glove as shown below. This makes it impossible to get all the fingers, thumb and palm around the handle, as the ball physically stops that happening. Because it is made from soft rubber it squashes nicely in the hand. This then encourages the batter to get the feel of a softer bottom-hand grip, and experience all the benefits this brings.

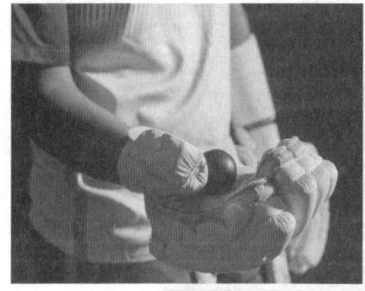

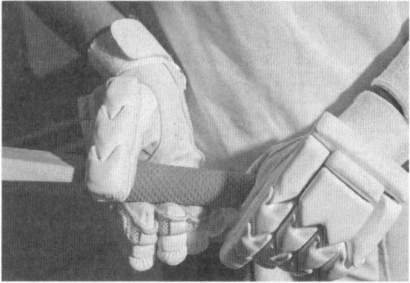

This can be worn in place for drills, nets and matches if required. The Australian batter and wicketkeeper Adam Gilchrist famously did this in the 2007 World Cup Final, scoring 149 off 104 balls!

Progression:
A form of competition is introduced.
   Batter uses a thin bat.

Alternative use of cricket mat surfaces

Equipment:
   Cricket mat
   Cones
   Discs
   Towels

Description:
A good method of manufacturing practice that is suitable to replicate batting on a spinning wicket is to turn the mat upside down, or for replicating batting on a poor, deteriorating pitch, debris can be scattered randomly underneath the normal-surfaced cricket mat. Both methods are described below.

By turning the mat upside down the rubber geometric base is now the batting surface, which will allow the ball to grip more on contact. Use this with a group of spinners or a Merlyn spin bowling machine, and you create a very challenging environment for the batter to play in.

By randomly scattering debris below the mat you create an uneven surface, containing bumps and hollows, which cause the ball to deviate both vertically and laterally, replicating batting on a poor or deteriorating pitch. Towels, discs, cones, etc. can be used depending on the degree of unpredictability you desire. Use this with a group of bowlers or a bowling machine and you create a very challenging environment for the batter to play in. It is important to determine how unpredictable the surface is before the batter starts playing, as this could be painful for the batter otherwise. A few practice deliveries are recommended. An alternative is to change the type of ball being used.

Progression:
A form of competition is introduced.
   Batter uses a thin bat.

Catapult fire

Equipment:
   Catapult
   Tennis balls

Description:
This is another alternative to feeding the ball quickly to a batter, replicating facing fast bowling. Different types of ball can be used, and the line and length of fire should be randomised for realism.

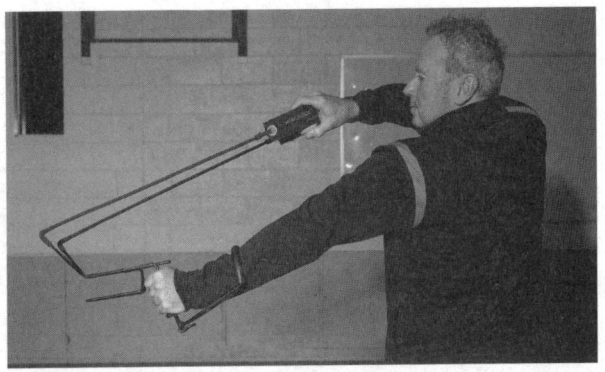

Progression:
A form of competition is introduced.
   Batter uses a thin bat.

Rapid-fire front-foot drive drop feed

Equipment:
   Tennis balls
   Numbered tennis balls

Description:
This is a very simple but effective drill for assessing a player learning the front-foot drive, or one who is having technical difficulties with it. The player is set up in the reverse chaining position of front-foot contact and drop feeds are fed to them quickly one after the other. The frequency, called 'rapid-fire', should be at the point the batter reaches back to the top of their backswing, after completing a front-foot check drive. The ball is hit on its first bounce. The batter's front foot should remain stationary throughout, the head, knee-bend, etc. all being in the correct position at point of contact with the ball.

Progression:

A form of competition is introduced where the batter has to complete hitting a certain number of balls without stopping.

Numbered tennis balls are introduced and the player has to call the correct number out as they hit the ball.

Batter hits top hand or bottom hand only.

Batter uses a thin bat.

Dropping tennis ball from chin

Equipment:
Tennis ball

Description:

A good way of highlighting to the batter the important relationship between their head and front-foot position is to use this simple procedure. After driving, the batter is asked to stand completely still. The coach then drops a tennis ball vertically from the batter's chin. Where the ball hits the ground is confirmation of the chin position in relation to the front-foot toes. This can be assessed by both batter and coach, and subsequent approval or remedial work can take place.

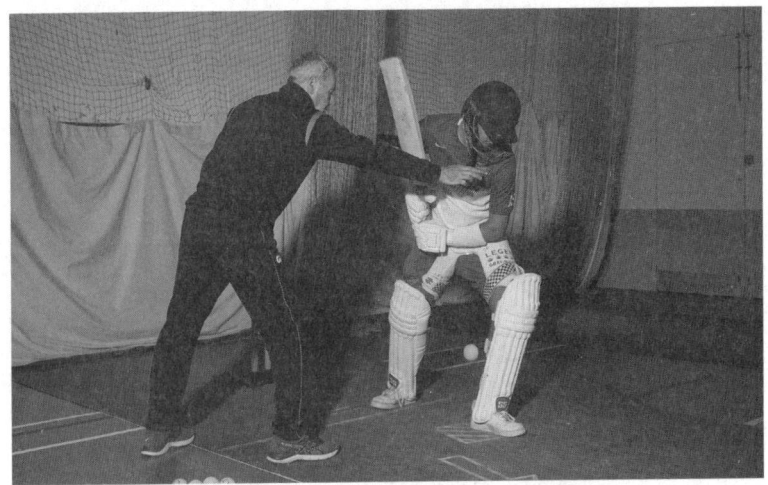

Ideally the chin should be positioned inside the line of the front foot, approximately level with it, if the ball is to be hit along the floor. If the batter intends to hit in the air, the chin should be positioned approximately midway between front and back foot.

Further confirmation of head and front-foot shot relationship

Equipment:
  1 cricket ball

Description:
Another visual method of showing the batter the important relationship between their head and front-foot position is to use this next simple procedure. The batter puts a ball on the floor and stands over it, with it in the middle of the body, their feet directly under their hips. This means that the ball is directly under their head – as in this photo:

Keeping the front foot completely still, they now move their back foot back far enough for them to be in a front-foot drive position, ensuring that the head is still over the ball. They should now have adopted a good knee-bend over their front foot. The distance laterally between front foot and head should be distance of approximately 4–5 inches. This is a great distance for playing the shot in a well-balanced way, ensuring the head is directly over the ball, while not being too close to be obstructed by the pads, and not too far from the ball that they are reaching for it, etc.

Progression:
This principle can be adopted for the cover drive, off drive, straight drive and on drive.

Visual confirmation of the benefits of moving across to the line of the ball

Equipment:
  1 cricket ball
  Plastic stumps and base

Description:
This form of visual confirmation can be very powerful for players who have a more visual learning style. A stump base is placed next to off stump, thus indicating stumps 1 to 6. The ball is placed on a driving length outside the off stump, on the line of stump 5. Stumps are laid on the floor either side of the ball, on a trajectory heading straight towards stump 5. This indicates the line of the ball. The batter is asked to play an imaginary drive, but to move their front foot to the line of leg stump. A stump is now placed on the floor heading in the direction of the foot/body weight. Immediately it can be seen that the ball line and the body weight line do not intersect. They in fact almost run parallel like a 'dual carriageway', one line going in one direction, the other in the opposite direction. Because the head, foot and shoulder are away from the ball, most of the power in the shot is made by the arms only, reaching out for the ball. There is also an increased chance of being dismissed because of this, as in this photo:

The batter is now asked to replay the imaginary drive, but this time positioning their front foot on a line just outside off stump (stump 3.5). The alignment stump is now repositioned to the front foot/body weight direction. It can now be seen that the body weight clearly intersects the line of the ball, producing a much stronger hitting position. In addition to the benefit just mentioned, the lead shoulder is now utilised in the shot, where it was not in the first open-chest example.

*Front-foot shot – two-hand catching drill
(encouraging good foot and head positioning)*

Equipment:
 1 tennis ball

Description:
A very good way of encouraging young players to get across to the line of the ball, simultaneously putting the head into a low position, is to start them off in their stance position without a bat in their hands. The coach stands approximately 3m away and underarm throws a full toss feed to the batter, outside off stump at knee height. The batter moves their front foot towards the ball, creates a base, and reaches down to catch the ball in both hands, trying to ensure their head is above the ball. Ask the batter to remain still after catching so that an assessment of technique can be made by player and coach.

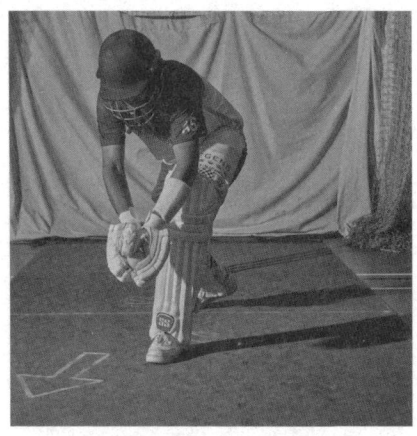

*Front-foot shot – one-hand reverse catching drill
(encouraging good top hand, elbow and shoulder positioning)*

Equipment:
1 tennis ball

Description:
A very good way of encouraging young players to get their top hand, shoulder and elbow across towards the line of the ball is to once again start them off in their stance position without a bat in their hands. The coach stands approximately 3m away and underarm throws a full toss feed to the batter, outside off stump just above knee height. The batter moves their front foot towards the ball, creates a base and reaches down to catch the ball in their top hand, which catches the ball in a reverse position. The batter tries to ensure their head is above the ball. Ask the batter to remain still after catching so that an assessment of top hand, shoulder and elbow alignment can be made by player and coach. This is a great way of getting the shoulder and elbow into the correct position.

*Bat dimensions used to visually enhance
a batter's front-foot drive and defensive shape*

Equipment:

The batter's own bat

Description:

While all batters are different technically, there are some shot shapes that are fundamentally the same for all batters. Irrespective of their size, there is obviously always a direct correlation between the height of the batter and their bat size. With this in mind, and while by no means a perfect science, there appears to be another correlation between their bat size and the shapes the batter makes when playing front-foot drives and front-foot defensive shots. These are shown below and should be used for guidance, as many players respond to a visual verification rather than just words.

The batter lays the bat on the floor and stands next to it in their normal stance, back-foot big toe aligned with the end of the handle. The batter's front foot strides forward and the toes of the front foot finish at the toe of the bat.

While in this front-foot base position, the batter should be looking for an angle of roughly 90 degrees or more from the heel of their front foot up to their knee.

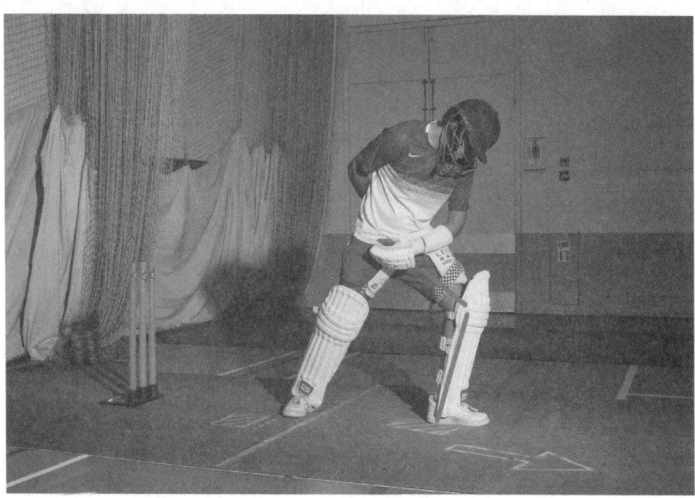

There should also be an angle of roughly 45 degrees from knee to groin.

Holding this shape, the final approximate measurement can be made by turning the bat upside down, holding it vertically, placing the handle splice at knee level. The bottom of the helmet grill of the batter should be near to the toe of the upturned bat. This gets the head forward and lower over the ball, which is certainly useful for all batters to try to achieve.

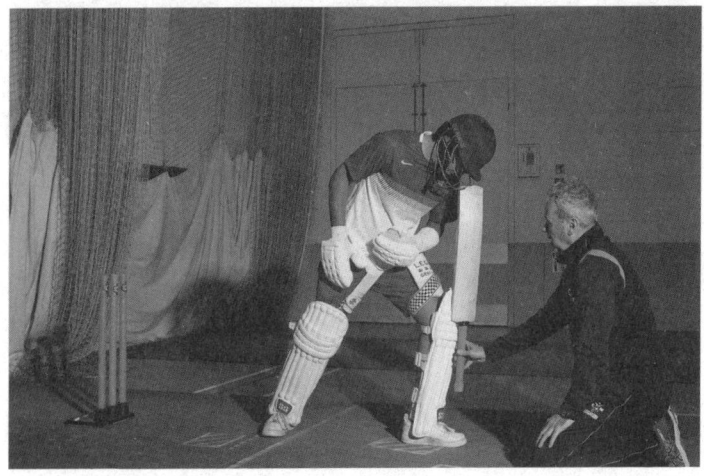

Using a sidearm feeder (dog-stick)

Equipment:
1 sidearm (dog-stick)

Description:
The sidearm or dog-stick is a very common form of delivering the ball to a batter. Most players now own one, as their training partners usually enjoy batting against it. The ball can be delivered replicating a fast bowler, gentle seamer, or spinner. Therefore, it is useful to have some knowledge on how to use one. Many instructional videos appear on the internet showing how to throw the ball, which the reader should consult. Do practise before using with a player – they take a while to master.

The ball positioning for four types of delivery, as seen by the batter, are shown opposite:

Away swing delivery (red side of ball replicates the shiny side)

Inswing delivery (red side of ball replicates the shiny side)

Off spin delivery

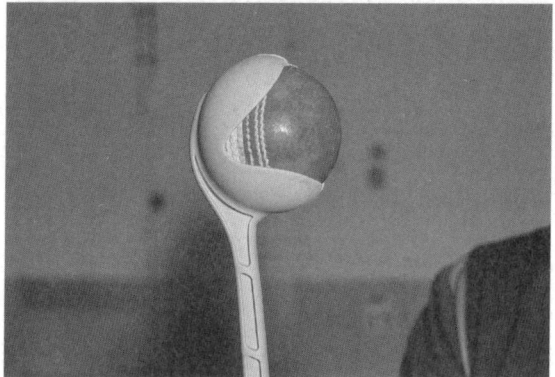

Leg spin delivery

*Encouraging the batter not to step
away from the ball down the leg side*

Equipment:
Cones
Discs
Mat
Plastic stumps
Soft gym mat barrier

Description:
Very often, particularly when younger players start making the transition from soft ball to hard ball cricket, some players can be scared of the ball, starting to back away from it, stepping down the leg side. To counter this, a simple drill is to place some form of physical barrier behind them, to reduce the instances of them retreating from the ball. The barrier should be safe and positioned at an appropriate distance behind them, and can be constructed of cones, discs, mats, plastic stumps or soft gym mat barrier.

It is advisable to have the barrier a fair distance from the batter at first, allowing them some immediate success at confronting this new fear, yet enough failures to have to work a little harder at keeping their stance position.

Progression:

Introduce a points-scoring game, coach scoring points if the batter backs away and steps on the barrier, batter scoring points if they do not.

Move the barrier progressively closer to the batter.

Off-side and leg-side games using two sets of stumps

Equipment:
   3 sets of plastic stumps

Description:

This game can be played with either an off-side bias or leg-side one. The pitch is set up as usual to the correct age-group length, with a set of stumps at both ends. One end will be the batting end, the other will be the bowling. For an off-side game, an additional set of stumps is added to the off side of the batting stumps. For a leg-side game, an additional set of stumps is added to the leg side of the batting stumps. The coach should be aware of any left-handed batters and bat them together. These arrangements are shown below:

The bowlers can bowl at both sets of stumps at the batter's end, with all normal methods of dismissal in play. However, the bowler can take a 'bowled' wicket if any of the six stumps are hit. However, lbw can only be given if in front of the normal set of stumps. This game encourages the bowler to bowl off side for an off-side game, and leg side for a leg-side game. The game also makes the batters play at everything bowled at them, thus improving their play both sides of the wicket accordingly. The batters only score runs if they hit to the appropriate side.

Keeping the ball down

Equipment:
 Plastic stumps
 Coloured twine

Description:
A very good way of encouraging batters to keep the ball down is to thread plastic stumps into the netting and instruct them to hit everything along the ground or below the line. Plastic stumps are great because they can be threaded in fairly quickly and can be easily seen. Coloured twine is also a great method.

Progression:
Introduce a points-scoring game, the coach scoring points if the batter hits the ball above the line, the batter scoring points if they hit it below the line.

Lower the line for increased difficulty.

The batter uses a thin bat.

This can be done as a drill or part of a live net session, etc.

Tactical development

The majority of the practices and drills above focus on the technical development of various shots (although some overlap to the tactical as well), but it is very important – especially as the season draws closer – to focus on a player's tactical awareness development as well. This can be done on a one-to-one player/coach basis with throw-downs, sidearm or machine work and it can also be done by setting scenarios and challenges in net practices with live bowling.

Technical and tactical scoring games principles

Equipment:
Whiteboard or marking pad

Description:
Technical and tactical practice games form an essential part of a player's development, and there are many, many types that can be employed. Numerous development areas can be worked on, with scoring systems, etc. engineered to enhance the player's progress. These can range from gapping games, specific match scenarios, batter vs coach scoring games, indoor matches, combat games between players, out when you are out games, etc. The options are endless. It is essential that the players have full clarification of the rules, so in addition to verbal instructions it is useful to have the rules in written form too. This adds structure and more formality to the session. A set of rules for a combat game is shown opposite and overleaf:

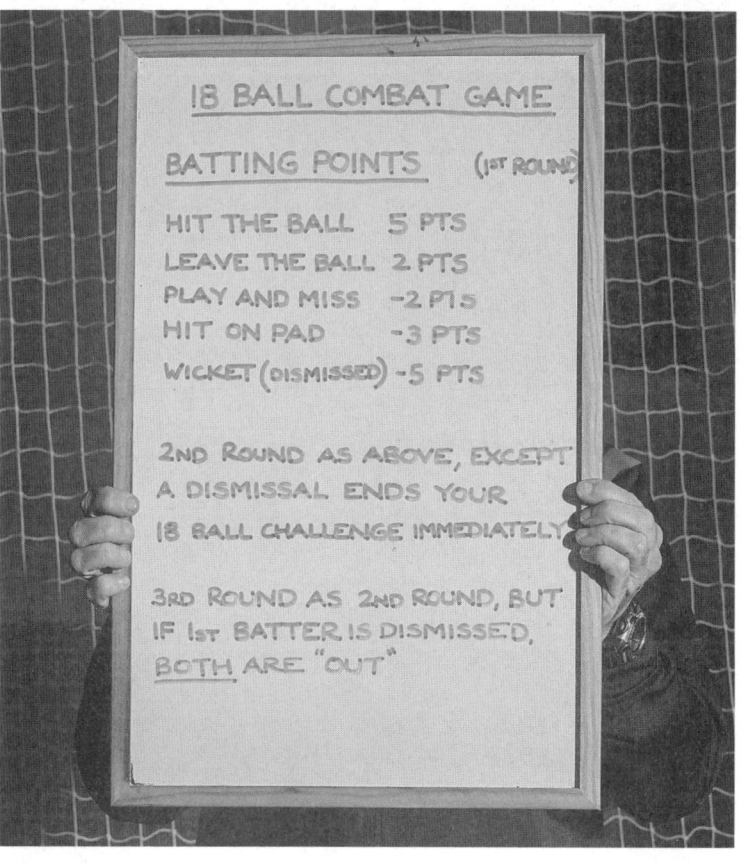

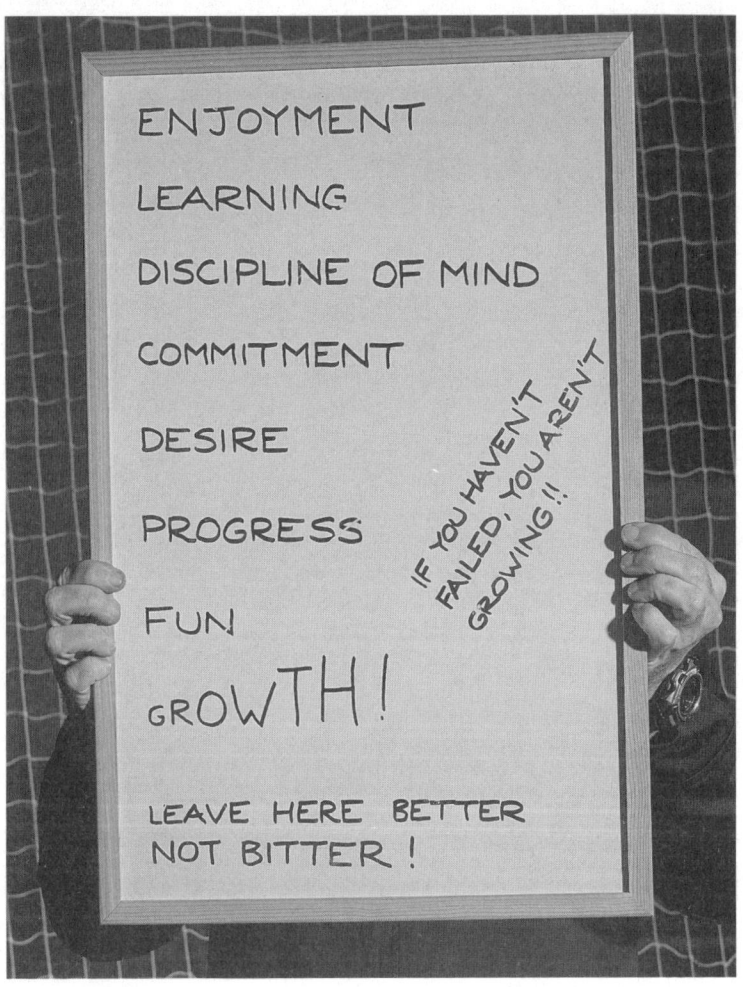

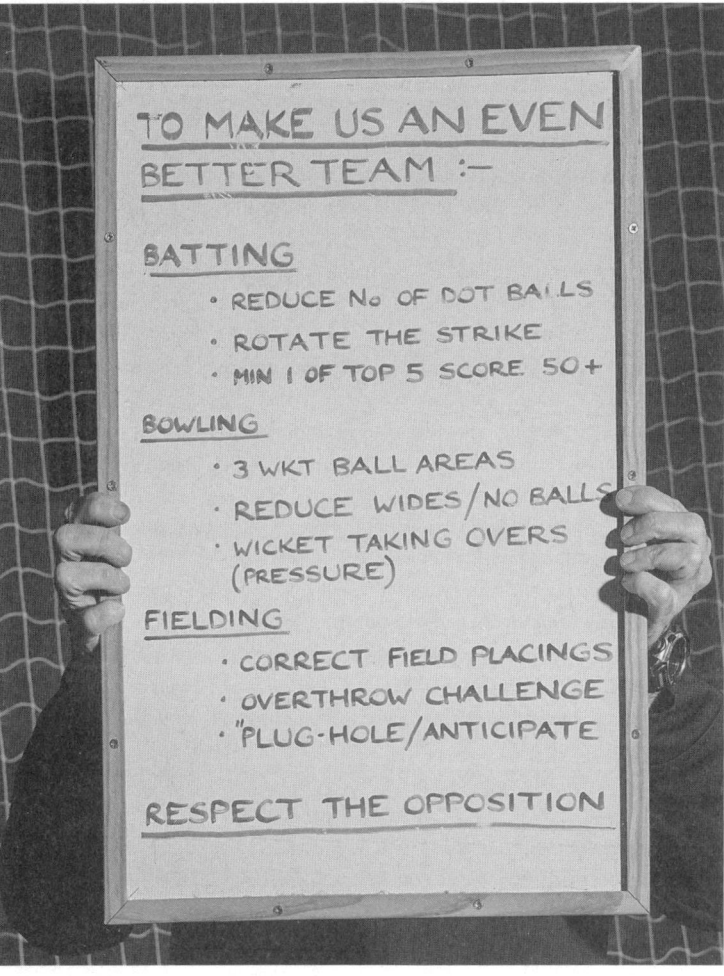

Scenario nets and bowling machine work

Equipment:
- 9 cones to mark fielding positions
- Whiteboard or paper to draw fields on
- Enough cricket balls for the bowlers

Description:
Ask the batter what scenario they would like for their session. Encourage them to choose something that is relative to where they usually bat in the team. For example use overs 10–30 for a middle-order player in a 40-over limited-overs game match.

With the bowlers set a field for each bowler type relative to the scenario and relay this to the batter. Draw the field on a whiteboard pad to show the batter and, if possible, mark the field placings with cones. After each ball, runs are awarded or not as the case may be by the coach and they will also decide on whether a batter is out caught or by other dismissals. Bowlers need to appeal for a decision to be given. This adds realism and you can discuss the importance of not appealing excessively and how to get on an umpire's good side.

If a batter is adjudged to be out at any stage, then runs are deducted from their total. If the emphasis of the practice is more on crease occupation, then have a relatively high number of runs deducted for each dismissal. If the emphasis is more on risk taking and faster run scoring, then have a lower number.

If throwing, using a sidearm or a bowling machine, it is still possible to set scenario sessions as you can make adjustments of pace, swing and line with each type of feed. A bowling machine has a bar on it where you can adjust the line without touching the settings and making it obvious to the batter.

Note for coaches

Encourage the virtue of honesty with scenario sessions. Did that ball hit the gap for runs? Did a catch go to the fielder or was it in the gap? The value of the practice diminishes if the player consistently argues with you every ball. You need to remind them that the umpire's decision is final on whether a ball is runs or out (in this case the umpire is you!) and they are therefore learning to have respect for the umpire as well.

Progression:

Pick scenarios that will take the batters out of their comfort zone, such as an opening batter to practise batting at the end of an innings.

Let the bowlers pick the scenario.

Use batters in pairs so they must run at match intensity to be awarded runs.

If the session is on a machine do six balls of one bowling type and then shift to six balls of a different pace and/or swing to mimic facing a different bowler each end (remember to adjust the field placings accordingly).

From there you can introduce further bowling types and even shift the machine to the other side of the wicket to mimic left-arm seamers/spinner.

Add zones that are worth double runs if there is an area of the ground you particularly want to emphasise that the batters look to score in.

Combat/competition nets

A very effective way to get the competitive juices flowing (and ramp up the realism of your practice) is to set up net sessions or one vs one or two vs two practices where the players are pitted against each other. If the players you are working with do not bowl as well as bat, then they can compete against each other with you as the feeder – throwing, sidearm or machine.

If you have a squad for your session, a really effective net practice is to split the group in half and nominate a captain for each team. With your knowledge of the players try to make the two groups as close in ability as possible to ensure a close contest. The captains choose the batting order for their team and each batter bats for an allotted period of time in the opposition's net.

The opposition must set a field for each bowling type (aided by the coach of that lane) and let the batters know this. Cones can be used to mark field placings. As with the scenario net, runs are awarded and dismissal judgements are made by the coach. If a batter is adjudged to be out at any stage, then runs are deducted from their total. If the emphasis of the practice is more on crease occupation, then have a relatively high number of runs that are deducted for each dismissal. If the emphasis is more on risk taking and faster run scoring, then have a lower number. The team with the most runs after all batters have batted wins.

If the coach has picked the teams fairly, then hopefully it will be close going into the last pair of batters. At this stage you could say that they receive exactly the same number of balls each. You could of course set a scenario where a batter is out if dismissed and the winning team is simply the team with the most wickets after an allotted time. If the scores are level, have a bowl-out! The session's value is even more enhanced if you have enough players for the batters to bat in pairs in the opposition net and they have to run between the wickets at match intensity to be awarded runs.

Rewards for winning are a good incentive for the players, as are forfeits for the losing team. An effective forfeit is simply making the losing team pack away at the end and the winning team can head back to the changing room.

Where it is one vs one or two vs two, the players can bowl against each other for an allotted time and runs/dismissals are decided by them, with the winner the one with the most runs/fewest dismissals as decided by the contest parameters the coach has set up. If batting against a feed or machine then it is important both batters receive the same number of deliveries to make the contest fair.

Note for coaches

Do remember to review with each batter at the end of their net. A really good question to ask is: if you were to play that scenario again, would you have done anything differently? Encourage honest reflection and, hopefully, they will come up with some good answers themselves. If it has not gone well it may be prudent to wait until the end of the session to ask this question, once emotions have died down.

Combat game – hit, leave, miss, wicket

Another form of combat game is the hit, leave, miss, wicket game. Once again, batters are competing against each other, whether it is individually, pairs or teams. This can be done using opposition bowlers or either seam or spin bowling machines, performed ideally in a net environment. It may be necessary for the machine to be randomly adjusted so that the batter is challenged on every delivery, unless there is a natural variation in the bowling machine deliveries.

Each batter faces an agreed number of balls, for instance 18, and their performance is judged on the results from the following scoring system, highest score (team or individual) wins:

Hit the ball: 5 points
Leave the ball :2 points
Play and miss: -2 points
Hit on the pad: -3 points
Wicket (dismissed): -5 points

Introduce jeopardy by adding the rule that if a batter is out they immediately stop their 18-ball challenge, even if it is their first attempt.

This game also highlights any technical difficulties a batter may have against a particular bowler bowling at a certain speed, a method of swing, type of spin, line and length of delivery, over or around the wicket, left arm/right arm, new ball/old ball, etc.

Out when out nets (or practices)

There is no better way to mimic match play than having an 'out when you are out' net to ensure a batter is properly focused and that they concentrate fully on each ball. Just like a match they cannot afford to switch off and make a mistake, thus working the mental skills required for batting as well as the tactical.

Although this practice is definitely more suited to practising the skills required for crease occupation in longer format cricket, any type of scenario can still be applied – after all, if you need ten an over in a match you are still out if you get out. For better players this is a really good way for them to identify a scoring rate they can achieve without taking very high risks every ball. It will help identify which shots are their 'go to' shots for boundaries and the importance of hitting the gaps and running well.

For younger and lower ability players, a grace period can be offered at the start, such as five minutes of batting allowed before the 'out when you are out' kicks in. Further incentives can be awarded if the batter achieves a certain time without being dismissed. This could be in the form of a can of Coke or that the player then gets five minutes of T20 batting or a scenario of their choice once they have achieved their allotted time.

> **Note for coaches**
> If you have a good batter who simply gives their wicket away too often, then apply the 'out when you are out' rule to as many practices as you can with the player. If they 'nick' off the first ball during a machine, then call the session to an end and ask them to come back next time with a greater focus.

Escalating target net or practice

On a machine, sidearm or in a net, this is a very good drill to get your batters thinking about the tactical changes they need to make as the run rate increases.

Description:
Set the batter(s) a runs per over target. Start low. The coach or bowlers set the field and the batters have to try to score that allotted number of runs off six balls. If successful, then the rate goes up by one. Keep going until there is a failure and remember to change the field as appropriate. Once there is a failure, discuss with the batter(s) what they could do differently next time round. Discuss this through with them and then set the same runs per over target as the one they have just failed and then keep increasing it for an allotted number of overs/deliveries.

> **Note for coaches**
> Once the rate hits six an over then the players will need to start looking for a boundary an over. Young players can often think they can achieve six an over with singles but there is always likely to be a dot ball or two within an over. Encourage them to look for this boundary at the start of the over to take the pressure off themselves and apply it to the bowler.

Progression:
Make a competition between the batters to see who can get up to the highest achieved runs per over before a dismissal or a certain number of overs.

Use a thin bat.

> **Note for coaches**
> Scenario sessions, combat sessions and escalating target sessions can all be done in the middle with live fielders and bowlers.

Leaving the ball game

This game ideally involves two teams competing against each other in a net, both taking their turn to bat and bowl. This can also be undertaken with two teams of batters playing against a bowling machine, either seam or spin. It may be necessary for the machine to be randomly adjusted unless there is a natural variation in the bowling machine deliveries, so that the batter does not leave every ball safely. The principle of the game is to leave as many balls as possible.

If it is carried out against bowlers, the batters score points for every ball they successfully leave. Bowlers score points if they make the batter play the ball, mainly by getting the ball to pitch on a line and length appropriate for hitting the stumps, getting an lbw, or a catch behind the wicket (three wicket ball). Bowlers also get points for taking wickets, or alternatively batters lose points for getting out. Both batters and bowlers benefit from this game.

This is a good game for encouraging batters to leave the ball where safe to do so, therefore a good form of practising a discipline that can often be overlooked. This is such an important element of building an innings, particularly if opening the batting when the ball is new, or for a situation where a batter may be batting out for a draw.

Batting games

Detailed below are some games that introduce young players to the batting skills involved in cricket. They are a great introduction to the game of cricket, particularly to players having never played before, and include many of the skills needed specifically for batters. They are great fun too.

- Diamond Cricket (twinkl.co.uk)
- Lords Game (sportplan.net)

- Non-Stop Cricket (twinkl.co.uk)
- Cricket Rounders (sportplan.net)

Hand-eye-foot coordination

Seeing the ball early is such an important part of batting and run scoring and the better players can improve their hand-eye-foot coordination to the greater variety of strokes they will be able to play. All the drills below will improve your hand-eye-foot coordination.

Ladder work

Equipment:
 2–3m agility ladder

Description:
Place the ladder as shown in the photo with the batter lined up at the end. The first time through, the batter traverses face-on, placing both feet at pace in the gaps between the rungs of the ladder. Once completed, they jog back to the start of the ladder. Second time through, they do this side-on and then the third time through side-on again, facing the opposite direction. Fourth and fifth times they can do one foot in, one foot out on one side and then work in the opposite direction.

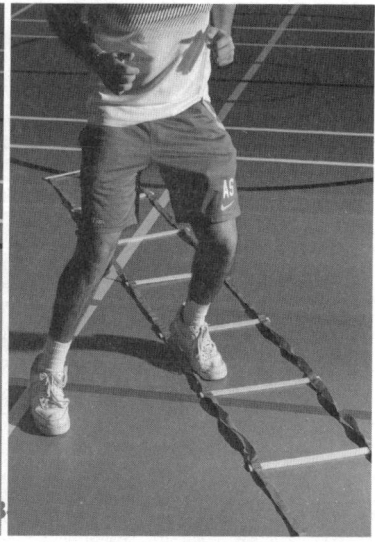

Progression:
Increase the pace and difficulty of the footwork.

Perform movements backwards.

Introduce movements that replicate footwork for front- and back-foot shots.

Fast feet cone work

Equipment:
8 cones

Description:
Place eight cones in a straight line touching each other. Starting at the left cone 1, place the left foot gently on the cone, with the right foot behind on the floor. Jump to the right, swapping feet around so that the right foot is now gently on cone 2, left foot behind. Repeat, gently putting the left foot on cone 3, right foot behind. Repeat to the end of cones. The aim is to traverse the full length of the cones as quickly and as lightly as possible. Go back to cone 1 and repeat.

Progression:
Complete one length of eight cones, then jump and spin around in mid-air to traverse down the other side of the cones. Continue repeating.

Reposition the cones into a random, scattered arrangement and repeat the jump and swapping feet manoeuvre, traversing in forwards, backwards and sideways directions.

Skipping rope footwork

Equipment:
Skipping rope

Description:
A skipping rope is another way of enhancing a batter's footwork and agility. These are commonly used in all sports that require quick footwork. How often do you see boxers training with a skipping rope?

Progression:
Research more complicated skipping jumps. Many can be found on the internet.

Balloons

Equipment:
  4 balloons

Description:
The batter adopts a set position and has to keep one balloon up in the air by tapping it up using either hand. The coach adds a second balloon, and the batter now has to control two balloons using either hand. The coach then adds a third and fourth balloon.

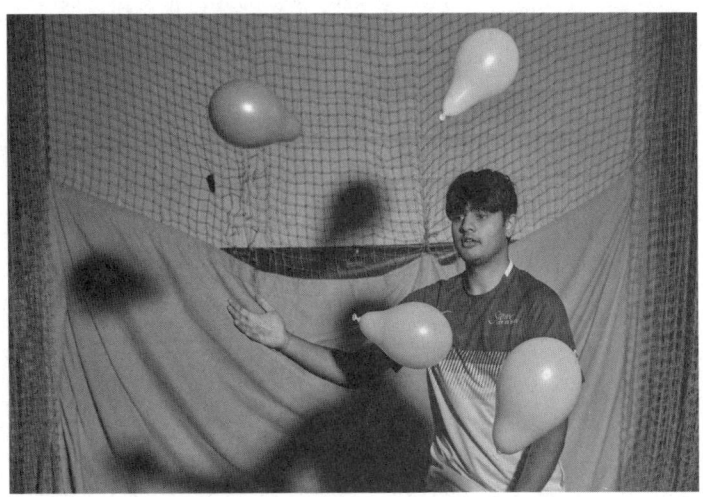

Progression:
Coach records time for being able to control two, three or four balloons.
   Add more balloons.
   Attempt the drill using one hand only.

Hoops and hurdles

Equipment:
   Hoops and hurdles

Description:
The coach lays out a group of hoops on the ground. The batter randomly jumps into one, landing on both feet, keeping their balance, staying inside the cone. Repeat into the next hoop, then continue to repeat.

   The coach lays out a symmetrical group of low hurdles. The batter jumps over one hurdle, and immediately jumps over another, landing on two feet. Continue to repeat, ensuring good balance.

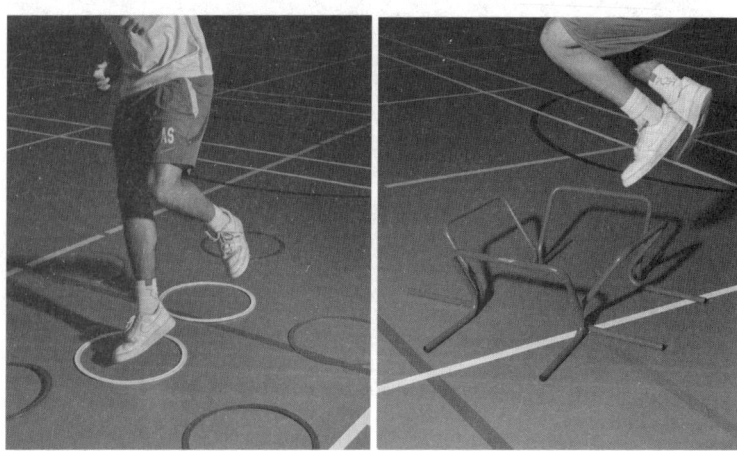

Progression:
Hoop drill – batter lands on two feet and then adopts a one-legged Superman position, ensuring they do not overbalance and fall out of the hoop. Batter then lands on one leg and adopts a one-legged Superman position. Coach increases the distance between hoops.

Hurdles drill – batter lands on one foot only. Batter performs all dynamics jumping off one foot only, alternating regularly.

Playing cards

Equipment:
Pack of playing cards

Description:
The batter adopts a set position, approximately 2m from the coach, who holds a single playing card and throws it vertically up into the air. The batter attempts to catch it before it hits the ground. The batter could also do this drill on their own by throwing the cards themself.

Progression:

Coach puts two cards into their hand, one card black and one red. They call a colour for the player to catch. The coach throws them together and the batter has to identify the correct card and catch it before it hits the floor.

Then progress to using two cards, both the same colour, but different numbers.

Progress to three cards, two with numbers on, the third being a royal. Call the royal, etc.

Same colour, different suits, etc.

Boxing gloves

Equipment:

Boxing gloves and boxing pads

Description:

The batter wears boxing gloves and the coach wears boxing pads. The batter punches the coach's pads in a planned routine.

Progression:
The coach constantly moves the pads around and keeps amending the hitting sequence previously agreed with the player.

Extend duration of drill to increase stamina.

Bat keep 'em ups

Equipment:
 1 soft or hard ball
 1 bat

Description:
Initially, using the flat bat face only see how many times you can bounce the ball in the middle of the bat in a minute.

Progression:
Move from flat bat face to edge of the bat, to back of the bat, to other edge, back to flat bat face. How many taps until you fail?

Add hitting with toe of the bat and top of the handle.

Ball drop

Equipment:
Two of the following: tennis balls, plastic stumps, squash balls, cricket bats

Description:
The coach stands with a tennis ball in each hand and fully extends their arms to each side, as high as possible. The batter is approximately 0.5m away, facing the coach, holding a plastic stump in each hand, fully extended similar to the coach. The coach then drops one of the balls, and the batter attempts to touch the ball with the plastic stump nearest to it. The coach should just let the ball drop, not use a slight throwing action, as this gives the catcher a visual clue!

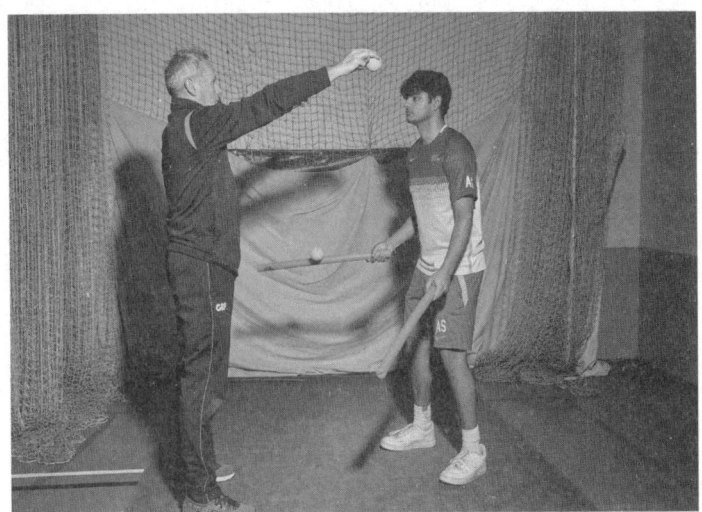

Progression:

Lower the arms of the coach feeding.

The batter has their hands close together in front of them as the ball is released, then quickly tries to hit the ball with same side stump.

Reduce ball size to squash balls.

Increase plastic stumps up to real bats for strength work.

Watching birds and insects

Description:
A very good way of training your eyes is to watch birds or insects in flight, particularly during the summer months. Swallows, swifts and house martins always fly very quickly in random directions, so pick one and keep your eyes fully focused on it, no matter how far away or close it is to you. Do the same for insects and butterflies. There are also many eye reaction-time games to be found on the internet that will enhance your vision and reactions.

One-eyed catching

Equipment:
1 soft ball

Description:
Ask two batters to stand a metre apart in a catching position. Ask them to cover one eye with one hand. They then throw and catch using one hand for ten repetitions. Repeat the throw, changing the covered eye and throwing hand. Repeat three times.

Progression:
Increase the distance between the players.

Time how many they can complete in a minute.

Back to zero – set the players a target to reach. If they drop one, they go back to zero until they complete the set number of repetitions.

Introduce a bat for one player, who has to keep one eye closed throughout playing the shot.

Multi-ball catching

Equipment:
2–5 soft balls

Description:
Ask your batters to stand a metre apart. One will have both balls. A ball at a time is thrown from the right hand of one player to the left hand of the other player, who then does the same thing. Keep them going for a minute. If successful with two balls, move to three and keep adding to stretch them.

Progression:

Increase the distance between the players.

Competition – how many can they complete in a minute?

Back to zero – set the players a target to reach. If they drop one, they go back to zero until they complete the set number of repetitions.

Use a variety of different balls (shapes and sizes).

Eye-focus string

Equipment:

5 metres of string with markers set half a metre apart

Description:

The batters have to stand facing each other holding the string at either end, pulled tight at eye level. The batters focus their eyes on each marker one at a time, working along the string and back again. They are not allowed to move on to the next marker until properly in focus. Repeat three times.

Progression:

Give each marker a number. The batters take it in turns to call a number and the other batter has to focus on that marker. Repeat ten times.

Do with one eye closed and alternate eyes used.

Reaction ball work

Equipment:

1 reaction ball

Description:

Have the players standing two metres apart – one with a bat and the other throwing the ball underarm into the middle space between them. The reaction ball will deviate in direction. The batter has to react to the bounce to hit the ball (defensive push only).

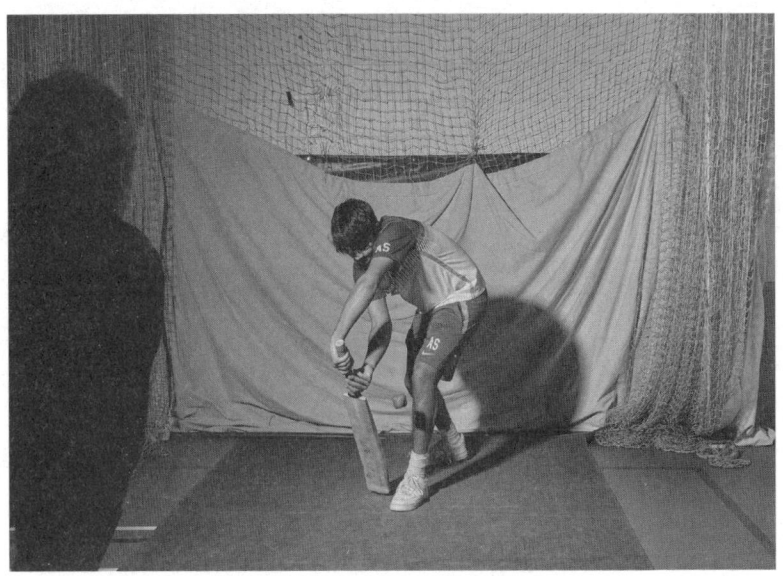

Progression:

Throw the ball closer to each other.

Overarm throws to increase the pace of the throw.

Set a target for the ball to be hit through.

Turn and hit

Equipment:
1 soft ball
2 cones

Description:
Set up two cones and ask your batter to stand in the ready position facing away from you. On your call they turn quickly into a ready position facing you as you throw the ball at them. The batter has to react and try to hit the ball. Repeat ten times.

Progression:
Reduce the distance between the coach and batter.
Vary the pace and direction of the feed.
Add targets for the batter to hit through.

Two coloured balls decision-making drill

Equipment:
Two different coloured tennis balls

Description:
The coach stands 6m away from the batter, holding two different coloured tennis balls in one hand. The coach prompts the batter by calling out the coloured ball they would like them to hit. They are simultaneously thrown (underarm or overarm) towards the batter at a pace, line and length appropriate for the shot being practised. The batter attempts to play the coloured ball selected, while ignoring the other ball totally. This drill can be used safely for almost all shots, and is a great drill for reactions, decision-making, movement, balance and technique.

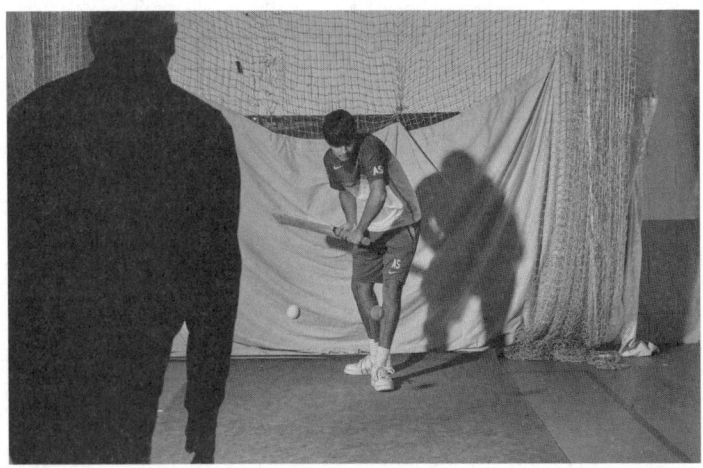

Progression:

Introduce a points-scoring game.

Add a third coloured ball.

Batter uses a thin bat.

Coach puts a single ball in each hand, hiding them behind their back. They then nominate a colour and simultaneously throw both balls underarm towards the batter, who hits the nominated ball.

Further progression can take the form of 'not' hitting the nominated colour, but the other one.

Batter starts with their back to the coach, turning around as the coach calls the colour.

Add targets to hit through.

Hidden wall rebound batting

Equipment:
Tennis ball
Set of plastic stumps
Reaction ball
Power ball
Thin bat

Description:
The batter is set up in their stance approximately 4m back from a wall, in front of a set of plastic stumps. The player is looking at the wall as though that is where the ball will be bowled from. The coach is a further 1m behind the stumps, set up slightly to the batter's off side. The coach throws the ball at various speeds, on to the rebound wall, ensuring that the ball bounces before it reaches the batter, who then plays the appropriate shot. Repeat numerous times. The batter could play this game on their own, throwing the ball and quickly getting into position to play a shot of their choice.

Progression:
Coach throws the ball at different positions on the wall, ensuring that the batter has to play different lines and lengths.

Coach can reposition themselves down the leg side of the batter to change the angle of delivery.

A form of competition can be introduced. The batter scores points for well executed shots, good balance and stable bases, and the coach scores points for wickets, play and misses, unstable bases, etc.

Match scenarios can be introduced and assessed accordingly.

Coach could set an imaginary field.

Introduce numbered tennis balls.

Reaction ball or power ball introduced.

Batter plays with a thin bat.

Shots could be played top hand only.

Bucket hit

Equipment:
One or more buckets
10 soft balls

Description:
Ask your players to stand two metres apart. One player has a bat in the stance position. Position the bucket off side or leg side two metres away. The player without the bat feeds ten balls to the batter and they see how many balls they can get into the bucket. Swap batters after ten balls.

Progression:
Use more buckets in different positions.
Move the buckets further away.
Increase the distance between the players.
Vary the direction and pace of the throws.

Dominant eye testing

Determining a batter's dominant eye is very important, as it could have a bearing on their stance, how well they see the ball and how well they play certain shots. This is called ocular dominance. Many methods of carrying out a quick and effective test can be found on the internet, one of which is listed below:

Cut out a 75mm equilateral triangle from a piece of cardboard. Look at an object and bring the open triangle up in front of your eyes, sighting centrally at the object. Close your left eye. If the object disappears you are left-eye dominant. If you now close your right eye the object should remain. The opposite should happen if you are right-eye dominant.

Many reports have been written comparing ocular dominance with hand dominance, defining the descriptions and the effect this could have on 'side-on' sports such as cricket, baseball, golf, shooting and archery. These should be researched further to enhance understanding.

Training on your own

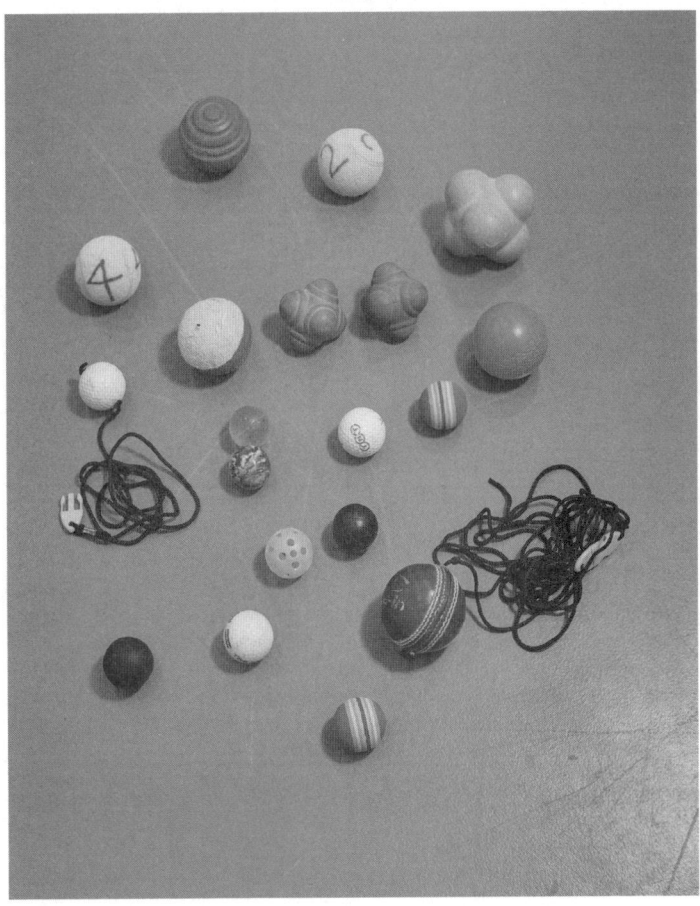

Many of the drills indicated in the previous hand-eye-foot coordination section are applicable to this section, so should be viewed and added to the individual training regime where necessary.

Drop feed hits

Drop feeds are predominantly used for practising front-foot shots. The batter drops or gently throws the ball vertically from a low height, landing in an accurate position for the shot being practised, the batter then hits the ball after one or two bounces. This form of practising alone is ideal for any front-foot shot.

Size, weight and type of ball should always be appropriate to the batter hitting. Use of target cones help in reducing the ball being hit in random directions. This practice method is usually carried out in a net, but if not, the hitting zones should be in a safe area and appropriately protected. The batter can drop the ball further away to simulate advancing down the wicket.

Reaction ball

Equipment:
1 reaction ball

Description:
The batter underarm throws the reaction ball at a wall, ensuring it lands predominantly on a good length. Upon pitching, the ball is likely to deviate a

lot, so this is good practice at playing the spinning ball, turning and bouncing off a worn pitch. The batter may play a range of shots, both attacking and defending, front foot or back foot, but successfully reacting to the unpredictability of the ball is their main objective.

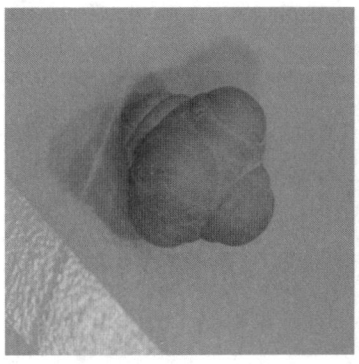 

Progression:
Introduce a points-scoring game for good technique in playing the unpredictable reaction ball. The batter scores points if they play the ball late, keeping it on the floor, or successfully leaving the ball. They lose points if they do not, they play and miss or get out in some way.

The batter can serve the ball as fast or as slow as they can, or reduce the throwing distance. Introduce cones as close-in catching fielders.

Batters could use thin bats.

Shots could be played top hand only.

Top-hand-only hits

Equipment:
Tennis balls
Plastic stumps

Description:
A common way to enhance a batter's top-hand strength is for them to hit balls or play shadow shots holding the bat in their top hand only. It is essential that the

batter keeps the same grip as they would for a normal two-handed shot and does not change it due to the bat being harder to control in one hand. For example, the batter adopts a base associated with a cover drive and lifts the bat to the top of its backswing (a ball is not required). The downswing is commenced, continuing through to the full check drive follow-through. This can be done continuously without stopping for ten strokes. The batter's aim is for complete control of the bat throughout the shadow shot. To check on the line of swing, this can be done over a line in a sports hall, joints in patio slabs, etc. Additionally, the batter's downswing to follow-through could be aligned to pass between a set of plastic stumps, where the middle stump has been removed.

The batter can then drop feed a tennis ball to themselves, releasing it from their bottom hand, driving it with their top hand only.

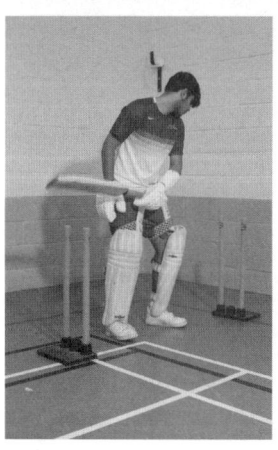

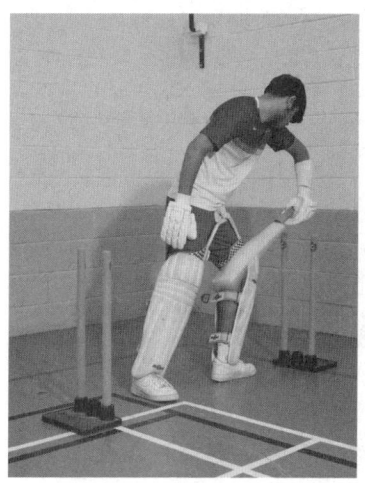 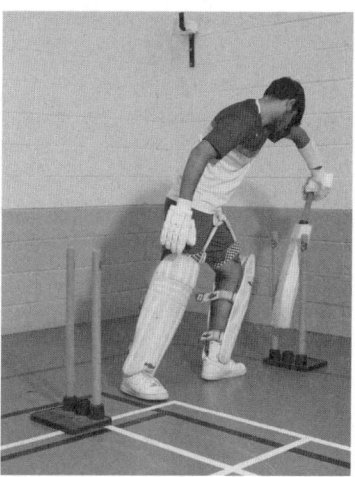

Progression:
The batter doubles the number of shadow hits.

The batter steps into the shadow hit from their stance position and repeats this when drop feeding the ball.

A coach bobble feeds a ball towards the batter, who steps into the drive and hits the ball.

The batter could use a thin bat, but that is much lighter, so the strengthening of the top-hand shot is lost at the expense of watching and focusing on the ball more.

A scoring game can be introduced where the batter scores a point for hitting the ball through a targeted coned area, etc.

Use this drill for any shot, either front- or back-foot.

Bottom-hand-only hits

Equipment:
Tennis balls
Plastic stumps

Description:
A common way to enhance a batter's feel for the shape and grip of their bottom

hand is to hit balls or play shadow shots holding the bat in their bottom hand only. It is essential that the batter keeps the same grip as they would for a normal two-handed shot and does not change it due to the bat being harder to control in one hand. For example, the batter adopts a base associated with a cover drive and lifts the bat to the top of its backswing (a ball is not required). The downswing is commenced, continuing through to the full check drive follow-through. This can be done continuously without stopping for ten strokes. The batter's aim is for complete control of the bat throughout the shadow shot. To check on the line of swing, this can be done over a line in a sports hall, joints in patio slabs, etc. Additionally, the batter's downswing to follow-through could be aligned to pass between a set of plastic stumps, where the middle stump has been removed.

The batter can then drop feed a tennis ball to themselves, releasing it from their top hand, driving it with their bottom hand only.

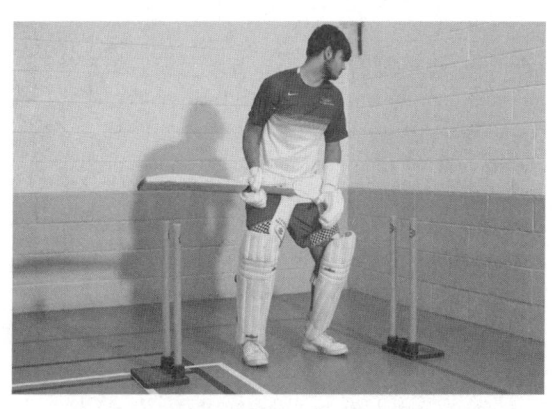

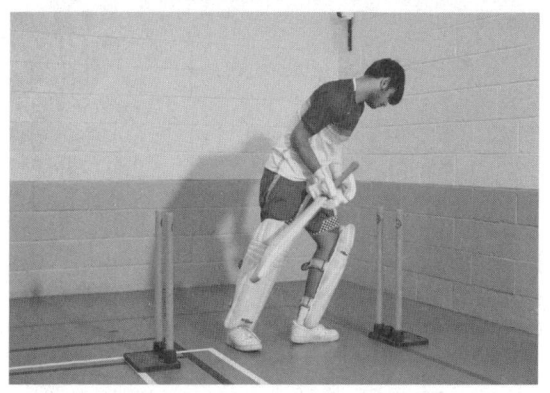

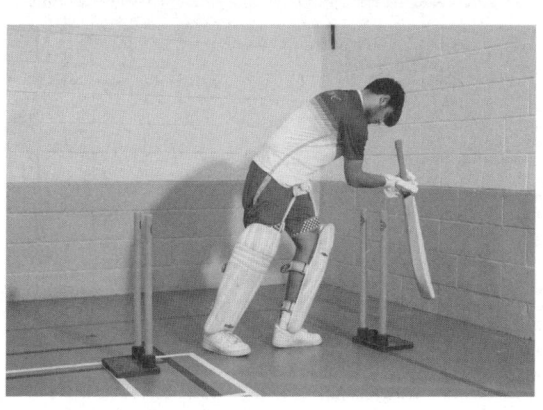

Progression:

The batter doubles the number of shadow hits.

The batter steps into the shadow hit from their stance position and repeats this when drop feeding the ball.

A coach bobble feeds a ball towards the batter, who steps into the drive and hits the ball.

The batter could use a thin bat, but that is much lighter, so the feel of the bottom-hand shot is lost at the expense of watching and focusing on the ball more.

A scoring game can be introduced where the batter scores a point for hitting the ball through a targeted coned area, etc.

Use this drill for any shot, either front- or back-foot.

Batting with a thin bat

There are many advantages to batting with a thin bat as part of a batter's practice regime. The foremost one is that as the bat can be less than half the width of a conventional one, it is obviously harder to hit the ball consistently in the middle of the bat. This then puts more emphasis on watching the ball and having a solid technique. This will apply to every shot executed. Another advantage is that because the bat is lighter there is more chance that the batter will have better top-hand control through all the shots. This may well contribute to a batter playing surprisingly well with a thinner bat, and discovering that a light bat could be an advantage in most cases. To wield a heavy bat you have to be extremely strong!

Batting with a short bat

There are many advantages to batting with a short bat as part of a batter's practice regime. The foremost one is that as the bat can be half the length of a conventional one, it is obviously harder to hit the ball consistently in the middle of the bat. This then puts more emphasis on watching the ball and having a solid technique. This is particularly applicable for players who, when playing on the front foot, fail to get low enough over the ball. This type of bat is a great coaching aid in encouraging them to get their head lower over the ball, coupled with a longer forward front-foot stride.

Another advantage is that because the bat is lighter there is more chance that the batter will have better top-hand control through all the shots. This may well contribute to a batter playing surprisingly well with a shorter bat, and discovering that a light bat could be an advantage in most cases. To wield a heavy bat you have to be extremely strong!

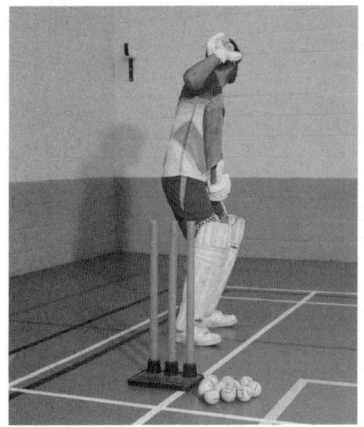 

Numbered tennis balls rebound hitting

Equipment:
12 numbered tennis balls

Description:
The batter is set up approximately 4m back from a wall, facing directly towards it. Behind them is a collection of 12 tennis balls randomly lying on the floor. Each tennis ball has a large number written on it four times in felt-tip pen, equally spaced around the ball. Balls are numbered 1 to 6, and there should be two of each. Without looking at the ball, the batter picks one up and overarm throws it against the wall at pace, ensuring it bounces once in front of them. After appropriately playing the ball, the player calls out the number they saw written on it as it was moving. This is a great drill for enhancing watching the ball.

Progression:
Balls are thrown from a position nearer to the wall.

Line and lengths are altered to increase the difficulty in identification, such as yorker, good length, short.

Shots could be played top hand only.

This drill can also be performed with a coach feed.

It is vital that when throwing, the batter keeps in a side-on position, as this will enable the shots to be played correctly. If a front-on position is accidentally used, the batter will get into a bad habit of presenting themselves in a chest-/front-on position when executing their shots.

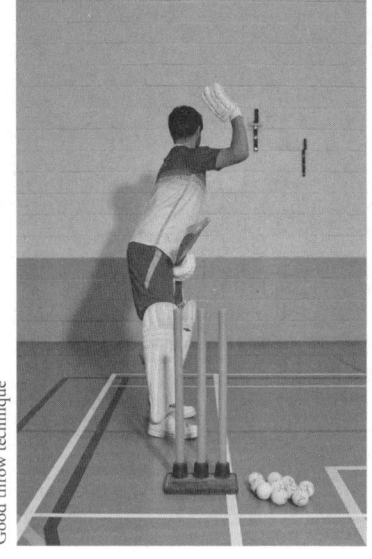

Good throw technique

Bad throw technique

Crazy Net and Katchet board rebound hitting

Equipment:
Tennis ball
Numbered tennis balls
Set of plastic stumps

Crazy Net
Katchet board
Shower mat

Description:
The batter stands in their stance in front of the stumps, located approximately 4–5m back from a wall, facing directly towards the Crazy Net resting against it. The player overarm throws the ball on to the net, playing an appropriate shot to the rebound. Repeat numerous times. This drill can also be performed with a coach feed.

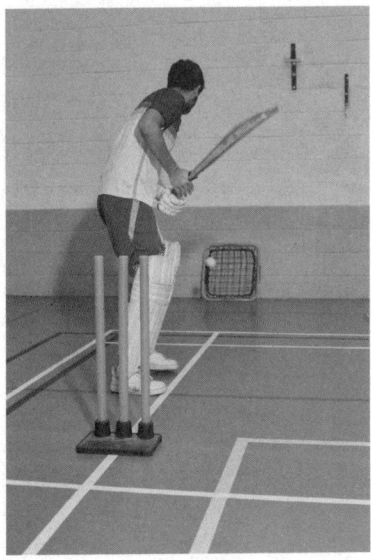

The batter stands in their stance in front of the stumps, located approximately 4–5m back from a wall, facing directly towards it. A Katchet board is placed approximately 2m from the wall, facing the batter. The player overarm throws the ball on to the wall. The ball rebounds off the board and the batter plays an appropriate shot to the rebound. Repeat numerous times. This drill can also be performed with a coach feed.

The batter stands in their stance in front of the stumps, located approximately 4–5m back from of a wall, facing directly towards it. A shower mat is placed approximately 2m from the wall, facing the batter. The player overarm throws the ball on to the wall. The ball rebounds off the mat and the batter plays an appropriate shot to the rebound. Repeat numerous times. This drill can also be performed with a coach feed.

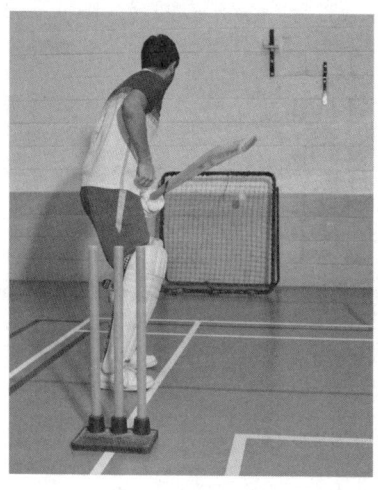

Progression:
Numbered tennis balls for an identification game could be introduced.
   Shots could be played top hand only.

Batting rebound tennis

Equipment:
   Tennis ball
   Cricket bat
   Thin bat
   Squash ball

Description:
The batter is set up approximately 1m back from a wall, facing directly towards it. They hit the ball against the wall using their bat, keeping the ball from dropping on to the floor. Repeat numerous times. The batter should be set in a comfortable position, keeping their feet still if possible. They could initially be set in a front-foot position, then change the repetition to back-foot hits. This drill is carried out alone.

Progression:

The batter hits the ball at different heights or positions on the wall, ensuring they keep the ball from hitting the floor.

A form of competition can be introduced.

The batter moves nearer to the wall while the drill is in progress or moves further away, while keeping the ball active.

A timed game could be introduced to record how long it takes to do 20 hits.

The ball could be hit into the corners of a sports hall, rebounding back at different angles.

The drill could be adapted so the ball must hit the floor once before being hit.

A squash ball could be used.

A thin bat could be used.

Cricket ball and golf ball hung from a cord line

Equipment:

Cricket ball and golf ball with cord line attached

Description:

This is a very simple but effective drill in encouraging a batter to present the full face of the bat to the ball. The cord is securely attached to a high prominent feature, and the ball is allowed to hang at an appropriate height for the intended shot. The batter then softly or moderately hits the ball, executing the intended shot, endeavouring to hit it square on. If successful, the ball should swing straight back on the same line. The shots are repeated until control of the ball is lost.

 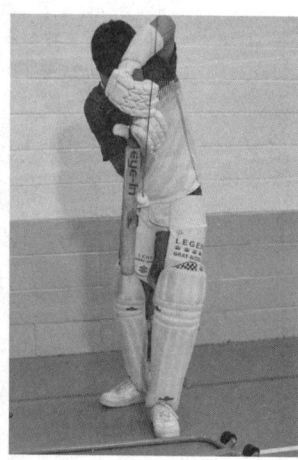

Progression:
A form of competition is introduced where the batter has to keep improving the number of continuous hits.

Batter hits top hand or bottom hand only.

Batter uses a thin bat.

Bat keepie uppies

Equipment:
1 soft or hard ball
1 bat

Description:
Initially, using the flat bat face only, see how many times you can bounce the ball in the middle of the bat in a minute.

Progression:
Move from flat bat face to edge of the bat, to back of the bat, to other edge, back to flat bat face. How many taps until you fail?
Add hitting with toe of the bat and top of the handle.

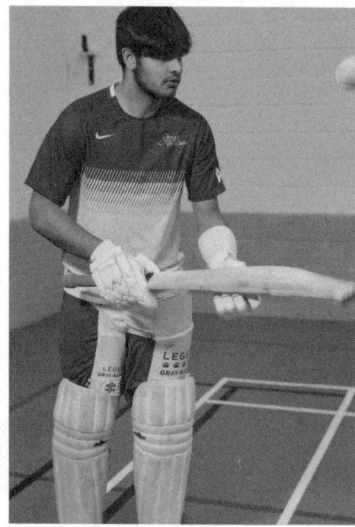

Front-foot shot, one-hand reverse catch drill
(encouraging good top-hand, elbow and shoulder positioning)

Equipment:
 1 tennis ball

Description:
The batter stands approximately 3m away from a wall and underarm throws a full toss feed on to it, rebounding on a line outside off stump just above knee height. The batter moves their front foot towards the ball, creates a base and reaches down to catch it in their top hand, which catches the ball in a reverse position. The batter tries to ensure the head is above the ball. The batter is to remain still after catching so that an assessment of top-hand, shoulder and elbow alignment can be made. This is a great way of getting the shoulder and elbow into the correct position.

Wrist and forearm strengthening

Equipment:
Tennis ball or wrist squeeze-grip

Description:
It is so important that a batter has strong wrists and forearms, especially for the top hand, which is the one that should provide the most control. These simple methods are very effective at achieving this. The batter squeezes the tennis ball or wrist squeeze-grip for a set number of repetitions, rests for a minute then repeats.

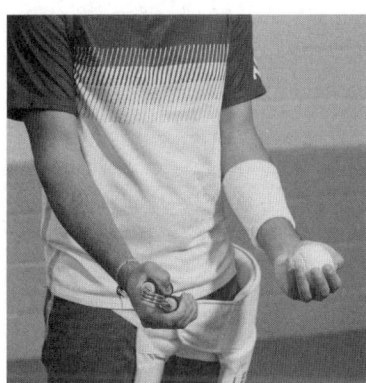

Progression:
The batter increases the number of repetitions and the duration progressively over time.

Mirror batting

A very simple but effective method of training alone is to shadow shots in front of a mirror, preferably a full-height one. This is almost like a live video camera, with slow motion, play and pause control at your fingertips! It is perfect for assessing stance, triggers, head position, balance, foot movement, backswing, base, bat contact shapes, and follow-through.

Running between the wickets

Equipment:
   8 cones (4 red, 4 white)

Description:
The pitch is set out in accordance with the relevant age-group dimensions. A pair of white cones is set across the full width of the popping crease at both ends. A pair of red cones is positioned approximately 1.5m away from the white ones, parallel to them down the pitch at both ends. The batter runs a two. On the completion of the first run, the batter stops at the red cone and stretches their bat over the white cone line. They then complete the second run, ensuring they start to slide their bat in from the red cones until it passes the white cones.

Progression:

The batter could run more than a two.

The stretching/turning distance could be lengthened to encourage a low turning technique.

The batter could roll a ball out in a certain direction and call for a certain number of runs to be taken, ensuring that they do not turn blind at the completion of each run.

The batter could actually hit a tennis ball for realism and run a certain number of runs.

Players could wear full kit when practising this drill for realism.

Pre-match

As stated in Chapter 8, so much of pre-match preparation is a player's preference and most often done with another batter giving each other underarm full toss feeds, throw-downs or dog-stick practice (as detailed earlier in this chapter). These are the forms most commonly used to work through shots and feel the ball in the middle of the bat to build confidence before a day's play. However, it also possible to work through your shots (front and back foot) while giving a wicketkeeper some catching practice or hitting balls into the outfield for fielders to field the ball.

Waiting to bat

Unless a player is opening the batting, they could potentially quite commonly be arriving at the wicket after a period of inactivity. The warm-up may have taken place in excess of 20 overs ago, so the batter is at a disadvantage in terms of being active and both mentally and physically switched on. On the way to the wicket you generally see batters playing air shots, swinging their arms and bat, doing short bursts of footwork movements, opening their eyes wide, etc. They are attempting to switch on to the task ahead as quickly as possible. The upcoming task entails ball-watching, assessing, deciding, reacting, moving, stopping, hitting, running, etc. This is why the batter is most vulnerable when immediately arriving at the wicket.

While waiting to go into bat there are a few things a batter can do to prepare for their upcoming innings. Some very simple methods are highlighted below. Some other appropriate quick warm-ups are also included earlier in this chapter, such as watching birds and insects, and mirror batting.

Some batters enjoy doing some footwork warm-ups, using either sports ladders or skipping ropes. These activities are great for getting the feet moving quickly and activating the motor system of the player. Some intermittently do a few press-ups or squeeze a tennis ball, etc. Once again, the focus is on the individual and what works for them.

Additionally, another simple warm-up exercise is to do bat-tap keepie uppies. This involves the continuous hitting upwards of a cricket ball, tennis ball, squash ball, golf ball, marble, etc. off the face of the bat held in a horizontal plane. The ball is continuously hit to a height of approximately 6–8 inches off the middle sweet spot of the bat. As the player becomes more skilful at this, they can alternately revolve the bat between the middle of the bat and the outside/inside edges, trying to ensure complete control of the ball. They could progress to just hitting the ball with the two edges of the bat. This simple drill is great for improving hand-eye coordination. Why not try it with two tennis balls at once, or even turn the bat around backwards!

The previously described examples should be done intermittently while waiting to bat, because you do not want to be too exhausted when arriving at the crease either.

Another suggestion for helping the eyes to focus while waiting to bat – whether reading, looking at your phone, or watching the match – is to turn away and focus on an object that is approximately 22yds away from you for a while, then focus back on to where you were looking. Then repeat a few times. This helps focus your eyes on the distance that the bowler will be bowling at you from if you are playing on a full-size pitch and warms the muscles up that control your eyes.

Note for coaches/players

Some batters may prefer to sit in a corner listening to music through their headphones. Others sit and watch the match, gaining information about the pitch, bowlers, etc. Everyone is different, so it is important that the batter discovers what best works for them regarding the mental and physical preparation for batting.

Introduction to video analysis

Mobile phones, tablets and iPads are commonplace today, so these offer a great opportunity for recording, assessing and making technical changes to batters, young or old, experienced or inexperienced. They also provide an accurate record of a player's level of play at a particular moment in time and, if the player has access to the footage, encourages them to take ownership of their own analysis. This brief introduction to video analysis may give the parent, or inexperienced person, a basic introduction to some fundamental areas to look at, which may help with the development of their player.

In most cases a potential flaw in technique will be compared with a proven successful method by the use of photos. Some apps enable a side-by-side comparison with a player playing the shot correctly and these can be synced together so a player and coach can compare from start to finish of the shot being practised.

Note for coaches/players

Remember that video analysis can only highlight flaws in technique – it cannot correct them. This can only be done by adopting the appropriate drills and high repetition.

The following pages contain some examples of areas of technique that are common and can be easily identified using video analysis.

The grip

It is so important that the bottom hand does not grip the handle too tightly, otherwise known as 'strangling'. The bat should be gripped mainly with the thumb and first two fingers, which ensures a softer grip and helps with hitting both sides of the wicket, a straighter bat path, and keeping the ball down where necessary.

Tight bottom hand grip

Soft bottom hand grip

The stance

A common fault is when the head is leaning over too much, taking it past the line of the toes. When this occurs, body weight can fall to the off side, which can be disastrous for the batter for many reasons. It is vital that a balanced position is held. A great way of showing this flaw is to pretend to feed the ball but do not let go of it or feed it into the bowling machine. This is called a 'dummy' feed. If the head is moving to the off side, the batter's heels will come up off the ground; they may even stumble over to that side. It is so important to have a head that is still, level and balanced.

Backswing too far from body

Often a batter may hold their bat too far away from their body, as if they are playing baseball. This can be detrimental to their backswing, balance and downswing direction, caused by an excessive looping effect while executing a downswing prior to attempting to hit the ball. The batter should be encouraged to have their bat closer to their body, thus having more control over backswing and downswing bat paths.

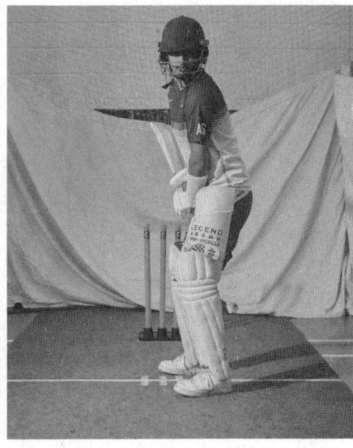

Backswing behind body

Another common fault is when the batter takes the bat behind the body in the backswing. This can be detrimental to their backswing, balance and downswing direction. This can sometimes indicate that the batter has an excessively firm bottom-hand grip, which pulls the bat back and around. The batter should be encouraged to have their bat straighter, either pointing at off stump or in a direction aligned with the wicketkeeper. This will achieve more control over backswing and downswing bat paths, reducing the possibility of having to hit around the body to access the ball.

Front-foot position closing off body in stance

Sometimes a batter will have their front foot slightly in front of their back foot when in their stance, which is called 'closing themselves off'. This can also happen after a batter has completed their trigger, should they have one. This can hinder a player working balls into the leg side, as they may have to play around their front leg to hit the ball when it is bowled straight or on their legs. This can also lead to lots of potential lbw dismissals. The batter should be encouraged to rearrange their feet so that they are level, or the front foot is slightly behind the back foot, in a slightly 'open' stance.

Front foot not pointing down the pitch for an on drive

Some batters find playing the on drive difficult, regularly getting hit on the pads. A common reason for this is that they try to hit the ball with their front foot still in a side-on set-up position when it lands ready to hit the ball. They often have to hit around their front leg, which impedes a free hit at the ball. Again, they may be susceptible to lbw decisions. A successful way of playing the on drive is to point the front foot straight down the pitch or towards mid-off as the front foot lands in position, which ensures that the hips open up, allowing a much straighter bat path to be presented to the ball.

Front foot too far away from line of ball

A very common theme with batters is when they fail to get their front foot near enough to the line of the ball. This can mean they miss the ball regularly, do not hit it very hard, or either get bowled or caught behind a lot. It is crucial that a batter gets their front foot across as well as forward to play the line of the ball relevant to where it will be once it reaches them. Video analysis can highlight when a batter is stepping forward but not across to the line of the ball. If they do not get to the line, then the head and hands are always reaching for the ball. Keeping their front shoulder and elbow pointing at the ball will help with this alignment. Remember, the upper half of the body does the hitting, and the lower part gets it into position to do so. The feet are the servants of the hands.

Back foot too far away from the line of the ball

Also common is when batters fail to get their back foot near enough to the line of the ball when playing a back-foot shot, which often means that the bat is angled, so neither horizontal (cut shot) nor vertical (defence/drive). This can lead to top edges or bottom edges that can often cannon into the stumps.

As most balls will be bowled on a line between middle stump and outside off stump it is crucial that a batter gets their back foot across to play that line. A great position to be in for any back-foot shot is to have the stumps completely covered by the batter's legs as the play it. By doing this, the batter is also able to direct more balls into the leg side. Keeping their front shoulder and elbow pointing at the ball will help with this alignment. Commonly, a batter will step backwards but not across.

No backswing

Sometimes a lack of power when hitting the ball can be attributed to a batter not having a backswing. Because there is no pendulum effect set up by a backswing, the batter tends to push at the ball quickly rather than hitting it naturally. They can often be late in the shot too, missing the ball regularly. It is critical that the bat is swung backwards to get it going forwards. This does not have to be a big movement, but just enough to initiate a positive downswing. Pick a reference point, such as the top of the stumps, and see where the batter's gloves are throughout the shot. If they do not go higher, there is no backswing; if they do go higher, a backswing does exist and the player should hit the ball more cleanly.

Squared-up or chest-on – front foot

Many batters have a habit of getting squared-up or playing chest-on. This means that their front shoulder opens up too much, and they end up hitting the ball while their chest faces the ball. This is a particular problem when hitting to the off side, as the shoulders have already rotated, leaving them redundant, power only being supplied by the arms. Players who do this may also reach for the ball, hitting upwards regularly. To counter this, the batter should try to point the front shoulder and elbow at the line of the ball when stepping towards it; pushing their helmet grill into the shoulder will help with this. Now, when striking the ball, the shoulders are still engaged in the shot, so upon rotation apply more power to the hit.

Squared-up or chest-on – back foot

Many batters have a habit of getting squared-up or playing chest-on. This means that their front shoulder opens up too much and they end up hitting the ball while their chest faces the ball. This is a particular problem when hitting to the off side, as the shoulders have already rotated, leaving them redundant, power only being supplied by the arms. Players who do this may also reach for the ball, hitting upwards regularly. To counter this, the batter should try to point the front shoulder and elbow at the line of the ball when stepping back and across to it; pushing their helmet grill into the shoulder will help with this. It is critical that they keep their back foot parallel with the crease line. This keeps them in a much better side-on position, enabling a strong base to be attained. Now, when striking the ball, the shoulders are still engaged in the shot, so upon rotation apply more power to the hit.

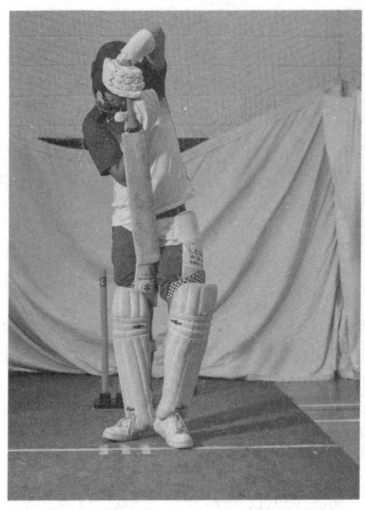
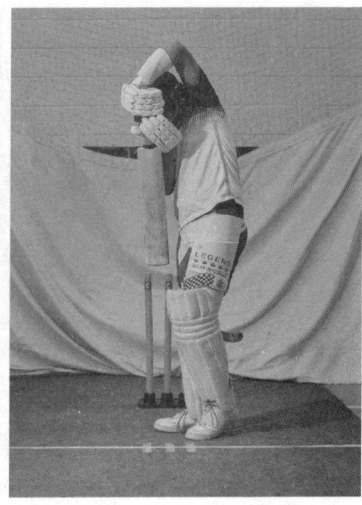

Hitting the ball along the ground or in the air

To be confident of purposely hitting the ball downwards or upwards, it is essential that the batter understands the simple mechanics involved in achieving this regarding the bat. To keep the ball down, it is critical that the bat handle is ahead of the blade at the point of ball contact. Conversely, if the batter wants to hit the ball upwards, the bat handle will be behind the blade at the point of ball contact. Timing, head position, body balance and base stabilising are all factors in determining a successful outcome. Additionally, if the ball is to be hit down, the contact is made with the head forward, with the ball under the eyes. If the ball is to be hit upwards, the head is to be set back as the ball is hit in front of the eyes.

Getting squared-up coming down the pitch

There will be many occasions when a batter advances down the pitch to get nearer to the pitch of the ball. Invariably this manoeuvre is done quickly and over a distance of a few metres. The batter starts off in their stance, which is mostly side-on. While advancing down the pitch, a common fault is that the batter may open up their body into a chest-on position in their quest to get to the ball quickly. They almost run at it. This then puts their whole shot at risk, from failing to set a solid base, making their shoulders redundant, etc. A side-on position at contact is more desirable in most cases, particularly as more power can be generated by the shoulder rotation inherent in this position. Therefore the batter should try to advance down the pitch in a side-on manner at all times.

Falling over when playing the sweep shot

A common fault when playing the sweep shot is for the batter to fall over as they hit the ball. This is generally caused by an unstable base alignment. As with driving off the front foot, the front knee must be bent to provide a solid base and keep the head forwards towards the ball. Some players also like to have their back knee on the ground to help provide an even better base. If the ball is being hit from a middle stump line, the batter simply goes down the pitch into a front-foot lunge, ensuring they keep their head low and forwards over a bent front knee. The greatest width of their body is their shoulders when viewed from the bowler's end. The bat goes out to the off side of the batter before coming down on to the ball as the shot is made. Overbalancing is normally caused when the batter does not bend the front knee enough and approaches the ball at an angle, so the greater width of their body is from the toes of the front foot to the heel of the back foot. The batter is at an angle to the path of the ball in a potentially unstable position. Now when the bat is

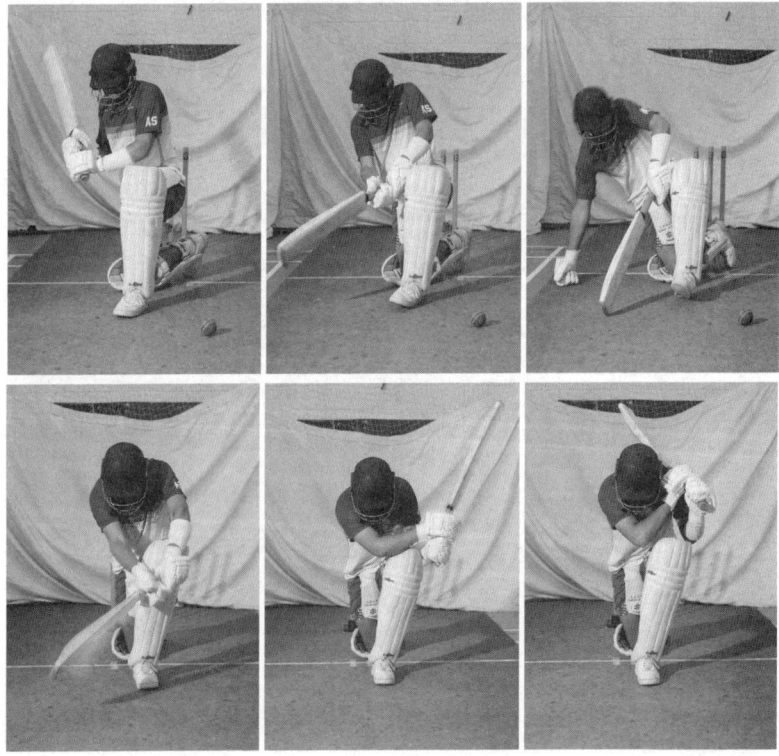

taken over to the off side to initiate the shot, the weight of the bat, coupled with the misaligned base angle, causes the batter to fall over.

With the sweep it also common for a batter to flinch with their head (usually towards the off side), take their eyes off the ball and overbalance.

Drill and practice safety awareness

We previously highlighted the form of progression for practising in a fixed batting practice session. These were: hitting off a batting tee, drop feed, full toss feed, bobble feed, throw-down feed, bowling machine feed. Progressing on from these, the final forms of practice are sidearm feeds, nets, indoor matches, outdoor middle practice, and outdoor matches.

All of these have potential danger and safety issues inherent within them, so it is vital that these are highlighted, whether you are a player, parent or coach. It is not just the batter who should be kept safe, but also the coach, feeder, parent and spectators. With all of the feeds below a coach must take into account the following:

- The size, weight and type of ball should always be appropriate to the batter hitting. Use of target cones helps in reducing the ball being hit in random directions.
- When giving instructions about the hitting drill to the batter, it is always wise to check that they have totally understood it by asking them to repeat what they are about to do. This 'checking for understanding' invariably allows the session to take place in a much safer environment.
- Ideally the feeds will be carried out in a net, but if not, the hitting zones should be in a safe area and appropriately protected.

Hitting off a batting tee

Rubber batting tees are predominantly used for practising front-foot shots to a stationary ball, although they can also be used for back-foot shots when placed on top of a plastic stump. The coach should always be positioned to the off side of the batter, a minimum of an arm's length away from the player when placing the ball on the tee and throughout the shot. They should never position themselves to the leg side at any time, as they could be hit by the batter when following through with their shot.

The coach or feeder should never stand directly in front of the batter, no matter how far away, as they may be hit by the ball or the batter may accidentally let go of the bat. The feeder must be aware of left-handed batters in multiple player sessions, as the feeder will have to switch feeding sides to avoid being hit by the batter's follow-through, etc.

Drop feed

Drop feeds are predominantly used for practising front-foot shots. The feeder drops the ball vertically from a low appropriate height, landing in an accurate position for the shot being practised. The batter then hits the ball after one or two bounces. The coach should always be positioned to the off side of the batter, a minimum of an arm's length away from the player when dropping the ball and throughout the shot. They should never position themselves to the leg side at any time, as they could be hit by the batter when following through with their shot.

The coach or feeder should never stand directly in front of the batter, no matter how far away, as they may be hit by the ball or bat, or the batter may accidentally let go of the bat. The feeder must be aware of left-handed batters in multiple player sessions, as the feeder will have to switch feeding sides to avoid being hit by the batters follow-through, etc.

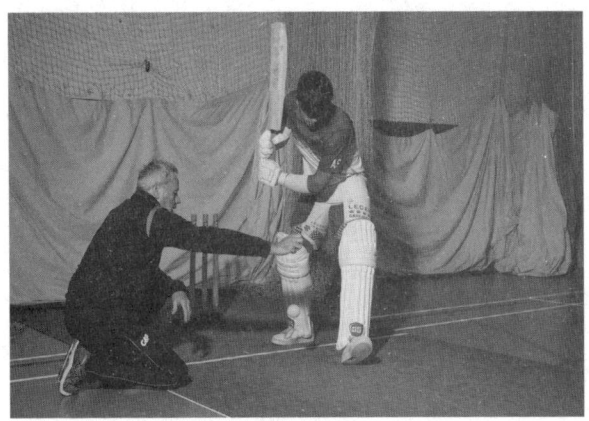

Full toss feed

Full toss feeds are predominantly thrown underarm and are used for practising both front- and back-foot shots. The feeder throws the ball at an appropriate height, targeted accurately for the shot being practised; the batter then hits the ball. The ball is always thrown from a position in front of the batter, on a line similar to that of a normal bowler. The coach should always position themselves in an appropriate and safe manner, never endangering themselves by being too close to the batter, just in case the ball comes straight back at them, or the batter accidentally lets go of the bat.

The feeder must be aware of left-handed batters in multiple player sessions, as the feeder will have to switch hitting zones.

Bobble feed

Bobble feeds are predominantly thrown underarm and are used for practising front-foot shots. The feeder throws the ball, ensuring it bounces at least twice before it reaches the batter. The ball should arrive at an appropriate height, targeted accurately for the shot being practised; the batter then hits the ball. The ball is always thrown from a position in front of the batter, on a line similar to that of a normal bowler. The coach should always position themselves in an appropriate and safe manner, never endangering themselves by being too close to the batter, just in case the ball comes straight back at them, or the batter accidentally lets go of the bat. The feeder must be aware of left-handed batters in multiple player sessions, as the feeder will have to switch hitting zones.

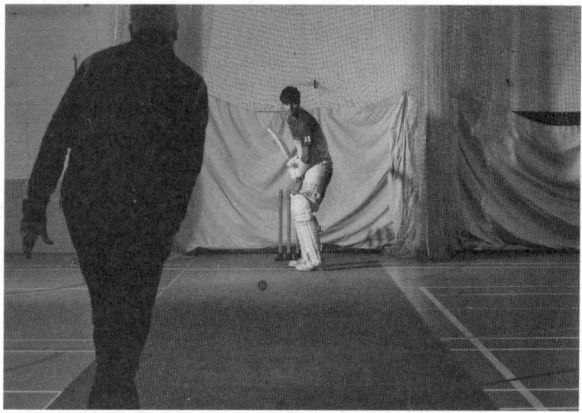

A firm and level surface is needed for this feed, as the ball needs to be accurately presented to the batter.

Throw-down feed

Throw-down feeds are thrown overarm and are used for practising both front- and back-foot shots. The ball should arrive at a line and length targeted accurately for the shot being practised; the batter then hits the ball. The ball is always thrown from a position in front of the batter, on a line similar to that of a normal bowler. The coach should always position themselves in an appropriate and safe manner, never endangering themselves by being too close to the batter, just in case the ball comes straight back at them, or the batter accidentally lets go of the bat. The feeder must be aware of left-handed batters in multiple player sessions, as the feeder will have to switch hitting zones.

Bowling machine feed

Safety is paramount when using bowling machines. Ensure that it is safely and securely positioned in a stable way and at an appropriate distance away from the batter about to take strike. All electrical connections and wiring must be checked for condition and safety, and all speed and direction controls, whether electrical or manual, checked to ensure they are working correctly. The machine safety/service sticker should be clearly seen for inspection. If the machine starts to smell, overheating is suspected, or there are any other safety issues, it should be switched off immediately and taken out of use. A warning message should be securely attached to the machine until it is repaired. The route of the electrical cable should always be checked in case it is a trip hazard. Step-ladders or fold-out steps are commonly used with bowling machines to elevate the feeder up to the ball feed height, so these must be in a safe and stable condition too.

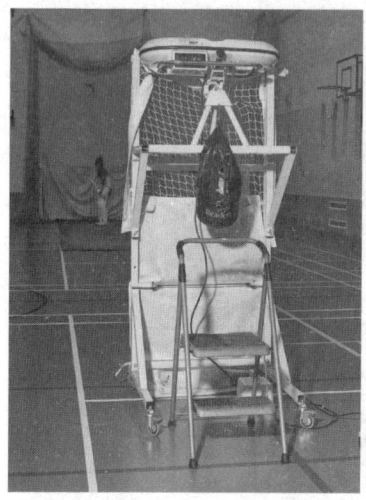
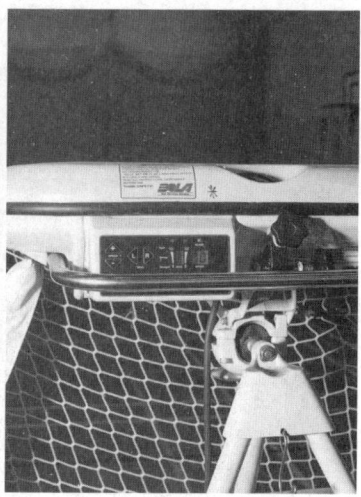

Before commencing feeding, the nets should be checked for safety issues (see separate section), and the playing surface should be inspected for any damage, holes, tears or interference debris. The area in front of and around the sides of the machine should also be clear of objects, as these could easily cause the ball to be deflected towards the person feeding the machine. Additionally, the safety of all players and spectators must always be considered. Integral plastic screens, metal cages or netting are essential forms of protection for the feeder; even the use of a batting helmet may be appropriate on occasions.

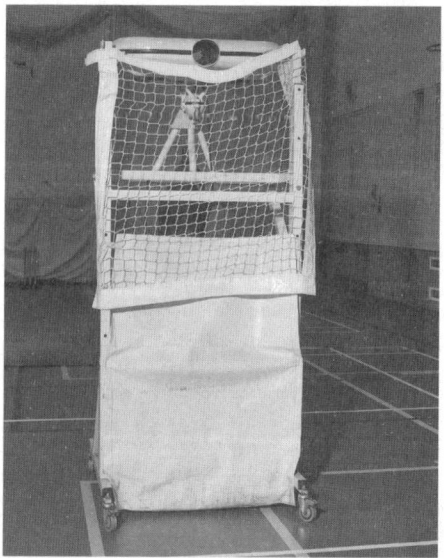

The speed, line, length, swing, etc. should all be appropriate to the playing surface, and also safe for the batter on strike. Always give the batter a 'sighter' before they take strike, so that both feeder and batter are happy with the feed delivery. Better to start too slow than too fast when feeding for the pull or hook shot. There may only be one ball fed in the session otherwise!

Bowling machine balls come in different weights and colours, so it is very important that the type of ball is appropriate for the batter facing. When practising against fast, short-pitched bowling, it is prudent to use the lighter weight balls, as these do not have the same impact on a batter that heavier balls do should they get hit by it. Some batters may even struggle to see certain coloured balls if they have colour blindness issues.

There are also bowling machines designed specifically for use with tennis balls, which can be useful for practising against short-pitched bowling, general faster bowling, or when working with younger batters.

Wet balls can become a dangerous safety issue if the machine is being used outside, as they come out of the machine at random angles and pace, so they should never be fed into the machine. Wet balls should be thoroughly dried with a towel before being fed into the machine. The condition of the balls should be checked regularly for damage, and the weight/type of ball should be appropriate for the machine and batter. It goes without saying that the feeder should never put their hands in the machine at any time!

Before the ball is fed into the machine, the feeder should extend their arm fully above their head, and then gently lower it, feeding the ball into the machine. This procedure gives the batter time to set themselves and get into a rhythm for the ball release. The feeder should hold the ball above their head and never commence the lowering until the batter is fully ready.

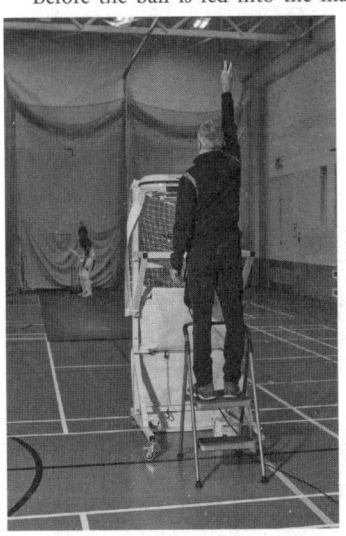

The batter should be made fully aware of bowling machine procedures by clear, concise safety instructions.

While the practice session is in progress, the feeder should make the batter aware of any balls that have rolled into a location in the direct vicinity of the batter's feet, thus avoiding a potential twisted or broken ankle. The feeder should also continually assess whether any balls lying on the playing surface are a potential deflection danger to the batter. The feeder should also be aware of this danger when stepping backwards off the access step-ladder etc.

The feeder should also be aware of activity in adjacent nets, ensuring that they do not feed the machine at inappropriately unsafe moments, such as when a player in an adjacent net is picking up balls from the separating net area, or when a shot from an adjacent net causes the net to bulge across the eyeline of the batter they are serving to.

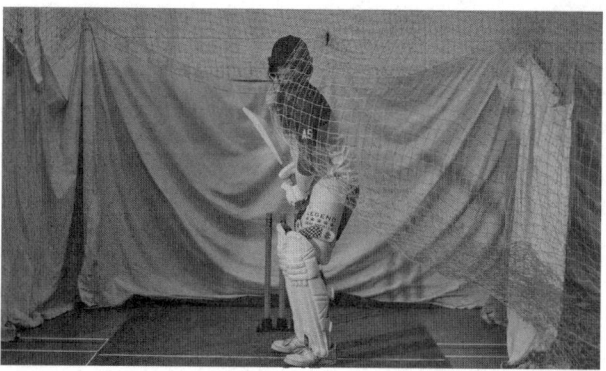

Finally, the protection of other players and spectators is essential at all times, so on occasions it may be prudent to attach the end of the nets to the bowling machine in some way, so that the majority of balls are contained within the individual net.

All the above details apply to the use of the Merlyn spin bowling machine too, although the feeding interval is normally automated, then activated with an associated audible beep. The machine can be operated manually if desired. It is essential that the automated feed is turned off if the coach wants to intervene before all the balls are fed and to walk down the net to talk to the batter. If not, the coach or batter will receive a very painful reminder that the machine is still feeding balls!

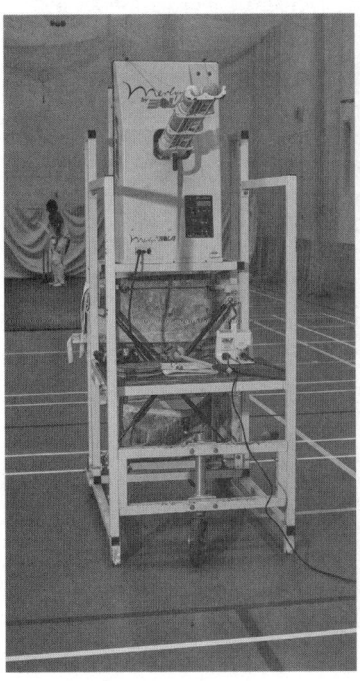
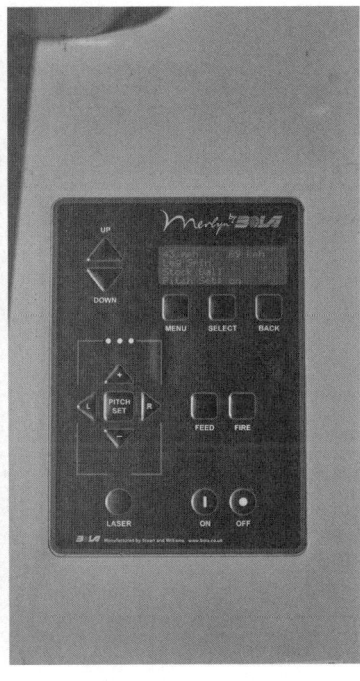

Sidearm (dog-stick) feed

Sidearm (dog-stick) feeds replicate a bowler's delivery and are thrown overarm, used for practising both front- and back-foot shots. They can be delivered at great pace or replicating a slow spin bowler. They are a great help to the coach/feeder, as they are easier on the arm/shoulder, etc. because less force is required to deliver the ball. The ball is normally thrown predominantly at the point where a bowler would normally release from and is usually used in a net situation. It is a great form of variable practice. Sidearms can also be used in fielding practice as an alternative to hitting skyers and boundary ground fielding sessions. When using the sidearm, the user should be vigilant and aware of the proximity of other players, particularly in the backswing and release of the ball.

Occasionally when working with high-performance players practising power or range hitting, and there are no physical methods of coach protection, such as nets, cage, screens, crash mats, it may be prudent to wear a helmet, or even the full range of batting protection to provide a degree of protection if the ball is hit back at you. If in doubt, the coach or feeder should leave the practice lane.

The sidearm ball holder's head and shaft should be regularly inspected for cracks and damage.

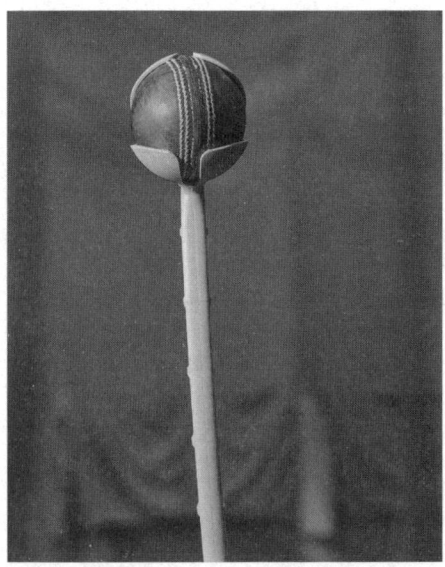

Safety when coaching and batting in nets

Cricket nets are the most common environment that players train in, taking place all year round, both indoors and outdoors. Safety of all players, coaches and spectators is once again paramount at all times. The main safety issues concern the playing surface, the nets themselves and the players within the nets. Having a safety plan greatly reduces the chance of safety issues surfacing.

Before the net training commences, the playing surface should be inspected for any damage, holes, tears, water ingress, etc., which would make the surface unsafe and unpredictable. Additionally, any interference debris should be removed from the whole net area, including bowler's run-ups, etc. Pitch distances should be clearly marked, with creases indicated appropriately for the age of the players training.

Simultaneously, the nets themselves should be fully extended and the implications of their extent assessed. If the net length is short, this will have implications on where kit is placed and where the batters will pad-up. The batters should always pad-up in a safe area behind or to the side of the nets, clear of the ball-hitting areas not protected by the nets. Batters should never pad-up behind the bowler's arm. It may also have a bearing on the safety of spectators too, so they should never watch from behind the bowler's arm, or in any area within the hitting zone of the batter.

The main concern with the nets is the condition of them, particularly if they have any holes in them. If a ball is hit through one, the consequences could be catastrophic, particularly if the ball hits a coach not wearing any protective equipment. Nets should be thoroughly inspected before every session, and if any holes are found they should be temporarily but securely repaired with cable ties, or the net should be condemned and not used again until permanent repair is facilitated, or new nets are installed. This applies to side and rear nets, plus the roof, if one exists. The nets should also be securely fixed to their upper runners, and to the ground where necessary.

Finally, the players are obviously most vulnerable to safety concerns as soon as the nets become active. Limiting the number of players in the net is a good way of improving the safety of the session. Six is normally the maximum size limit. Any more than this and the players can easily become distracted, start talking and messing around, culminating in them not concentrating and watching the batter and the ball. This can have disastrous effects.

Good

Bad

All players should be made fully aware of net batting, bowling, ball retrieval, waiting and padding-up procedures by clear, concise safety instructions prior to this taking place. Batters should always retrieve the ball from the net in a safe way and return it by gently throwing it back to the bowler in an underarm motion. They should never hit the ball back. If the ball is sitting in the separation net between two lanes, the correct procedure is for the batter to firstly assess the action in the other net, wait for the shot to be played, then either retrieve the ball by dragging it with their bat or pushing the net away with their bat and dragging the ball towards them with their foot. They should never directly lean down into the net to pick the ball up, as impact injury to the head or hand can easily happen. This obviously applies to bowlers too.

A batter should make sure they are wearing their complete protective equipment and that it is in full working order. Players' boot laces should always be done up when in the net environment.

A bowler should never bowl a ball while there is another bowler still in the net in front of the bowler's wicket. They should wait for them to be back past the bowler's stumps, with the retreating bowler always looking back at, or preferably walking backwards looking at the striking batter. There should be a distinct bowling order, which is strictly adhered to throughout the duration of the net. While waiting to bowl, the bowlers should concentrate and never turn their back on or look away from the batters hitting the ball. This could have a disastrous and catastrophic effect upon the bowler!

Finally, it is essential that the coach is positioned safely within the net, continually concentrating on the running of the net, for both the players and their own safety. They must be in such a position that the net session can be stopped immediately through loud, clear instructions, should a safety issue present itself.

Useful coaching quotes to remember

Listed below are a collection of batting coaching and motivational quotes to remember, which may strike a chord or be a good prompt for batters. They are in no particular order, but are relevant to the technical, tactical, physical, mental and lifestyle elements of a player profile. It may be worth remembering where they are located in the book. They are:

- Heart in the oven, head in the freezer
- Train hard, play easy
- Hard work beats talent when talent fails to work hard
- Never give up, whether you are winning or losing
- Failsafe, it is safe to fail
- Fear of failure or fear of success?
- FEAR – False Evidence Appearing Real
- FAIL – First Attempt In Learning
- Believe and you will receive
- Pressure makes diamonds
- 3 Ps – Preparation, Perseverance, Patience
- PRIDE – Personal Responsibility In Developing Excellence
- Plumbing teamwork – are you a drain or a radiator?
- A=1%, Z=26%, ATTITUDE = 100%
- Get as near to the ball, or as far away
- Smell your gloves
- A leave is a good shot if it is the right shot
- Fail to prepare, prepare to fail
- Do not confuse positive mindset with an aggressive mindset
- Defend with a view to attack, attack with a view to defend
- Rotate, Accumulate, Accelerate, Dominate
- Gears 1, 2, 3
- Move-stop-hit
- Paralysis by analysis
- Downswing or upswing?
- Who is winning? Why?
- Head, shoulders, knees and toes
- Feet are the servants of the body
- Risk, reward
- Was it fun? What did you learn?

ABOUT THE AUTHORS

JAMES KNOTT

Having come through the junior ranks at Kent, James played professional cricket for MCC Young Cricketers, Surrey and Somerset for eight years between 1994 and 2001, making 24 appearances for Surrey's 1st XI. Following on from that he played nine years of Minor Counties cricket for Bedfordshire, captaining for three of those. He made several appearances for the representative Minor Counties XI and also the ECB XI (England Amateurs) that won the European Championships in 2004.

As a coach, James has been the Head of Cricket at Stowe School since 2004, finishing top of the schools' cricket league twice, finishing semi-finalists of the National T20 twice and quarter-finalists once. Several pupils have gone on to play professional cricket in that time – Mark Nelson (Northants), Graeme White (Northants, Notts & England Lions), Ben Howgego (Northants), Liam Gough (MCC YC & Essex), with the most high-profile being Ben Duckett (Northants, Notts & England Test, ODI & T20i). Several others have gone on to MCCU programmes at Loughborough (Adam King, James Cronie and Olly Clarke), Cambridge (Jack Keeping), Oxford (John Gurney) and Durham (Rufus Easdale).

ANDY O'CONNOR

Andy came through the junior system at Northants, playing for both the Academy and 2nd XI. The remainder of his 25-year playing career consisted of playing in the Birmingham League, and predominantly the Northamptonshire

Premier League, also representing the county in the Northants Amateur League XI.

Andy is an ECB Level 3 coach and is also a member of the Northamptonshire ECB Coach Education team. He is part of the junior coaching set-up at Northants, having coached most age groups, both boys and girls. He is currently coach of the new U18s Boys squad, having coached the U17 Boys team during their ECB National Championship three-day and one-day cup-winning seasons of 2017 and 2019. Andy was head coach of the Northants Women's squad, the Steelettos, for eight seasons, and also headed up the Northants Girls Emerging Players Programme (EPP), while also working with the boys Academy and EPP Coaching teams. He was also head coach at the Moulton College Cricket Academy for five years, one of the students being Olly Stone (Northants, Warwickshire, & England), and others moving on to MCCU cricket.

Andy has been a coach at Stowe School for the past five years, seeing some cricketers progress to MCCU and county 2nd XI cricket. In 2010 Andy was voted National Chance to Shine MCC Spirit of Cricket Coach of the Year.

James and Andy have previously co-authored the book *Wicketkeeping: A Comprehensive Modern Guide for Cricket Players and Coaches.*

In addition to their current commitments, James and Andy have their own coaching business – Cricket Coaching Masterclass – www.cricketcoachingmasterclass.co.uk

ABOUT THE PLAYERS & COACHES

ADAM HOLLIOAKE

Adam played for Surrey and England as a batting all-rounder. He captained Surrey from 1997 until 2003, winning three County Championships, and led the England cricket team in one-day internationals. He was named one of the Wisden Cricketers of the Year in 2003. Adam has had coaching stints in England and Australia, and is currently the Queensland batting coach.

GRAHAM GOOCH

Graham's first-class cricket career spanned four decades from 1972 to 2000. He captained Essex and England and was one of the most successful international batsmen of his generation, becoming the most prolific run scorer of all time, with 67,057 runs across first-class and limited-overs games. His List A cricket tally of 22,211 runs is also a record. He is one of only 25 players to have scored over 100 first-class centuries. After 118 Tests, aged 42, he retired into coaching with Essex, before becoming England batting coach in 2012.

BEN DUCKETT

Ben Duckett's youth cricket saw him play as a batsman/wicketkeeper for Northamptonshire CCC and Stowe School. After signing professionally Ben kept wicket less regularly and began to focus more on his batting. He had incredible success early in his career with 2016 being his best season to date. That year he scored over 1,300 first-class runs and won the T20 Blast with

Northants. This led to him being named as the young cricketer of the year by both the Cricket Writers' Club and the Professional Cricketers' Association (PCA). He was also named PCA Player of the Year – the first player to win both PCA awards in the same season. To date Ben has played four Test matches, three ODIs and one T20i for England, as well as franchise T20 cricket around the world.

SIR GEOFFREY BOYCOTT

Sir Geoffrey is one of England's most successful batsmen of all time. In a career spanning 24 years for Yorkshire and England he scored 151 centuries in first-class cricket. He famously scored his 100th against Australia at his home ground of Headingley. In total he scored over 8,000 runs in Test matches at an average of 47.72. Upon retiring Sir Geoffrey has had many coaching roles and has built a successful career as a commentator.

JULIAN WOOD

Julian played first-class cricket for Hampshire in the late 80s and early 90s before having a long stint in Minor Counties cricket for Berkshire. He is now the cricket professional at Bradfield College. He specialises in coaching power hitting and has had stints working globally with the world's best players with various T20 franchises. Julian also runs his own coaching business: The Julian Wood Cricket Academy (jwcricketacademy.com).

MARK BUTCHER

Mark played 71 Test matches for England, mainly as an opening left-handed batsman. He played county cricket for Surrey from 1992 until his retirement in 2009 and scored over 17,000 first-class runs. Mark is now a commentator and musician.

JAMES CRONIE

James is a batsman/off-spinner on the Northants Academy and has played in their 2nd XI. James finished A-levels at Stowe School in 2021 and now studying financial mathematics at Loughborough University. He has represented the Midlands at both the ECB Bunbury Festival and the Super 4s, as well as training with England U19s.

AADI SHARMA

Aadi is currently doing his GCSEs at Stowe School and is on the Northants Academy, having come through the Bucks pathway. He was the leading run scorer for the South & West at the ECB Bunbury Festival in 2021.

ACKNOWLEDGEMENTS

...e to thank the many players and coaches who gave up their time ...wledge to contribute to this book – Sir Geoffrey Boycott, Graham ...k Butcher, Julian Wood and Ben Duckett. They were very giving ...us with their time and we are extremely grateful to them all.

...thanks to James Cronie and Aadi Sharma, our two batters, who ...ent several days in batting gear while the photographs were taken. ...bat maker Gary Sandford from Choice Cricket, for his contribution ...manufacture and maintenance, and for supplying items for the batting ...pment section.

Special thanks goes to Jonathan Glynn-Smith and Leah Band @ ...oweStudio100 for their hard work taking such high-quality photos over the ...our-day shoot, and then for several days further enhancing the images you see in this book.

Thank you also to the Stowe School Headmaster, Dr Anthony Wallersteiner, who allowed us to use the Stowe School Cricket facilities for the photographs. Also thanks to Steve Curley, the head groundsman there, and his team of ground staff.

Finally, a big thank you to Peter Burns and his team at Polaris Publishing for their help in developing the book, and to our agent, David Luxton, for his invaluable support and advice.

We would also like to thank all of those who have helped us on our cricketing journey throughout the years that led us to this point: our families, our friends, our team-mates, our co-workers, other teachers and other coaches. They have all inspired, encouraged, challenged and shared their knowledge and experiences with us over many years, and without all of that accumulated knowledge, this book would never have been written.

Lastly, a huge thank you to you the reader for buying this book. We very much hope you enjoy it and, whether a player or coach, that it helps you on your own cricketing journey.

Andrew O'Connor

James Knott